Producing Pop

Producing Pop

Culture and Conflict in the Popular Music Industry

Keith Negus

A member of the Hodder Headline Group
LONDON • NEW YORK • SYDNEY • AUCKLAND

First published in Great Britain 1992 by Edward Arnold
Reprinted 1999 by Arnold
a member of the Hodder Headline Group
338 Euston Road, London NW1 3BH

Copublished in the United States of America by
Oxford University Press Inc.,
198 Madison Avenue, New York 10016

British Library Cataloguing in Publication Data
Negus, Keith
    Producing Pop: Culture and Conflict in
    the Popular Music Industry
    I. Title
    338.4778163

Library of Congress Cataloging-in-Publication Data
A catalog record for this book is available from the Library of Congress

ISBN 0 340 57512 3

6 7 8 9 10

Typeset in 10/11 Paladium by Colset Private Ltd, Singapore
Printed and bound in Great Britain by Athenæum Press Ltd,
Gateshead, Tyne & Wear

Contents

INTRODUCTION

Between the Artist and Audience

In August 1991 the Polygram group – one of the world's largest recorded music producers and publishers – issued an interim report to shareholders in which president Alain Levy set out the corporation's strategy; emphasising that the key to future growth lay in the company's ability to find and successfully develop new recording artists. Levy added that although new acts do not usually make a significant contribution to the company until the second or third album, 'it is the initial discovery and subsequent nurturing of the artist which is the critical phase'.

In this book I am taking the 'critical phase' which Levy identifies – the discovery and development of recording artists – as my central theme, and using it as an organising principle to provide a more general account of the recording industry and production of pop music. My focus is on personnel within the music business, rather than the artists or audiences, and my aim is to describe how a particular group of workers – who I have characterised as 'cultural intermediaries' (Bourdieu, 1986) – actively contribute to the sounds and images of pop. Although often invisible behind star names and audience styles, recording industry personnel work at a point where the tensions between artists, consumers and entertainment corporations meet and result in a range of working practices, ideological divisions and conflicts. This book is about these practices, divisions and conflicts.

In emphasising the active work of recording industry personnel in this way I am, in many respects, offering an implicit defence of the music business against various forms of sociological and journalistic cynicism, with its emphasis on corruption and exploitation, and steering a deliberate course away from the pessimistic laments of mechanical determinists and economic reductionists. The music industry is an untidy place where working practices frequently do not fit easily into the sharp distinctions and clear-cut boundaries of organizational theory and systems analysis. As Jacques Attali has remarked; when observed from the outside the music business appears as 'an ordinary consumer industry', yet it is 'a strange industry on the borderline between the most sophisticated marketing and the most unpredictable of cottage industries' (1985, pp 102–103). So often these idiosyncratic and unpredictable aspects have been lost as the recording industry has been reduced to a closed mechanical assembly line, filtering products to the public according to organizational conventions or the commercial logic of capitalism. This book is a conscious attempt to move away from viewing the music business as a series of bureaucratic boxes and cybernetic systems through which products are transmitted from producers to consumers. Instead I will be emphasising the cultural worlds being lived and constantly re-made, and highlighting the webs of relationships and multiple dialogues along and around which the musical and visual identities of pop artists are composed and communicated.

In taking the day-to-day work of recording industry personnel seriously, and highlighting the human activity involved I am certainly not about to embark on a celebration of the endless possibilities provided by the products of popular culture. This has become a feature of postmodern theorising and subcultural writing in recent years. Such orientations tend to over-emphasize the activities of audiences and prioritise the way in which musical sounds and technologies have been used in the act of consumption. Instead, this book is a critique of the way in which the recording industry has come to favour certain types of music, particular working practices and quite specific ways of acquiring, marketing and promoting recording artists.

The research for this book was carried out between 1988 and 1992, and a large part of the discussion is based on interviews with personnel in Britain and the United States during this period. In most cases where I have used quotes in the text I have cited individuals anonymously and referred to their position in general terms. I have done this for two reasons: Firstly, because many of the people I spoke to were very forthcoming and forthright in their views and explanations, and clearly did not want many of the things which they told me attributed to themselves or their company by name. But, secondly, I have used quotations to make general observations or illustrate specific issues which arise within the industry, rather than to make a point about any individual. I have occasionally cited named individuals, with permission, when it seemed relevant, and I have used quotes which have appeared in the trade or music press (I have kept references to a minimum, however, and have deliberately avoided using a plethora of footnotes on the assumption that most readers will not need to know the source of every quote or assertion; for more details see the bibliography at the end).

A large part of this book resonates with the voices of the recording industry personnel I have spoken to. I would like to thank everyone who gave up their time to describe their work and patiently assisted me in clarifying many of the ideas I am putting forward – in doing so they became an integral part of this book. Many thanks to the following people who were working at these companies or organisations when I visited them. In Britain; Brian Shepherd at A & M Records; Philip Vaughan at the Association of Professional Recording Studios (APRS); Graham Jelfs at Beggars Banquet; Gareth Harris, Dave Harper and Lisa Anderson at BMG Records; Paul Curran at BMG Music Publishing; Peter Scaping and Jeremy Silver at the British Phonographic Industry (BPI); Jonathan Morrish, Muff Winwood and Bobbie Coppen at CBS/Sony; Sharon Chevin at Sharon Chevin Public Relations; Berni Kilmartin and Mike Allen at Chrysalis Records; Bruce Craigie at Chrysalis Music Publishing; Ed Bicknell at Damage Management; Terri Anderson, Andrew Pryor, Amanda Rabbs and Ian Hampson at EMI; Mark Kingston at the International Federation of the

Phonographic Industry (IFPI); Amanda Freeman at Island Records; Keith Blackhurst and Pete Hadfield at Kollectiv Management/Deconstruction Records; Colin Bell at London Records; Bob Fisher and Phil Smith at MCA; Martin Nelson at Phonogram; Graham Carpenter at Polydor; Pam Sherratt at Polygram; David Howells at PWL Ltd; David Lewis at Qualitative Research and Planning in Music; Malcolm Buckland at Rough Trade; Guy Moot at SBK Songs/EMI Publishing; Peter Felstead at Second Vision Management; Jeremy Lascelles at Virgin; Malcolm Dunbar at WEA and Paul Brown at Worlds End Management. For informal discussions about their experience of the recording industry thanks go to; Graham Sacher, Paul Dean, Bill Johnson, Phil Hardy, Gary Hawkins, Roberta Kirkue and Colin Hall. For additional information via telephone or post I would like to thank; Lesley Bray and Philip Molden at the Performing Right Society; Paul Campbell and Claire Shirley at Sony UK; and Peter Wareham at BMG Records.

For speaking to me in the United States I would like to thank; Alison Donald and Jean Riggins at Capitol; the marketing staff at Chrysalis in New York; Ken Antonelli at EMI; Valerie Killigrew at Polygram; Nick Cucci at Rough Trade; Jacquie Perryman, Jean Rousseau and Aaron at Virgin; Mary Brown at Warner-Chappell; Jill Dell'Abate and Jennifer Cohen at WEA and Marques Wyatt, freelance disc jockey and mixer. Special thanks for assistance in arranging interviews in the United States go to; Trish Heimers at the Recording Industry Association of America (RIAA); Sue Satriano at Capitol; Tracy Bledsoe and Michael Moran at WEA. For putting me up and putting up with me in Los Angeles thanks to Lou Thornton.

A number of colleagues and friends have mediated between my first tentative garbled drafts and the final chapters of this book. I would like to thank Paul Gilroy and Jean Seaton for the excellent guidance and support which they gave me throughout my writing and research when this was a Ph.D study, and for their encouragement and suggestions as it turned into a book. Special thanks are also due to Paul du Gay for providing valuable criticisms and information, enduring my anxieties and uncertainties and offering continual support and encouragement during our endless discussions over the past three years. For a very constructive critique which helped clarify my thinking for the final version I would like to thank Simon Frith. For spotting errors and making detailed and perceptive comments on an earlier version of Chapter 2, thanks go to Paul Théberge; and in a similar way for reading a number of chapters and offering some very useful suggestions for Chapter 7, I would like to thank Sara Cohen. For discussing a number of working ideas and putting me right on dance clubs I would like to thank Sarah Thornton. For the hours of discussion and dialectics in the kitchen I would like to thank Eddie Dorfman. For helping me clarify various working notes, ideas and misconceptions throughout my research and writing I would like to thank Paul Rutten, Larry Shore, Ron Moy and everyone, too numerous to mention, who made comments during seminars at The Institute of Popular Music, Liverpool University and at the International Association for the Study of Popular Music Conference in Berlin during July 1991. I would like to thank the Economic and Social Research Council for financing my research, Norman Ginsberg for improving my intellectual efficiency with his technical guidance and knowledge of computers, and James Curran for encouraging me to embark on this project in the first place. Special thanks to Jean Croot for listening to hours of rambling semi-coherent monologues and providing endless support and encouragement over the years. Thanks also to Lesley Riddle at Edward Arnold for her enthusiasm, suggestions and advice. Last but not least, for making it easier to cope during the eight day weeks of writing and thinking I would like to thank Dave for the soul and the dancing; Bill for the rocking and recording; and Chris and Phil for injecting a bit of blunt reality (and occasionally a bout of surreality) into the proceedings and letting me know when I was talking nonsense.

As I want to emphasise the way in which pop music arises from a constant dialogue between production and consumption, I have arranged the chapters in this book to build up a picture of the recording industry by circling from the abstract global strategies of the corporations, to the day-to-day relationships between people working together in acquiring and developing artists. The first two chapters provide a series of contexts for the detailed discussions which follow, by outlining the ways in which the music business is part of a global network of entertainment industries and by highlighting the technological influences and constraints within which contemporary pop music is composed and communicated. Chapter 3 focuses on the distinctive working practices and prejudices of artist and repertoire staff, and draws attention to the historical and social circumstances which have informed these priorities. Artist and repertoire staff must work closely with other departments within a record company and Chapter 4 provides an immediate contrast by looking at the different orientations of marketing staff and the way in which record companies attempt to establish a point of identification between artists and audiences in order to sell recordings. Chapter 5 describes the practices and problems involved in producing the sounds and images in the studio and for music videos. It looks at the way in which the technologies described in Chapter 2 are practically employed in the production of pop. In Chapter 6 I discuss how these sounds and identities are influenced by the radio stations of Britain and North America. Chapter 7 describes the contribution which press officers make to the process of artist development, and Chapter 8 brings together the threads from all of these discussions and outlines the conflicts which emerge between different occupational groups and between artists and record companies.

1

FEEDING THE WORLD

Popular Music and
the Global Entertainment Industry

Music industry staff who are involved in acquiring, developing and marketing artists are not simply working for record companies. As Tony Powell, the managing director of MCA Records remarked in 1991: 'Record companies don't see themselves as record companies anymore. They see themselves as entertainment companies.' Since the latter part of the 1980s these companies have been explicitly defining themselves as 'global' organisations. The major labels involved in recording popular music are no longer merely seeking local musicians, singers or songwriters. The phonogram industry, as it is sometimes quaintly called, is concerned with developing global personalities which can be communicated across multiple media; through recordings, videos, films, television, magazines, books and via advertising, product endorsement and sponsorship over a range of consumer merchandise. The quest is for entertainment icons whose sounds and images can be inserted into the media and communication networks which are spanning the globe. As the twentieth century ends, the music business is one integral component of an increasingly global network of inter-connected leisure and entertainment industries.

This chapter is neither a comprehensive account of this emerging and changing entertainment complex, nor a detailed description of the world recording industry. More modestly it is an introductory sketch of what 'the world' looks like from an office or studio in the recording industry. My aim is to provide an indication of the global character of popular music production and consumption and, as a prelude to later chapters, to outline the corporate setting within which the day-to-day work of recording industry personnel takes place.

The Major Corporations Involved in Producing Popular Music

In recent years approximately 70 per cent of the recorded popular music sold in the world has been produced, manufactured and distributed by five major companies: EMI Music, Polygram, Sony Music Entertainment, Warner Music International and the BMG Music Group (see Appendix 1 on recording industry statistics). These companies are in turn owned by large transnational

corporations which have interests encompassing a range of leisure and entertainment media, electronic and industrial manufacturing enterprises and firms
providing domestic products and services.

EMI is, at the time of writing, owned by the British-based company Thorn-
EMI, which has interests in lighting, the rental of domestic appliances, musical
and electrical retail outlets, security systems, computer software and electronic
technology. Polygram is part of the Dutch-based Philips corporation, which
like EMI, owns companies manufacturing lighting equipment and a range of
electronic consumer products and technological systems used in communication, medicine, industrial manufacturing and defence. Sony Music is a division
of the Japanese Sony Corporation, a leading manufacturer of domestic and
industrial audio and visual products, semiconductors, telecommunications
equipment and the owner of Columbia Pictures in Hollywood. Warner Music
is part of the Time-Warner conglomerate which, although not a manufacturer
of equipment and hardware, is the largest entertainment corporation in the
world with interests in film, cable, television and publishing. BMG Music is a
subsidiary of the Bertelsmann group of Germany which, despite maintaining
a low corporate profile, was the largest media conglomerate prior to the Time-
Warner merger in 1989. Bertelsmann's interests include newspapers, magazine
and book publishing, record clubs and cable television networks.

A further significant share of the world market for recorded popular music
(somewhere between 12 and 15 per cent) has been taken by two other leisure
and entertainment groups: The Music Corporation of America (MCA) and
the UK-based Virgin Music Group. In discussions of the recording industry
these companies have often been treated separately from the 'big five' because
they have not manufactured and distributed their own discs or tapes. Instead
they have relied on various arrangements with one or more of the companies mentioned above. However, with corporations adopting more flexible
approaches to manufacturing, and increasingly engaging in joint ventures, this
has not impeded their expansion. MCA has a number of leisure interests,
most notably Universal Studios, and in 1990 was acquired by Matshushita,
the corporation which developed and introduced the VHS video recorder and
which owns companies manufacturing electronic goods ranging from batteries
to industrial robots. Virgin started as a mail order record business in 1970 and
rapidly expanded into a group of companies involved in home entertainment
retailing, long-haul air travel, broadcasting, publishing and film production.
By 1990 Virgin was operating 120 companies in 30 countries worldwide and
following 14 months of talks sold its music group to Thorn-EMI in March 1992
for £150 million.

The dominance of recorded popular music by a small number of large corporations is not a recent phenomenon, nor is the way in which these companies
have developed interests in a range of related entertainment industries and
technologies (the latter point I shall discuss further in Chapter 2). During
its formative years the recording industry developed within a world economy
which was shifting from business activity organised around multi-divisional
national companies, to one dominated by transnational corporations operating
across national boundaries (Hymer, 1979). In this setting the leading record
companies set their goals internationally from the very beginning and in
the early years of the twentieth century established local factories and

networks of subsidiaries in a large number of countries around the world (Gronow, 1983).

Most of the major companies involved in producing popular music in the 1990s have arrived at their current form as a result of a complex history of acquisitions and mergers, technological changes, and booms and slumps connected to wider changes in the world economy, and can trace their origins back to the beginning of the twentieth century. In the 1910s the industry in America was largely controlled by the Victor Talking Machine Company (later to become RCA, then BMG), and Columbia (to become CBS, then Sony). In Europe there was strong competition between British and German firms, most notably between the British Gramophone Company and Lindstrom. On a world scale this early period came to be dominated by two Anglo-American businesses; The Victor Talking Machine Company of New Jersey in the United States, and The Gramophone Company of Middlesex, England. Their influence was amplified by a cross ownership arrangement in which the Victor Talking Machine Company acquired a 50 per cent stake in the Gramophone Company and an agreement which enabled them to further their mutual interests by dividing the world between them; Victor operated in the Americas and Far East, whilst Gramophone serviced the rest of the world (Gronow, 1983). Well into the 1920s these two companies dominated the manufacture and distribution of popular music.

In 1931, following a series of mergers, the Gramophone Company was reformed as Electrical & Musical Industries (EMI) and during the 1930s EMI began to grow to prominence in Britain. By the end of the 1930s EMI and Decca (formed in 1929) manufactured the majority of recordings made in Britain and controlled their distribution to retailers (Frith, 1988a). By the middle of the 1950s the Anglo-American music industry was dominated by RCA Victor, Columbia, EMI-Capitol and Decca, and during this decade the total size of the market for recorded popular music in the United States and Europe, and throughout the world, expanded dramatically. Given impetus by a consumer boom and increase in disposable income amongst teenagers of the post-war baby boom generation, the size of the market for popular music in North America grew by approximately ten times between 1954 and 1973. During this period eight companies regularly accounted for between 83 and 85 per cent of the sales of recordings (Chapple & Garofalo, 1977).

A comprehensive history of the recording industry in the twentieth century has yet to be written and it is not my intention to begin developing one here. I merely want to note two characteristics which laid the foundations for the way in which commercial and artistic policies have subsequently developed. Firstly, the recording industry was initially formed in North America and Europe. This is where key manufacturing operations and retail practices evolved and were concentrated, and where artistic and commercial policies developed. Secondly, since its earliest days the recording industry has been dominated by a few major corporations which have increasingly developed connections with a range of related media and technologies.

Since the middle of the 1980s companies have been consolidating and building on these trends through the related strategies of geographical expansion – in search of markets outside of their North Atlantic and European national bases; and by pursuing ever more mergers, acquisitions and joint ventures within the fields of communication and entertainment in response to the increasing opportunities for 'media synergy'.

Mergers, Acquisitions and the Dream of Media Synergy

The late 1980s and early 1990s were a time of frenetic merger and acquisition activity in the music related industries. Acknowledging the importance of revenue derived from owning the copyright on music publishing, EMI acquired the catalogue of SBK Songs and absorbed the staff into its organisation. In a similar way Warner Brothers combined with Chappell to form the world's largest publishing company with a catalogue of over 800,000 songs. EMI then leapfrogged over Warner-Chappell through the acquisition of the Filmtrax catalogue in December 1990. The Polygram group added the well established and critically acclaimed A & M and Island record labels to their roster, and EMI, likewise, acquired the highly respected labels of the Chrysalis and Virgin groups.

At the same time, the Sony Corporation, recognising the strategic importance of having access to performers and their musical material, acquired CBS Records, whilst Matshushita, for similar reasons, acquired MCA. Meanwhile, the electronics company JVC was forming Victory Music and acquiring David Bowie's band Tin Machine, and the Walt Disney Company was signing Queen and their lucrative back catalogue to its recently launched Hollywood Records label.

These deals were typical of business activity throughout the media, leisure and communication industries, and a further twist was added to all of this as these corporations began to operate 'non competitive strategic alliances'. Already I have noted that the Victor Talking Machine Company and Gramophone Company agreed to divide the world between them early in the twentieth century. More recently Sony and Philips have had close ties for a number of years and cooperated to research and develop audio cassettes, compact discs and digital compact cassettes. In a similar way Philips, owners of the Polygram group, have had a long standing alliance with Matshushita, owners of MCA, and in 1990 Time-Warner and Sony agreed to work together in the direct marketing of music and home video products on a worldwide basis.

These acquisitions and joint ventures have partly been motivated by the need to diversify in industries in which the popularity of cultural goods has always been unpredictable, and hence to share the investment and risk involved in developing new products and constructing markets. More recently these movements have been a calculated response to the increasing possibilities of 'media synergy' – a 'dream' which the *Nation* magazine caricatured as follows:

> Giant Corporation Inc. owns subsidiaries in every medium. One of its magazines buys (or commissions) an article that can be expanded into a book, whose author is widely interviewed in the company magazines and on its broadcast stations. The book is turned into a screenplay for the company movie studios, and the film is automatically booked into the company's chain of theatres. The movie has a sound track that is released on the company's record label. The vocalist is turned into an instant celebrity by cover features in the company magazines and interviews on

its television stations. The recording is played on the company's chain of Top 40 radio stations. The movie is eventually issued by the firm's videocassette division and shown on company television stations. After that, rerun rights to the movie are sold to other television stations around the world (Bagdikian, 1989, p 813).

'Synergy' refers to a strategy of diversifying into directly related technologies and areas of entertainment and using the opportunities that this provides for extending the exposure of specific pieces of music and artists. During the 1960s and 1970s recording corporations often bought businesses involved in supplying quite unrelated products and services such as car parks, children's toys and real estate. Since the middle of the 1980s, however, entertainment groups have been more concerned with diversifying into related fields, and a number of major companies including Sony and EMI divested unrelated interests which had been acquired during previous decades.

Synergy is not only motivated by the desire to gain maximum revenue from the inter-connections which various leisure industries provide for presenting artists across multiple media. It is also a recognition that technological changes have been converging to the point where the potential exists for computer software, video, discs and tapes to be combined and used on one 'multimedia' self-contained home entertainment system.

Staff within record companies are very aware of these connections. Although pop has always depended on visual images for promotion and audience identification these changes have contributed to the displacement of sound as a central focus, and accelerated the re-organisation of record companies as components of entertainment corporations. The personnel who are engaged in acquiring, developing and presenting recording artists are increasingly contributing to an entire entertainment package – a 'total star text' (Dyer, 1991) – around an individual or group, which involves far more than just music. In doing so staff are faced with a whole range of issues and decisions about the positioning of artists in various media and the construction of images which move beyond just sound production – and this is an issue which I shall return to later in this book as I describe in more detail how the composition of the sounds and visions of contemporary pop occurs across webs of occupational and organisational groupings and divisions. Here I want to move on to consider the 'global' dimensions of the recording industry.

Feeding the Global Village

Like a repetitive powerchord running through the pages of its 1989 annual report, Time Warner Inc informed its shareholders, over and over again, in lurid lemon print: 'There is a global hunger for Information and Entertainment'. In smaller print corporate thought could be followed through a series of flow chart diagrams which announced that: 'Feeding the appetite for information and entertainment – Doesn't satisfy the hunger – It increases it.' This metaphor, coming at the end of a decade in which there had been famines, starvation and 'global hunger' for the bare essentials of life in many of the poorest countries of the world, succinctly conveyed the company's 'global' intention of establishing 'a presence in all the world's important markets.' At the same time it inflected the 'Feed the World' messages of the charity records which were released during the 1980s with far less altruistic meanings.

An emphasis on 'the global', accompanied by images of the planet Earth, has appeared repetitively in the annual reports and advertising literature of entertainment corporations since the late 1980s. Like Time-Warner, Thorn-EMI informed its shareholders that the music division had been refocused into a 'truly global organisation'; and Bruce MacKenzie, senior vice president of Polygram, described his company as a 'European based global recording group'. At the same time Akio Morita, president of The Sony Corporation, was propounding his strategy of 'global localisation' and explaining that he had no time for 'the word multinational . . . If it means a company with many nationalities then that is not Sony. Sony is global.'

As these few selective quotes indicate, 'globalisation' had become a buzz-word, and was being regularly employed in business literature and journalism, and throughout a range of intellectual disciplines and discourses. Since its use by Theodore Levitt (1983) in an apocalyptic and influential rallying call to big business, in which he wrote of technology driving the planet towards a convergence and homogenisation of 'the world's needs and desires', the term has acquired a number of meanings, clustering around a common one-world theme. It has been variously employed to describe the homogenisation of tastes, 'cultural interrelatedness', the globalisation of markets, capital and the communications media, as prefix to ecological problems such as global warming, and more generally to refer to the ways in which the world might be becoming 'united' (Robertson, 1990).

Many proclamations of globalisation involve little more than political rhetoric, corporate dreaming, journalistic hyperbole or intellectual banality, and have promoted a view of the global based on quite recent and particular interests and experiences. When routinely trotted out by senior executives in entertainment companies, globalisation has tended to become a bland wallpaper term used to cover the cracks, conflicts and discontinuities in the world as the planet is reduced to a cosy 'global village'.

However, beyond the one-world rhetoric and the corporate dreams of world domination, there are a series of issues and debates which have clustered around this term, and these will become of increasing relevance to discussions of the production and consumption of popular music in the coming years. At a general level globalisation indicates a shift in thinking, and directs attention away from viewing the world in terms of discrete nation states towards a consideration of the relationships between geographical regions, and the economic, social and cultural movements across conventional boundaries which are becoming an increasing feature of the capitalist economy.

As Kevin Robins has pointed out, ' "Globalisation" is about the organisation of production and the exploitation of markets on a world scale' (1991, p 25). In its current form it is the latest stage of a long historical trend towards the concentration of industrial and finance capital and attempts by companies to overcome national boundaries. Modern corporations seek to operate in all markets simultaneously, rather than sequentially, and target consumers on the basis of demographics, habits and lifestyles, rather than straightforward geographical regions. This has been facilitated by the technologies of the mass media and telecommunications which have enabled corporations to impose what Robins has called 'an abstract electronic space' over and across pre-existing physical and social geographies. This is particularly noticeable in the music industry where the videos and recordings of major artists such as Michael Jackson and Madonna are consumed simultaneously throughout the world; their sounds and images rapidly communicating across linguistic frontiers and cultural boundaries. Robins has argued that globalisation breaks the link between culture and territory, and popular music – less dependent for its comprehension upon language, education and the acquisition of a sophisticated body of knowledge – is one of *the* forms of mass communication which has been able to do this most dramatically; constructing audiences around the common shared experience of a cultural event (such as the Mandela Freedom Concert), or an artist's lifestyle and identity, rather than a local social experience in a discrete time and place.

However, whilst these trends are evidently taking place, the breaking down of such time-place barriers is not occurring evenly across the planet, and the emergence of new abstract spaces has been accompanied by a re-affirmation of local identity. This has quite often taken the form of a reaction against the perceived threat of a homogenous, undifferentiated 'mass' culture being imposed from outside – with an accompanying tendency to idealise and romanticise the local as an authentic expression of folk culture, and to condemn the global as artificial and unauthentic. At a local level processes of globalisation in popular music are increasingly being experienced as a tension between progress and restoration; between the eclectic, syncretic forms of acculturated expression brought about by the meeting of various musical techniques, technologies and traditions; and a concomitant retreat into nostalgia, with attempts to preserve the imagined purity of the past by constructing idealised 'heritage' cultures (Frith (Ed) 1989; Robinson, Buck & Cuthbert, 1991; Wallis & Malm, 1984). Informing the resistance to a global mass culture in various parts of the world has been the recognition that, over the last thirty years, much of this has been Anglo-American in origin and content.

The Anglo-American Dominance of World Music and the Challenge of Europe

The globalisation of communications media and geographical expansion of transnational corporations has provided more opportunities for, and increased the significance of the marketing and promotion of recording artists across the planet. Motivated by the commercial desire to maximise the sales of an artist's recordings and to utilise the various media outlets available to the corporation, world sales potential has become an important consideration when a record company is deciding whether to acquire an artist. But, it has also become more necessary as higher revenues have been required to recoup the escalating costs involved in producing, manufacturing and marketing popular music.

The approach to what constitutes the 'rest of the world' inevitably varies according to the size and position of different countries. For North American record companies the money gained from overseas sales provides an additional source of income. As an international coordinator in the Los Angeles office of a British owned record company commented:

International sales are like money in your pocket without really having to do much. You can sell, potentially, from two, to five, to ten million records overseas and it's a heavy source of income. If you consider that you have no promotional overhead, no marketing overhead, you don't even package it. All the marketing and promotion costs are covered by each territory. The only thing you do is supply the tape, and the money you make is on your royalties basically. It's an internal company licensing deal, which is a great source of revenue. Say you make two to three dollars on the licensing, that's 20 to 30 million dollars. It's phenomenal.

For British record labels the revenue from sales to the rest of the world, particularly to North America and Europe, is a more important source of income. Revenue derived from British sales alone is often not sufficient to cover the overheads and costs involved. In 1990 one managing director who I spoke to in London remarked: 'Our investments are so high that we wouldn't dream of existing on UK sales alone. We have to have international sales. I have to think globally all the time.'

When 'thinking globally' record industry personnel are increasingly viewing the world as a series of pan-regional blocs, such as USA/Canada, Europe, and Japan/south east Asia. However, staff still tend to use a heuristic model of the world divided into primary, secondary and tertiary markets. These divisions correspond to the economic sales potential of existing national territories, incorporate judgments about the strategic importance of specific areas, and are influenced by assessments of countries considered to be politically unstable or difficult to extract currency out of. In general the offices of the major companies have been established in the most important markets. In regions considered to be less significant or markets considered unstable (at the time of my research recording industry staff in Britain and the USA mentioned countries in Latin America, eastern Europe and Africa) most companies have tended to work through local companies; either licensing their entire catalogue to a regional label or arranging ad-hoc deals by assigning specific artists and recordings to different companies.

In terms of total retail sales the primary markets for popular music are the United States, Japan, Germany, United Kingdom, and France (Table 1). In recent years these territories have regularly accounted for about 70 per cent of the total world sales of recorded music.

In the past, sales in Europe – taken as a whole – have been less than those of North America, which has been the most important source of both revenue and repertoire for the recording industry. However, in 1988 sales in the EC countries began to creep above those of the United States and two years later retail sales in Europe climbed to 35 per cent, whilst sales in North America accounted for 31 per cent of the total.

A number of commentators have viewed this as an indication of a significant shift in the relative importance of North America within the world recording industry; an opinion which has been given added weight by the moves towards greater European integration and the collapse of the previously inaccessible communist states of eastern Europe. There is no doubt that Europe, as both a market and cultural space, will become increasingly important to the recording industry throughout the 1990s, and already MTV Europe and various satellite operators are attempting to construct a distinctive European identity as part of their broadcasting strategies.

Table 1. World Sales of Records and Tapes in Selected Markets 1990.

	retail value $ millions	per cent of total
USA	7,541.1	31
Japan	2,981.8	12
Germany	2,273.9	9
UK	2,117.5	9
France	1,665.8	7
Netherlands	643.0	3
Canada	608.8	3
Italy	581.8	2
Spain	521.5	2
Australia	476.3	2
TOTAL	24,050.0	

Source: 'World Record Sales 1990'. International Federation of the Phonographic Industry, Press Information, 1 October 1991. (For a complete listing see Appendix 2.)

However, many staff members within the recording industry are sceptical about the claims made on behalf of Europe. They consider that the language and cultural differences, coupled with the different media and promotional systems which are currently in place, will continue to mark out very distinct boundaries to their markets for the foreseeable future. Processes of globalisation are operating unevenly in the recording industry and it is perhaps important to distinguish between the construction of Europe as an identifiable market involving the integration and harmonisation of retail practices, prices and distribution systems, which is proceeding rapidly; and, the emergence of Europe as a distinctive cultural identity and repertoire source, which is occurring clumsily across the existing cultural and national boundaries which have historically informed the way in which repertoire policies have developed and been organised. Here the dominance of Britain and the United States is likely to continue for some time, as it has become deeply embedded in the existing relations between record companies and label divisions throughout the world.

When marketing British artists 'international' staff liaise with personnel in company subdivisions or at licensed companies around the world. Their first task is to attempt to persuade staff in another territory to release the recordings of a British artist. Having achieved this, personnel in Britain then monitor the progress of an act or recording in each territory and assist in supplying information and any material required for promotion.

At the same time that staff in a British company are attempting to persuade sister companies to release material in other territories, representatives of these companies are trying to negotiate the release of their own artist's products in Britain. There is no mutual and equal exchange of acts, however; a point which is obscured in the figures cited above. Although showing the size of markets, these figures do not reveal the extent to which the world sales of recordings have been dominated by those made by North American and British artists. It is difficult to obtain concise and coherent statistics to illustrate this clearly. But, a variety of sources indicate similar patterns.

The German Federal Republic, prior to the uniting of Germany, was a typical example of the national record markets of Europe. Between 1985 and 1988 UK artists accounted for between 33 per cent and 40 per cent of the sales of all recordings (BPI, 1988, 1989), with American acts accounting for a further third. As one observer pointed out:

> Since the early 1960s, all new major trends (eg, rock 'n' roll, beat, rock) on the German market have been imported from Anglo-American popular cultural circles. West German impulses in the formation of both national and international musical innovations hardly exist . . . typically German pop songs (Schlager) still accounted for a 50 per cent share in the 1950s, its present [1979] share consists of a bare 10 per cent (Zeppenfeld, 1979, p 250).

The major exception to this trend in Europe is France which has been one of the few European countries to have a market which regularly includes a high percentage of domestic repertoire rather than one based predominantly on Anglo-American recordings (Hung & Morencos, 1990). The largest market outside of North America and Europe is Japan, and although British artists have not sold very large quantities of recordings in Japan, rising from only 2 per cent in 1985 to 8 per cent of sales in 1988, American artists have been more popular but domestic Japanese repertoire has accounted for between 70 and 75 per cent of the sales of records and tapes since the middle of the 1970s (BPI, 1988, 1989; Hung & Morencos, 1990). With the sales of recordings growing in South Korea and Taiwan, and the market for rock music expanding in Japan, the 'Pacific rim' will probably become an important market for recorded music in the coming years.

In the late 1970s Larry Shore (1983) carried out a detailed analysis of the *Billboard* charts of top selling records around the world and found that songs with English lyrics dominated the hit records in most countries. Not surprisingly this was most evident in regions where English was one of the main languages such as the USA, UK, Canada, Australia, New Zealand and South Africa. In these territories hit records in a language other than English were almost non-existent. Shore found the highest number of local hits to be in the Spanish speaking countries of South America and a 'medium to high ratio of local language hits' in France, Spain, Finland and Argentina. In Holland, Switzerland and Sweden less than 20 per cent of hits were local in origin. Britain and the United States were the only countries to have a mutual exchange of recordings, although the flow was greater from the United States into Britain. Shore concluded that there was 'a predominantly one-way flow of music from the United States, and to a lesser extent Britain, to other parts of the world' (1983, p 264).

The dominance of world markets by Anglo-American music and artists is reinforced by the way in which the American and British sales charts decisively influence the local policies of record companies and the decisions of radio programmers throughout the world. The comments of many members of staff I spoke to in Britain echoed the findings of a study carried out by Wallis and Malm in the 1970s which found that:

> British and American charts provide guidelines for phonogram licensees as regards which international repertoire is considered worth releasing in different territories. Disc jockeys the world over like to report on news from the British Top 40 or the

Billboard Hot Hundred. This applies to Sri Lanka and Kenya's English-language channels, to the light music output of the Scandinavian broadcasting monopolies [and] to most of the fifty FM stations in Chile (1984, p 250).

Hence, the world markets for popular music have been constructed to provide a series of opportunities for British and American artists across the globe. At the same time however, these opportunities are limited to those British acts which have already achieved success at home. This is less to do with the taste of consumers in different territories, than a direct consequence of the politics involved in making music available around the world. Success in Britain is used as a lever to negotiate the release of material in other territories. As the British managing director of the main record label of a European corporation explained;

> There is a lot to be said for a record going in at Number 1, or staying at Number 1 , or staying in the Top 5. It gives international credibility. The concept of success in other territories is very much flavoured by how we get on here in the UK. It's very important that you present the right picture to the outside world . . . To be credible you must establish yourself in your home market.

Due to the way in which the British charts set the agenda for record companies and radio stations across Europe, labels based in the United States tend to seek British success as part of their global strategies rather than simply to gain more sales. The United Kingdom, as well as being a trend-setting market, has been of strategic importance as a point of entry into Europe for American artists. In addition, Germany has developed as an important market for building a base from which to gain access to surrounding territories. The uniting of Germany in 1990 has increased both the size of the German market for popular music, and reinforced its strategic importance for gaining access to the changing economies of eastern Europe and the new independent states of the former Soviet Union (this latter region being eyed as a potentially massive new market by the entertainment industry).

If the dominance of Anglo-American repertoire around the world provides opportunities for successful British and North American artists to gain extra sales, at the same time it severely restricts the opportunities for local artists. Although the major corporations are – in theory – concerned with finding and developing local talent throughout the world, in practice this has taken second place to the marketing of acts from Britain and the United States. In many countries the balance of power within record companies has been firmly structured through the appointment of staff, investment and policy decisions to favour the marketing and promotion of 'international' acts, rather than the acquisition and development of local artists. This point was made by Paul Rutten (1991) who carried out research on the Dutch music industry at the turn of the decade and found that the main activities of the record companies, whether local or transnational, were organised around the distribution and marketing of foreign, mainly Anglo-American recordings.

This Anglo-American dominance of repertoire policy is well illustrated by the decision of Sony Music to establish a new label called Sony Music Soho Square in July 1991 as the 'first ever pan-European repertoire source'. Not only is the title of the label decidedly English, being named after the company's base in London from where the operations will be coordinated, but, the brief of this 'pan-European' operation is restricted to signing only English speaking artists in Europe. Such policies not only impede the prospects for local performers who do not sing in English, but increase the potential global influence of decisions made about the acquisition and development of artists in Britain and the United States.

Social Consumption and Copyright Revenue

So far I have outlined the way in which music produced by artists from Britain and the United States, and distributed by a small number of transnational entertainment corporations, has come to dominate the sales of recordings around the world, contributing to Anglo-American cultural hegemony, and limiting the opportunities for local and regional artists. However, at this point I want to disrupt this fairly straightforward argument slightly, and draw attention to a major difficulty involved in reading sales statistics as an indicator of both the consumption of music, and of musical practices in different regions of the world.

Official sales figures produced by the recording industry provide an increasingly limited and partial way of representing consumption patterns, and of understanding the music being created around the world, because they prioritise individual purchases of legally manufactured products. They give no indication of the way in which music is created and consumed in a variety of social settings, nor the way in which recordings are produced and distributed through unofficial channels such as the unauthorised manufacture of cassette tapes. As in other areas of the music industry, figures to illustrate these invisible patterns of production and consumption are difficult to obtain.

One indication can be gained by considering revenues derived from licensing the use of music through copyright legislation. As Simon Frith (1987c) has pointed out, entertainment corporations are increasingly organising their global strategies around the exploitation of rights and circulating musical commodities within the media in order to generate income. A considerable part of the turn-over of the music industry is now being derived from 'the exchange of immaterial items' based on the rights to produce a musical work or its performance (Fabbri, 1991).

In grappling with the paucity of figures available Franco Fabbri (1991) has argued that although Italy compares unfavourably with the markets in other countries when judged solely in terms of the sales of recordings, a consideration of the additional revenue derived from copyright would bring the country closer to its description as 'the fifth most industrialised power in the capitalist world' than sales figures alone suggest. A further dimension to Fabbri's argument – that official sales figures give a misleading indication of musical activity in Italy – can be added by considering the manufacture and distribution of illegally reproduced recordings. In July 1991 the trade magazine *Billboard* reported that a well established pirate operation in Italy was accounting for annual sales of approximately 20 million cassette tapes. Not only did this include a substantial amount of 'international' repertoire, it also contained a high proportion of music produced originally on local labels by Italian artists, indicating that the sales of recordings by native Italian artists might be higher than the official figures suggested.

Estimates of 'pirate' cassettes have to be approached with caution, bearing in mind the way they are used to support lobbying for both a blank tape levy and the prosecution of illegal entrepreneurs. But there is considerable evidence to suggest that a large amount of local musical activity around the world is organised around the illegal reproduction and distribution of existing recordings. And, a further activity – which has received little attention – is the way in which music is produced and consumed through the informal recording and circulation of sounds amongst music enthusiasts (Wallis & Malm, 1984).

It is the publishing divisions of entertainment corporations, and their contracted composers, who are accruing the revenue derived from the ownership of copyright and from licensing the use of recordings. It is the ideology of 'intellectual property' – that musical ideas have an owner who must be compensated every time they are used in a public place – which is being employed to legitimate this practice (Frith, 1987c). This can be a very confusing subject, but there are broadly three types of revenue which can be collected: 1) Performing rights: this is for the use of the musical material and collected on behalf of writers and publishers when music is performed or broadcast. 2) Mechanical rights: this must be paid to the copyright holder every time a particular song or piece of music is recorded, or as the archaic terminology stipulates, 'mechanically reproduced'. 3) Public performance rights: this must be paid for the privilege of broadcasting or playing the actual recording (rather than the song) in public.

Copyright revenues are collected by a loosely aligned network of musical licensing bodies throughout the world, such as The Performing Rights Society (PRS) in Britain, The American Society of Composers, Publishers and Authors (ASCAP) and Broadcast Music Incorporated (BMI) in the United States, Gesellschaft für Musikalische Aufführungs (GEMA) in Germany and the Société des Auteurs, Compositeurs et Editeurs de Musique (SACEM) in France. In 1989 calculations by the National Music Publishers Association of America suggested that the total music publishing revenues in the 'major global markets', which represented about 80 per cent of the total, were in excess of 3,000 million U.S. dollars. In the same year the British trade magazine *Music Week* estimated that the turnover of the publishing industry accounted for one-third of the total turn-over of the recording industry worldwide.

Entertainment corporations are increasingly attempting to gain the maximum revenue possible from exploiting the ownership of copyright; using the mass communications media available to place recordings across multiple sites, and lobbying for the licensing of ever more public spaces where music is being used (such as shops, clubs, restaurants, pubs and hairdressing salons) and supporting the deployment of copyright inspectors to enforce these policies and prosecute outlets engaging in the unlicensed use of music. During the late 1980s publishers and their collecting societies began escalating their lobbying for the introduction of 'intellectual property' agreements in geographical regions where they did not exist and for the harmonisation of licensing arrangements throughout the world. New legislation in countries which have had little formal copyright law and the greater surveillance of the public use of music will undoubtedly increase dramatically throughout the 1990s and into the twenty first century.

Whilst sales figures might conceal the various forms of social consumption and local musical activity which generate copyright revenue, the expansion and exploitation of rights and the ideology of intellectual ownership is being firmly pursued by the major corporations and within the context of their existing global policies. As Ed Murphy, president of the National Music Publishers Association of America declared, when interviewed for *Billboard* magazine in 1991:

> The world wide popularity of American music has led astute publishers to realise the importance of expanding the scope of their activities to an international level. However, this globalization cannot fully succeed without adequate protection of intellectual property by means of copyright law.

World Music in a Global Triad

The activities of transnational corporations have been concentrated within a 'triad' composed of the United States, Europe and Japan. This is where the majority of the world's production and consumption has been concentrated, and these three regions accounted for 85 per cent of all computer and consumer electronic products sold in the early 1980s and was where the high technology industries 'critical to wealth generation' during this period were situated (Ohmae, 1985). The recording industry, as part of a global entertainment network, is embedded within this triad. The policies of record companies are firmly part of a process contributing to a 'cleavage' between countries integrated within this pattern and those outside of it (Henderson, 1989), continuing a process of uneven development of the world economy, and reinforcing existing divisions whereby patterns of income, status and consumption radiate out from these centres (Hymer, 1979).

The dominant markets for popular music are in the USA, Europe and Japan. The location of hardware manufacturing plants and software recording facilities follow this pattern. The global production and consumption of popular music in the 1990s is defined by the North Atlantic Anglo-American cultural movements of sounds and images, and European, USA and Japanese dominance of finance capital and hardware on which to record and reproduce these sounds and images. This is the world of music which staff in the recording industry are looking out at, and I now want to turn to the more immediate experience of work within the corporations.

Splitting up the Corporations

Previously characterised and caricatured as cautious, cumbersome, and incapable of responding to audience tastes and musical changes, record companies have undergone a process of rationalisation, restructuring and decentralisation throughout the 1980s. The centralised monoliths attacked by critics in the 1970s have attempted to introduce systems of working in small teams which enable the staff involved in day-to-day decisions about which artists to acquire and develop to work in a more autonomous and less bureaucratic environment.

Virgin Records were one of the first record companies to do this. During the 1980s as the organisation began to expand following success with such artists as The Human League, Culture Club, Simple Minds and Phil Collins the company began to acquire a huge number of artists. There was music industry gossip that Virgin had acquired a roster in excess of 130 acts and, possibly apocryphal, anecdotes circulating about the managers of artists turning up at the company's premises to find that staff didn't know who they were. The company became cumbersome and the Virgin Music group re-organised. Retaining a Virgin label, it established a separate Associated Virgin Labels (AVL) division, which was composed of a constellation of satellite companies comprising Circa, Ten, Siren, EG, Enigma and Caroline. These subdivisions retained specific label identities and focused on acquiring and developing artists, whilst the administrative and strategic aspects of sales and promotion were coordinated through a central AVL division within the music group.

In a similar way the labels of the Polygram Group (Mercury, Polydor, London, Vertigo, Fontana, Verve, Island, A & M) were operating with 'maximum autonomy' according to what senior executives referred to as a 'federal' system. The company labels were spread throughout 29 different countries where they were given the 'creative freedom and responsibility' to sign and develop artists in their own particular territories. At the same time these labels and sub-divisions were sharing international marketing and administration systems, and were tied into a sophisticated infrastructure of manufacture and distribution.

Record companies are dependent on the delivery of new recordings from established artists and the ongoing acquisition of new acts and material, and must continually decide which projects to pursue and how much to invest in them. These changes are part of an attempt, by the expanding corporations, to manage the risk that this activity entails by dismantling hierarchical working practices and devolving tasks; spreading the decision-making across small units within the corporation. These working practices, which are similar to changes occurring throughout a wide range of high technology and service industries, have altered the immediate experience of work and the working environment. They have resulted in a proliferation of project groups and team-based working practices and contributed to a blurring of previous hierarchical distinctions (Sabel, 1990). These patterns of organisation enable the corporation to adapt and respond more quickly to local circumstances, languages, laws and markets. In the recording industry it means that staff in large companies confront less daily bureaucracy and can concentrate more of their energy on artistic decision-making.

However, this autonomy is tempered by what Don Cruickshank, one of the directors at the Virgin group, described as a 'loose-tight' approach; 'loose in terms of creative freedom, but tight in terms of financial control'. Splitting company operations into semi-autonomous divisions and labels makes it easier for corporate management to assess the creative activity, commercial success, management competence and ultimately the financial effectiveness of each component part. Control is exerted through monitoring and surveillance, rather than direct intervention into daily decision-making, enabling the corporation to identify and deal with any parts of the company which might not be achieving the desired goals and objectives.

A further way in which corporations have attempted to re-organise in order to manage the identification of new artists and products is by embarking on collaborative arrangements, joint ventures and licensing deals with small companies.

The Romance of Independence

Changes in post-war popular music have often been explained as a response to an antagonistic relationship between large bureaucratic major corporations and small economically independent companies. According to this argument the small independent companies have been more receptive to creative changes ('closer to the street') and have periodically challenged the practices and market dominance of the major corporations.

The ground-breaking independent record company – the 'indie' – imbued with connotations of a radical, alternative and more sincere way of producing music, has become part of the everyday theory of rock fans. It operated as a romantic ideology informing the buying habits of a student-based subcultural group in Britain during the 1980s, and resulted in the construction of an audience whose musical taste had been informed by making this direct connection between the value of the music and the record label releasing it. As a senior artist and repertoire manager at one label told me, when discussing different audiences for music in 1989: 'There's a whole indie section. Kids that will only buy records that are on an indie label . . . which is why we sometimes concoct labels to try and fool them.'

In the late 1980s a number of companies released material on 'bogus' independent labels in an attempt to target this audience, and in order to establish a market base for artists who required a certain 'street credibility'. This tactic did not necessarily fool the audience, but it did lead to some confusion and debate about the meaning of independence – did it refer to the record label, or a type of music and attitude? In the United States, where music which was being referred to as 'indie' in the UK was being categorised as 'alternative', similar practices were occurring. A number of commentators were denouncing the way in which 'alternative' had merely become a marketing term and were voicing criticisms similar to those in the UK about the use of 'phoney indies' by major labels.

However, the introduction of such labels by some companies did not become an integral part of record company practice – more a short term tactic at a particular moment. It also became less relevant as companies established more formal links with small labels and 'indie' began to lose its association with alternative music.

Whilst the dynamic between major and independent companies may partially explain some of the changes in popular music during the 1950s and early 1960s in the United States (Gillett, 1983; Chapple and Garofalo, 1977), and has a certain relevance when considering the punk period of 1976–78 in Britain (Laing, 1985b), and the music industry in 'small countries' during the 1970s (Wallis & Malm, 1984), it has tended to ossify into an ideological dogma which overemphasises the degree of conflict between two ideal types of company.

Phil Hardy (1984) has proposed a less oppositional three way grouping of companies into: Transnational corporations which have their own manufacturing and distribution facilities: Majors which are middle range companies using the manufacturing and distribution networks of the transnationals: and small independent companies which negotiate separate custom deals with manufacturers and distributors. Although this avoids simplistically reducing the dynamics of the music industry to a small independent versus major conglomerate dichotomy, this description itself has become a historical snapshot. In the following section I want to suggest that the concept of independence has become somewhat misleading, and characterise the recording industry as a web of major and minor companies.

Webs of Majors and Minors

Running parallel to the internal reorganisation of record companies has been the forging of external links between large corporate labels and small companies through investment arrangements, licensing deals and joint ventures. These connections have provided regionally based small companies with finance, arrangements for manufacture and distribution, and the opportunity to reach markets in other territories; and have given large corporations access to an external source of repertoire and enabled them to use small companies as 'research and development' divisions (Hardy, 1984). So, for example, the Food label negotiated a funding deal with EMI in 1988. This allowed Food to operate as a small autonomous label acquiring and developing the artists it chose, and at the same time provided access to higher levels of investment and more sophisticated marketing, distribution and promotion methods. EMI retained the first option to Food artists, and the right to review and renew their arrangements with Food every six months. In a similar way Alan McGhee relaunched his independent label Creation, renamed as Elevation and financed the label through an arrangement with Warner Music in Britain and EMI in the United States. McGhee contrasted working as a 'pure' independent to working through a corporation:

> Last year Creation gave The Weather Prophets £3,000 to live on; this year WEA, through Elevation is giving them £100,000. Equally, if their new LP had come out on Creation it would have sold about 40,000 copies. On Elevation I reckon it'll do somewhere between 100 and 150,000 (Kelly, 1987, p 30).

A slightly different approach was involved in a joint venture which brought together staff from different independent operations within the organisation of a major company. Promoter Mike Alway, head of Rough Trade Records Geoff Travis, and journalist Dave McCullough formed the Blanco Y Negro label in order to develop artists through WEA; a liaison, which in the words of Geoff Travis combined the 'maverick spirit with a sense of economics'. Other small companies were also forming complex links. The Newcastle-based label Kitchenware Records negotiated separate deals for each of its artists with major corporations; Prefab Sprout through Sony, Martin Stephenson through the London label of the Polygram group and The Fatima Mansions through MCA. The Rhythm King label established deals in which two major companies – EMI and Sony – would provide finance for the acquisition and development of artists.

Rock fans and critics have often been suspicious and critical of these types of arrangements, accusing both artists and labels of 'selling out'. However, the idea that independence inevitably provides an alternative and more sincere form of musical production – apart from romanticising both 'amateurishness' (Kelly, 1987) and petit-bourgeois entrepreneurial capitalism – is based on selecting a few 'pioneering' labels such as Atlantic, Island, Factory and Rough Trade as embodying an ethic in contrast to the dominant practices of the record industry at the time. This completely ignores the range of companies which have sheltered beneath the umbrella term of 'independent', and the values and practices these labels share with the larger corporations. Some small companies merely provide a specific type of music, often acquired through back catalogues and distributed by mail order, to a small, dedicated and often nostalgic audience (for 1960s psychedelia, folk, or rock 'n' roll). A few may well be attempting to engage in an aesthetically or ideologically alternative form of music making, but a large proportion of independent companies have been producing music with the aim of selling it on the commercial markets of the world. It is typical for a small company involved in developing and recording new artists to have been formed, not for any commitment to alternative music, but because they could not get material released by a major company. As Jazz Summers, who formed the Big Life label and who achieved success with Yazz, Lisa Stansfield and the Soup Dragons, remarked: 'I couldn't get Yazz signed and I got a bad deal for Coldcut, so I decided to do it myself. So we put together Big Life Records.'

Small companies, initially formed independently of major corporate capital, have undoubtedly played a role in popularising musical styles and opening up spaces within the music industry at specific moments in the past. However, as the conventional distinctions between small independent companies and large bureaucratic corporations have broken down it is misleading to maintain a view of independents as oppositional mavericks on the margins. A more flexible division, using less pejorative terminology, would be to distinguish between major and minor companies. Majors increasingly split into semi-autonomous working groups and label divisions, and minor companies connected to these by complex patterns of ownership, investment, licensing, formal and informal and sometimes deliberately obscured relationships. This has resulted in complex and confusing, continually shifting corporate constellations which are difficult to plot, as deals expire, new relationships are negotiated, new acquisitions made and joint ventures embarked upon. At the end of 1990 the trade magazine *Music Week* reported that 82 different labels were operating 'under the banner' of the Polygram group in the UK alone. Which companies are owned, part owned or licensed becomes difficult to ascertain. If it can be done, what it means in terms of working practices becomes equally hard to infer, as the distinctions between an inside and outside, and between centre and margins, has given way to a web of mutually dependent work groupings radiating out from multiple centres.

These organisational webs, of units within a company and connections to smaller companies, enable entertainment corporations to gain access to material and artists, and to operate a coordinating, monitoring and surveillance operation rather than just centralised control. The corporation can still shape the nature of these webs through the use and distribution of investment. But it is a tight-loose approach, rather than a rigidly hierarchical form of organisation; tight enough to ensure a degree of predictability and stability in dealing with collaborators, but loose enough to manoeuvre, redirect or even reverse company activity (Robins, 1991). This means that staff within major entertainment companies and the labels connected to them experience a large degree of autonomy in carrying out their daily work, and the bulk of this book is concerned with how staff work within and across these corporate webs.

In this chapter I have argued that the recording industry has become an integral element within a global process of entertainment production and consumption. I have sought to make three specific, but interrelated points:

1. The production and consumption of musical recordings, and exploitation of the rights to these recordings, has been dominated by a few major transnational corporations, frequently operating strategic mutual alliances to further their shared interests. These corporate groups have pursued increasingly global policies, and at the same time expanded their interests across various media and information technologies in response to the opportunities opened up by the prospect of media synergy.

2. The world markets for popular music, as defined and actively constructed by these corporations, have been dominated by Anglo-American recordings and artists. This has increased the global influence of artistic and commercial decisions made in Britain, the United States and more recently Europe and Japan, and systematically limited the commercial opportunities for local artists in regions throughout the world.

3. In order to deal with geographical expansion, and the increasingly complex artistic and commercial decisions involved in putting the sounds and images of pop together within this setting, the major corporations have reorganised and adopted more flexible working arrangements; based on internal subdivisions and a complexity of external connections which has resulted in webs of major and minor companies.

In Chapter 3 I will begin describing how staff work within these corporate webs. Before this, however, I want to provide a complementary discussion to this chapter by looking at the relationship between music and technology.

2

MUSIC MACHINES

Technology and Popular Music

Technologies for producing and reproducing sounds and images have decisively influenced the way in which popular music has been composed, communicated and consumed throughout the twentieth century, and have been central to the development of a global entertainment industry. This chapter is about the relationship between technology and popular music in three broad areas; the organisation of the recording industry, the composition of sounds and the consumption of music.

My aim is not to assess the impact of technology *on* popular music, as if technology was an external phenomenon exerting an influence on some pure and abstract form of expression known as music, but to suggest through my discussion that musical meanings and practices at any one time cannot be separated from their realisation in and through particular technologies, and the way in which specific groups and individuals have struggled to exert control over the use and definition of these technologies. This chapter is, therefore, a deliberate attempt to avoid the sharp division which has split recent discussions between pessimistic techno-phobes who condemn technology for contaminating the authentic character of human expression and corrupting musical skills, and optimistic techno-euphorics who have celebrated the 'appropriation' of technology in the act of consuming commodities. Before specifically addressing these two positions I shall briefly look at the way in which the recording industry has responded to technological changes throughout the twentieth century.

Technology and the Changing Recording Industry

Thomas Edison, after experimenting with telegraphy, telephones and electromagnetism, first demonstrated his cylindrical phonograph in December 1877, and shortly afterwards drew up the following list of possible applications:

1. Letter writing and all kinds of dictation without the aid of a stenographer.
2. Phonographic books that will speak to the blind without effort on their part.
3. The teaching of elocution.

4. The reproduction of music.
5. The 'family record' – a registry of sayings, reminiscences, by members of a family in their own voices, and of words of dying persons.
6. Music boxes and toys.
7. Clocks that would announce in articulate speech the time for going home, going to meals etc.
8. The preservation of language by exact reproduction of the manner of pronouncing.
9. Educational purposes; such as the preserving of the explanations made by a teacher, so that the pupil can refer to them at any moment, and spelling or other lessons placed upon the phonograph for convenience in committing to memory.
10. Connection with the telephone, so as to make that instrument an auxiliary in the transmission of permanent and invaluable records, instead of being the recipient of momentary and fleeting communications (Schicke, 1974, pp 12–13).

Frustrated with its shortcomings, Edison became more interested in the electric light and dismissed the phonograph as 'a mere toy with no commercial value'. However, when Bell Laboratories introduced an improved version of this machine, the cylindrical graphophone in 1886, Edison returned to his invention and began developing it as an office dictation device. Shortly afterwards a number of regional phonographic companies were formed in the United States, and began using the phonograph to produce recorded entertainment for penny arcades and amusement centres. Most notable was the 'nickel-in-the-slot' machine introduced by Louis Glass, a development which began pushing the phonograph in the direction of musical recording and entertainment rather than towards the other possibilities identified by Edison.

Hence, there was no inevitable logic to the way in which the recorded sound industry developed, as some writers have implied (Struthers, 1987). The initial technology introduced by Edison provided a range of possibilities, but its subsequent development, at least initially, was shaped by the competition between entrepreneurs, inventors and speculators, and the way in which the public responded to the machine. Phonographic technology was introduced following scientific investigations which also resulted in radio and television, and the subsequent use of the phonograph as an entertainment medium parallels the way in which radio and television evolved: Raymond Williams has pointed out that radio and television, unlike previous communication technologies, were primarily devised for transmission and reception as abstract processes. Not only did the supply of broadcasting facilities precede the demand; 'the means of communication preceded their content' (Williams, 1990, p 25).

In retrospect it can be argued that capitalist corporations have established a form of technology which has suited a 'commoditised entertainment industry', and have endeavoured to maintain the designs most conducive to exerting control over the producers and consumers of recordings (Struthers, 1987). However, this was by no means inevitable. Early technologies became available before their potential was realised and before they were subject to the pressure of capitalist competition and commodity production.

Discs and Cylinders

Back in the early 1890s a number of phonographic companies had been formed in the United States and were producing recordings on cylinders, with music categorised into such genres as 'Sentimental', 'Topical', 'Comic', 'Irish' and 'Negro', and the largest pay-as-you-listen phonograph salon in the world had been opened in Paris. Whilst an industry was beginning to form around the cylindrical phonograph, Emile Berliner had already developed a flat disc gramophone which played on a turntable and was predicting its future use as a home entertainment medium. The flat disc gramophone, first patented in 1887, was launched commercially by the United States Gramophone Company in 1895, and is conventionally identified as *the* technological development which led to the modern recording industry. However, it was not established immediately. In the same year in which it was launched Edison reassessed his initial reservations about the commercial potential of the phonograph and remarked; 'I will yet live to see the day when phonographs will be almost as common in houses as pianos and organs are today' (Schicke, 1974, p 34).

A period followed when no company or manufacturer held a monopoly of the technology of sound reproduction, and during which there was intense rivalry between cylinder and disc producers. Companies competed by making technical modifications which improved the sound quality, appearance and use of machines, and used the legal system to contest issues of ownership and to enforce patent rights. Complex disputes arose, initiated by different parties, over the use of technologies and of terminologies, and Berliner as one of the co-founders of The Victor Talking Machine Company initiated an aggressive advertising and promotion campaign.

The competition between the two technologies was played out until the combined influence of the economic recession of 1907 and the commercial pressures which led Edison and his associates to introduce a diamond disc phonograph in 1912 effectively sealed the fate of the cylinder. The disc gramophone was technically superior; it produced greater levels of sound, took up less storage space and discs could be duplicated more efficiently. It was also better suited to the capitalist system of production and distribution because it was harder to make pirate copies and, hence, the companies were able to control its manufacture more easily. Unlike cylinders, discs could not be manufactured anywhere, but required organised pressing plants (Read & Welch, 1976). This latter point is a theme which resonates throughout the history of recording, up to debates in the 1980s and 1990s about home taping and technology being used to infringe upon and steal 'intellectual property', and the attempts by record companies to derive revenue from all of the potential ways in which music may be reproduced.

Electrical Connections

After the 1914–18 war the expanding recording industry was given impetus by the introduction of the electrical microphone, a technology developed during the war and first used for musical recording by two former British Army Officers in 1920. Although recording companies were rather slow to begin using it, this device enabled sound to be picked up by a microphone and translated into electro-magnetic signals. It no longer required musicians or singers to crowd around a single acoustic recording horn and adjust the volume of their performance as the recorded signal could be boosted after the take. This immediately introduced a degree of flexibility into the recording process and provided an early technical supportive role for sound engineers.

During this period record companies were owned and run by engineers, inventors, and stock market speculators, who had little connection with the impresarios previously involved in publishing, theatres, performing and artist management (Frith, 1987a). These owners pursued electrical connections, rather than just artistic or entertainment options, because companies were dependent on the technologies of musical production and reproduction for the communication of recordings. Hence the recording industry initially developed as part of a wider 'electrical goods industry' (Frith, 1987b). Pekka Gronow has noted the way in which:

> The leading companies owed a considerable part of their success to technological innovation. They were not just record companies, they had to produce complete systems of recording technology. For the consumer, they offered both recordings and the equipment to play them on (and a critical observer of the cabinet phonographs of the 1910s might say that records were a sideline to help the sale of furniture). For the industry itself they had to develop recording equipment, mastering processes and presses (1983, p 55).

From its very earliest days the recording industry was organised around the connection between; a) industrial manufacturing equipment used to produce recordings; b) consumer furniture necessary to re-produce these recordings; c) the complex of equipment and devices necessary to coordinate this. The owners of record companies therefore sought to organise and exert control over the technologies of sound production and those of its consumption. This entailed the acquisition of basic components and technologies and considerable cross licensing, with companies frequently merging to acquire patents and gain access to technologies. These connections, between the record industry and electronics industry, were symbolised by the acquisitions which led to the merger in 1931 of the Gramophone Company and Columbia Gramophone to form Electrical and Musical Industries Ltd, known by its acronym of EMI.

Audio Visual Star Connections

The emergence of radio and the application of sound in the cinema were two further technological developments which changed the way in which music was experienced, and contributed to a further reorganisation of the recording industry. Companies initially structurating around the electrical connections of sound technologies now began to re-organise to become an integral part of a wider entertainment industry.

From its earliest days radio programmers used recorded music. Radio became a primary source of music listening and an important medium for marketing recordings (Barnard, 1989). The cinema provided a further opportunity for placing songs and recordings of music, and formal links began to be established between the entertainment media. Radio, recording and cinema were also related through the use of the electrical microphone. The microphone had been developed further by Western Electric and the company were able to claim a royalty on all electrical recordings and became the principal manufacturer of theatre talkie installations (Frith, 1987a). The connections between the film, music and radio industries began leading to the emergence of the record company professionals who were required to supervise and coordinate the production and placing of musical recordings across these media, and at the same time created the conditions for the emergence of the star system in its modern form.

Although the emergence of 'pop' is often identified with Elvis Presley, who was the first popular music star to appeal almost exclusively to a young teenage consumer, it was Bing Crosby who was the first modern star to be created via the connection between radio, records and film. In many respects Crosby became the archetypal pop star, and had a direct impact on the development of the mass-entertainment industry in these formative years. Through strategies adopted by Crosby himself, his brother and manager Everett, and Jack Knapp the general manager of the Brunswick Record Company, the Crosby persona was divided between records, radio and films and carefully promoted across these three media. Houlton has observed that:

> The consumption of one Crosby-commodity while satisfying one particular demand would also have the effect of increasing the demand for the other two commodities. Thus, when Bing Crosby made a radio broadcast it stimulated the sales of his records and attracted an audience for his films (1967, p 47).

Not only did Crosby use the available technologies of communication to constitute himself as a star across various media, he took an active interest in the development of electrically transmitted broadcasting and magnetic tape recording. Electro-magnetic tape equipment had initially been developed by German engineers during the Second World War. As the German patents were cancelled by the Allies as part of the war reparations, Crosby – realising the importance of this hardware to his future career – was able to use the institutions established around him to finance the development and introduction of the Ampex tape recorder; a machine which was launched commercially with Bing Crosby Enterprises as its first distributor (Houlton, 1967). In a similar way Bing Crosby's companies were actively involved in the early research and development of video tape recording and broadcasting equipment (Keen, 1987).

In producing their work, artists are consumers of the technology of musical production, and they always have certain requirements which manufacturers attempt to monitor and respond to. The early piano makers were keen to encourage established composers such as Liszt and Chopin to use and endorse their products (Chanan, 1988), as have been the manufacturers of drum kits, electric guitars and synthesizers. Successful and influential musicians such as Madonna and Pete Townsend, and 'user groups' composed of professional musicians and technicians, have regularly been utilised in the development of instrument technologies for both research design and marketing purposes (Théberge, 1990a, 1990b). In this way the technical and aesthetic requirements of musicians and performers has had a direct influence on the way technologies have been introduced, and the way in which they have been mediated through performance and product endorsement.

The Manipulation of Sound: Magnetic Tape, Multi-Track and Midi

Electro-magnetic tape and the tape recorder gradually replaced the technique of recording onto cumbersome wax master discs. Magnetic tape had a number of advantages. It produced sound of superior fidelity, it could be used and re-used, recordings of greater length could be made without interruption, and tapes could be cut and edited together. Tape was more economical and was soon being used in films, radio broadcasting and in record production.

During the 1950s two-track tape recording was developed and in 1958 the Shure Brothers company introduced a four-channel tape recorder, which very soon became an integral part of the recording industry. This enabled musicians to accompany themselves and to add to their own recordings by using the technique of over-dubbing. Many artists immediately began using this, and The Beatles' *Sergeant Pepper* album, recorded on two four-track tape recorders and released in 1967, has often been cited as the most popular example of the early imaginative use of overdubbing techniques in pop. Shortly afterwards the eight track recorder was introduced into studios, and during the 1970s studios increasingly used 16, 24, 32 and 48 track recording equipment.

Stereo sound was initially introduced to the public through recordings of classical music and sound effects but soon became integral to the techniques of mixing a musical recording, enabling sounds to be positioned between the two speakers to create various realistic or surrealistic effects. In the late 1970s digital recording techniques became available as a result of the development of cheap microprocessors and computer technology. Digital recording enabled even greater sound manipulation as it was no longer necessary to store sound on tape in wave form. Instead, sounds could be encoded within a computer memory in binary electrical pulses. This technique became built into synthesizers such as the Fairlight, Synclavier, and Emulator. These allowed sounds to be recorded and stored in a random access memory, manipulated and modified at will and then retrieved.

The introduction of a computer system known as MIDI (Musical Instrument Digital Interface) enabled various instruments to be connected up together, allowing composition to take place within a computer's memory without the need of an acoustic recording environment in the studio. Hence, a composition could be produced in a confined space via the technology and a mixing desk. 'Studio' quality recording can now take place in any location, and the digital signals can be transmitted over distances using both satellite and fibre optic technology.

Musical Dialogues Across Space and Time

These technological changes have transformed the organisation of popular music by creating the conditions where the composition of a musical event need not be confined to one performance recorded in 'real time' on a specific day at one location. Prior to multi-tracking techniques the relationship between sounds was controlled at the time of recording. The frequency responses of the recorded sounds could be equalised in postproduction, and the tape could be physically edited by cutting out unwanted noises and by splicing together pieces of tape. But the manipulation of the relationship *between* sounds was very limited (Tankel, 1990). Multi-tracking techniques and digital recording, however, have enabled pieces of sound to be added by a different person (or by the same person from a different source) as a musical composition is put together, using a different machine on a different day, or in another part of the world on the same day. As producer and musician Nile Rogers enthusiastically explained in the mid 1980s:

> We're working out systems where if somebody who lives in England, say, has a system similar to what I have, and he's got a track and he wants me to play on it, well, he can send it to me over the satellite to New York. My system can then pick it up. It will go down on tape. I can listen to it, put my guitar overdub on it, send it back to him, and it'll be all digital information. It will sound exactly the same as when I played it. And it'll be clear as a bell and it'll be dynamite. Right here in his home as if I were playing it with him. We just transfer the messages to each other digitally. The quality is perfect. Now, a lot of people would argue about that, but to me that's great, that's efficient. Now I don't have to go there and move into a hotel, and raise the $20,000 budget or even hassle with England. I think that's a great thing. In fact, that's more communication, not less. I can play on your record if you're anywhere (Fox, 1986, p 376).

These changes have been condemned for leading to a decline in the social character of musical practices. Popular music making, particularly in folk, jazz and rock, has often been eulogised as a collective form of expression based on interaction, personal exchanges and communication between musicians. Electronic technologies and multi-track recording techniques have been criticised for destroying this and 'abstracting' the individual from the performance. Frederickson, for example, has argued that technology has transformed traditional conventions of music making by separating musicians from one another; in place of musical dialogues, there is a perpetual monologue. Instead of communicating with others, the musician 'interfaces with a diskette' (1989, p 204).

The first problem with this type of argument is that music making has never been simply a collective act. Musical instruments have always been used for individual solitary expression and for collective composition. Apart from immediately enabling individuals such as Stevie Wonder (*Talking Book*), and Mike Oldfield (*Tubular Bells*) to realise critically acclaimed and commercially successful compositions in dialogue with themselves, multi-track (and then digital) technology has changed the character of the dialogue with other musicians, rather than simply replaced it with a monologue.

Multi-track recording and the diskette *does* provide the opportunity for a dialogue, although this perhaps takes the form of a 'simulation' of collective activity – a sequence of reactions with the passing backwards and forwards of tape or discs on which a track is being built up, rather than a pure 'interaction' (Théberge, 1989), as Chet Atkins and Mark Knopfler found when they recorded the LP *Neck and Neck* together in 1990. The composition of this album is interesting here because Knopfler spoke of attempting to gain 'an organic feel' and placed much emphasis on the use of 1930s and 1950s Martin and Gibson guitars. However, Knopfler himself acknowledged that the recording of the album was not equally as 'authentic'. The two musicians worked in their own small studios on different sides of the Atlantic rather than writing, performing and recording 'live' together (Denselow, 1990).

The Mediations of Sound and Vision

The audio-visual connections established by the meeting of music and cinema were extended by the advent of television. The introduction of consumer television coincided with the emergence of rock'n'roll and provided a medium for beaming the image of the performer into homes across the United States. Simon Frith (1988a) has pointed out that television became central to the way in which 'youth music' was understood and provided the imagery which explained rock and roll – Elvis Presley, in particular, became a youth icon through his appearances on network variety shows.

The introduction of consumer music video in the 1970s increased the importance of television for communicating the sounds and images of popular music. Video emerged through a complex process of research, experimentation and competition between different interests, punctuated with false starts and abandoned or neglected possibilities. As early as 1927 John Logie Baird had been experimenting with a video disc system. But it was not until the 1960s that the video tape system became possible, and the 1970s when it began to be introduced into the home (Keen, 1987).

Alan Durant (1984) has argued that, apart from its use during the twentieth century on radio and disc, music has always been experienced as part of the pleasure of seeing; and music video has been described as heir to older visual elements of performance and spectacle (Cubitt, 1991), and as marking a return to the main tradition of musical experience (Laing, 1985a). Although representing a 'return' to a particular tradition in some ways, the relationship between popular music and the star image as presented through films and then television has been given greater emphasis by the growth of video. Music video has become an essential element within the pop process and has been taken increasingly seriously by record companies due to its potential for simultaneously reaching diverse audiences around the world without needing the physical presence of the artist. Music video has therefore been another technology which has contributed to record company re-organisation, increasingly formalising the process of visual composition and generating a demand for yet more professional mediators – stylists, publicity and image experts and video directors.

Throughout the twentieth century the production of popular music has increasingly involved a process of composition in which sounds and images are combined, modified, mixed and communicated across space and time. This has required ever greater coordination, organisation and investment, and the involvement of increasing numbers of specialist recording industry staff. Technology has been central in the re-organisation of record companies into an elaborate entertainment industry, and generated the conditions which have required the ever greater involvement of staff to manage the production of sound and vision discussed here, and negotiate the organisational webs outlined in Chapter 1.

Technophobia: Technology as False

In the preceding discussion I have drawn attention to the way in which the technologies of multi-track and digital recording have changed the way in which music is composed, and altered the dialogues which occur between musicians. I now want to pursue this further by explicitly focusing on a form of techno-phobia which has often informed accounts of the relationship between popular music and technology.

Fears that technology has been steadily leading to a loss of the human and authentic qualities of musical creativity became widespread in a range of intellectual, artistic and professional discourses during the 1980s due to the way in which cheap synthesizers, samplers and computerised recording equipment were transforming studio-based composition and performance practices. Technology was seen to be replacing musicians with machines, enabling charlatans to create music by stealing other people's ideas and in the process leading to a decline in musical skills. The way in which reproductive technologies enabled artists to mime and 'lip-sync' to preprogrammed material led to accusations that record buyers and audiences attending public performances were being deceived and confused about the authentic origins of the musical material.

Such accusations are not particularly new. They are merely the latest episode in a longer running argument which has claimed that the use of technology in popular music has been steadily devaluing musicianship and alienating musicians from both their artistic creations and from audiences. This argument can be found throughout a range of writing over a number of years and has frequently been associated with a form of anti-technological purism (Middleton, 1990). Simon Frith (1986) has noted how 'the implication that technology is somehow false or falsifying' has been a recurring motif throughout twentieth-century popular music. From criticisms made by senior management at the BBC, of the way in which the microphone encouraged 'crooning' and not real singing, to the way in which folk audiences condemned the use of electric guitars and amplification equipment, and way rock critics attacked 'artificial ' synthesizer-based disco and dance music.

This type of reasoning can be traced back to the 'mass culture' critique of the 1920s and 1930s when it was argued that the technology of mechanical reproduction was resulting in standardised musical products which were being transmitted to listeners who were alienated from each other and estranged from the authentic source of the music (Frith, 1983). Threads of this approach can be traced back further to the romantic critique of industrial capitalism in the nineteenth century with its concern about machine manufacturing and industrialisation replacing spontaneous independent creation with formalised imitative work (Williams, 1963). In the following discussion I will suggest that variations on these arguments have an even longer genealogy.

Instrument Technologies and Composition

Musical composition and performance have always depended on the instrument technologies available; whether European classical music, orally transmitted folk music, music of the different regions of the African continent or contemporary popular music with its complex industrial networks of production and distribution. The character, conventions and reception of a particular music have been shaped by the machines of sound creation. Jacques Barzun has pointed out that, once people ceased to make music with the voice alone music became 'machine-ridden' and he described Orpheus's lyre as a machine, a symphony orchestra as a regular factory for making artificial sounds, and the piano as the 'most appalling contrivance of levers and wires this side of the steam engine' (quoted in Russcol, 1981, p 200).

In Europe the introduction of the lute in the sixteenth century and the pianoforte in the eighteenth century were decisive in transforming music, from a vocal-based harmony and tonality to a more rhythmical music based around timbre and dynamics. These new instruments introduced 'a new system of combination, creating an open field for a whole new exploration of the possible expressions of musical usage. Thus Beethoven's *Sonata No. 106*, the first piece written for the piano, would have been unthinkable on any other instrument' (Attali, 1985, p 35).

In the African-American musical tradition the dialogues between banjo playing slaves from west Africa and European guitarists decisively shaped the direction and conventions of American music. A complex musical interaction followed the meeting of these two instruments, both descended fron the lute and stringed instruments of western Asia and the Arab world. The guitar, being easier to manufacture, superseded the banjo and in both its commercially produced and home made form provided the mobile music machine which enabled the blues and country traditions to emerge. At the same time, African musical skills met the techniques of European classical music in America and explicitly influenced the work of composers such as Dvořák and Henri Herz (Grunfeld, 1974).

Guitars and keyboard instruments have played a central role in the composition of twentieth century music, particularly during the pop era since the Second World War. Between the mid 1950s and the late 1970s the electric guitar was *the* fetishised symbol of the rock era. Since the early 1980s electronic keyboards have been central to a range of dance and pop music, providing a different imagery and changing the conventions of composition and performance.

It is worth dwelling on the emergence of keyboard instruments, and in particular the piano, as just one example of the way in which instrument technologies have changed the experience of music and shaped the social and cultural contexts of composition and performance. It also provides a perspective on the relationship between music and technology somewhat broader than the recent focus on electronic technologies and synthesizers. It allows a brief glimpse of debates – and despair – about music and technology to be seen reverberating back through time.

The Sound of Machinery and Musical Transvestism

In an essay first published in 1916 Edward Dent characterised the first keyboard instruments as 'labour saving devices': The organ enabled one person to admit air to several pipes simultaneously by the movement of a single key, and as the keyboard attained its modern form 'a single player could control at once as many as four or even more of these different sets of pipes . . . one man at the organ might control what would have been the work of four singers' (Dent, 1956, p 55). The adaptation of strings to the keyboard introduced even greater flexibility and composers began to arrange music previously written for separate instruments on one machine. The development of the piano increased these technical and musical possibilities further.

The first manufacturers of pianos were not attempting to create a new instrument, but were responding to requests from wealthy patrons to refine and improve the clavichord and harpsichord (Chanan, 1988; Ehrlich, 1976). However, the introduction of the hammer mechanism, unlike the plucked string of harpsichords, enabled the player to introduce dynamic changes by varying the amount of force applied to the keys. As a consequence 'orchestral' music began to be composed on and arranged for the piano, and the conventions of performing and aesthetic criteria by which a performance was judged began to change.

The music composed was more rhythmic due to the violent way in which the new machine created sound, and the performer began to assume the role of individual virtuoso seated at the instrument. Dramatic performance conventions began to be adopted; arms would be raised at the end of passages and the body would be hunched to accentuate the dynamics of the music. The piano enabled musicians to turn their performance into a visual spectacle and this was personified in Liszt (1811–86) who whilst seated at the instrument pulled faces, leapt up and down the keyboard, kicked away the piano stool, writhed like a python and moved his head back and forth like a man watching a game of tennis (Hildebrandt, 1988). With its scope for individual expression and dynamic range, the piano provided the technological possibilities for a new musical sensibility. It became 'the ideal instrument for the expression of musical romanticism', with its aesthetic of emotional effect, and sounds used for association, evocation and imitation (Parish, 1944).

When modern synthesizers are used to emulate 'real' instruments they are often criticised for not having the same quality or 'feel'. Musicians using them are accused of imitation or, occasionally, an act of outright deception. It is interesting to find similarities in the way in which early keyboard instruments were used. Edward Dent has described how the composer Byrd (1543–1623) incorporated 'trumpet effects' into his compositions for the virginal, and notes that a gradual change in trumpet style emerged as a result of:

> the trumpet effects in the harpsichord music of Purcell, Alessandro and Domenico Scarlatti down to Schubert, Mendelssohn and Chopin or later. It is absurd to suppose that a single sound on the harpsichord or pianoforte could ever be mistaken for the sound of a trumpet; but play a familiar and characteristic trumpet phrase, and any one can respond to the stimulus of association (1956, p 57).

The introduction of new instrument technologies changes the relationship of instruments and sounds to one another and results in complex patterns of influence and mimesis. Frederic Grunfeld has noted a similar change in the use of the guitar. A Spanish guitar manual published in 1799 informed its readers that the guitar 'can easily imitate other instruments, such as flutes, trumpets or oboes' (Grunfeld, 1974, p 140). For Grunfeld this is an ominous sign of an impending 'instrumental transvestism' which was to become a prominent characteristic of the European romantic era, and seems to have continued ever since. But the influences were often more subtle than straightforward imitation. In an account of the life and work of Scott Joplin, Preston (1989) described how the plucking technique used by banjo players directly influenced the way in which pianists played their instruments and contributed to the development of the characteristic style of ragtime music.

One classically trained record producer and arranger I spoke to when carrying out the research for this book complained that synthesizer players composing on computers were writing music according to the requirements of technology rather than with 'feeling and musicality'. In light of such a frequently made comment it is interesting to note what Dent has to say about Beethoven's use of the piano:

> Paradoxical as it may appear, it is to Beethoven's deafness that we owe his extraordinary development of the possibilities of the pianoforte. Totally indifferent as he must necessarily have been to the actual quality of sounds produced by the instrument, as compared with the same sounds produced by other instruments, he viewed the pianoforte in its true light, as a mechanical means by which one player could indicate in a convenient and sufficiently intelligible way the huge range of sounds offered by the orchestra (1956, p 60).

In a social history of the piano, Dieter Hildebrandt has also highlighted the technical way in which music was produced by this 'highly complex machine'. Referring to calculations by Pollini he notes that 8000 mechanical movements were required in just one and a half minutes of the playing of Chopin's *Eighth Prelude*, and that Schumann's *Toccata (Op. 7)* required 40 000 movements in just five minutes of playing. Beethoven's *Hammerklavier Sonata*, a title explicitly referring to the machinery involved – hammer keyboard – demanded almost a quarter of a million movements within the instrument. In awe, Hildebrandt stands back and views the piano as 'a monument to one and a half centuries of engineering genius. Tinkers and dreamers, carpenters and tanners, mechanics and musicians all played their part in this one small field of human endeavour' (1988, pp 151/2).

Electronic Technologies of Composition

In more recent discussions of recording and reproduction equipment it has been argued that the emergence of electronic technologies mark a significant and dramatic transition from the previous mechanical devices. What has occurred, according to one such writer, is a change from 'passive' and 'subservient' technology which acted as a vehicle for musical information to a 'functional interpenetration of art and technology' (Schlem, 1981, p 151). This type of argument, however, tends to overlook the way in which musical creation and technology have always been related. Technology has never been passive, neutral or natural. Music has, for centuries, been created through the interaction between 'art' and technology. As Richard Middleton has pointed out; 'technology and musical technique, content and meaning, generally develop together, dialectically' (Middleton, 1990, p 90). The piano introduced a new way of combining sounds using the mechanical engineering of the nineteenth century, and in a similar way studio technology has enabled composers to create musaics and musicollages using the electronic engineering of the twentieth century.

In this respect sound recording equipment is not just a means of reproducing musical works but is itself an instrument of composition. In the early years of the twentieth century the phonograph was overtly used as an instrument by avant-garde composers. During the 1930s the French composer Darius Milhaud, along with the German musicians Paul Hindemith and Ernst Toch, began to use variable speed phonographs in their work in order to alter the characteristics of pre-existing sounds; and Arthur Honegger was advocating a machine aesthetic, declaring that the future promised a music which would no longer be constrained by the human capabilities which limit the scope and duration of the sounds which are made (Ernst, 1977; Frederickson, 1989).

From early in the twentieth century sound recording and reproduction equipment were used by avant-garde composers as instruments of musical composition. It was not until the rock era that popular artists such as The Beatles and Frank Zappa began to employ these techniques, and then in a self-consciously mannered style derivative of the European art tradition. In later years technologies of musical recording and reproduction such as portable cassette players and record turntables were used, initially by black urban subcultures in the United States, to create the scratching and mixed sound collages of rap and hip hop (Toop, 1984). Like the guitar and keyboard instruments, twentieth-century recording and reproduction equipment has continually opened up new possibilities, required new skills, created new aesthetics and generated new social relations of musical production.

The Ever Declining Art of the Real Musician

The art of composing music has never been an act based solely on individual creative inspiration. It has always been a technical as well as a musical act. When the muse drops inspiration from the sky it usually meets the technical range and limitations of instruments and is expressed according to particular musical forms and conventions, whether a symphony, folk ballad or three-minute pop song.

In his essay on the piano in 1916 Edward Dent ultimately argued that the introduction of the piano, and in particular its use by Beethoven and Wagner, was responsible for ruining the art of singing. This is an assertion which sounds remarkably similar to the accusation that pop musicians using synthesizers, drum machines and samplers, have ruined the art of playing 'real' instruments. In turn, this is not so different to the responses of musicians and critics in the late sixteenth and early seventeenth centuries when the guitar began to replace the lute. Writers in France and Spain complained that the guitar no longer required the 'skills and disposition' of the lute and was leading to a decline in musical standards. In 1611 the Inquisitor Sebastián de Covarrubias wrote that the guitar was 'like a cowbell' which even a, 'stable boy who is not a musician' could play (Grunfeld, 1974, pp 91–106).

Musical composition and performance practice is not something which exists in some pure state (which has subsequently been corrupted) outside of its immediate realisation in and through particular technologies and techniques. Music machines have continually provided new opportunities for sound creation, changed the existing relationships between instruments, and changed the nature of musical skills. Undoubtedly certain existing skills have been made redundant as a result of technological change. But fresh skills and musical possibilities have been continually introduced. The argument that musical technologies are in some way false and lead to a decline in the skills of music making, accompanied by a nostalgia for what was seen as more real and authentic, is not new and has recurred throughout the history of European music.

Consumption and the Celebration of Technology

Alongside the pessimistic condemnations of musical technology has been a more optimistic strand of reasoning. This approach frequently derives from Walter Benjamin's essay on 'The Work of Art in the Age of Mechanical Reproduction' (1970). In this essay Benjamin was mainly concerned with the visual arts and argued that the technologies of reproduction were leading to a breakdown in the traditional authority of art. The loss of the 'aura' associated with an authentic original work could lead to a more democratic form of art in which possibilities would arise for participation in both its creation and appreciation. Writers drawing on this approach, often combined with a concept of symbolic resistance derived from youth subcultural theory (Hebdige, 1979), have tended to focus on the consumption of musical technologies. The emphasis has been on the way in which cheap recording equipment, instruments and portable cassette machines have 'decentralised' music making and provided opportunities for a wider range of people to participate in musical practices. Chambers has argued that it is in the act of consumption that opportunities arise for 'the continual appropriation of pop's technology and reproductive capacities' (1988, p 609). And in a moment of revolutionary euphoria Simon Frith declared that 'technological devices have been musicians' and audiences' most effective weapons in their continuous guerilla war against the cultural power of capital and the state' (1986, p 278).

New musical technologies have undoubtedly provided opportunities for appropriating and re-defining musical products, whether by home taping or scratching and re-mixing. Subjective identities are continually invested in and expressed through technologies such as record players, radios, video recorders and portable cassette players. Consumption is clearly not simply a passive activity. But this approach has tended to favour the way in which an individual, group or class can define a product through the meanings which emerge and are invested in it as it is appropriated and used. Little attention has been paid to the way in which the technology or product itself has shaped the experience of consumption. Whilst I do not wish to re-erect the image of consumers as passive victims of corporations and technology, in this section I want to use the example of the Sony Walkman to argue that any approach to consumption must trace the opportunities provided by commodities further back than simply their appearance on the market.

Consumer Technology: Listening to the Sound of Sony

In his memoirs and meditations on business philosophy Akio Morita, chairman and co-founder of the Sony corporation, discussed how he pursued the idea of the miniaturised portable cassette player, which came to be named the Walkman despite the reluctance of his project engineers, protestations from company accountants and a lack of enthusiasm from marketing staff (Morita et al, 1987). Not only were there reservations within the Sony corporation about the viability of a small portable cassette machine, Kozo Ohsone, one of the senior general managers at Sony, recalled that when the first Walkman was put on sale in July 1979 'our competitors, who are usually quick to market their own versions of our products, refrained from entering the market for almost a year, probably because they doubted that the Walkman would be popular with consumers' (1988, p 5). It was three months before the Walkman started selling, and as Yasuo Kuroki, the director of the Sony Design Centre also remarked, again emphasising the sense of uncertainty which surrounded its introduction; 'this was not a product we planned or launched carefully' (BBC, 1990).

Despite these initial doubts, considerable investment and effort was put into its marketing and within eight and a half years the Walkman had sold in excess of 35 million units around the world, with 85 different models being available from Sony, and countless others from their competitors. As Morita remarked:

> I do not believe that any amount of market research could have told us that the Sony Walkman would be successful, not to say a sensational hit that would spawn many imitators. And yet this small item has literally changed the music-listening habits of millions of people all around the world (1987, p 82)

The introduction of the Walkman involved the application of tape playback technology with the specific aim of creating a miniaturised, personal tape machine. Unlike early technical developments in phonography, radio and television, when different technologies were being developed by a range of entrepreneurs with no clear, agreed idea of their future application in entertainment, the Walkman was developed by a transnational corporation with quite specific intentions as to what it should be used for. It logically followed such technologies as portable gramophones, transistor radios and the car stereo – all of which enabled music to be consumed whilst on the move and provided a cultural context which informed its development and introduction. Regardless of the potential for competition with its precursors and despite the considerable uncertainty about its viability, Sony did not consider it necessary to assess its viability through market research. In this sense, it was not developed, initially, in response to identifiable public needs. As Morita explained when summing up a central tenet of Sony's philosophy; 'The public does not know what is possible, but we do. So instead of doing a lot of market research, we refine our thinking on a product and its use and try to create a market for it by educating and communicating with the public' (1987, p 79).

The Walkman is a technological device which has encoded within it a specific use and way of hearing music and has directly shaped the listening habits of millions of people. It has been celebrated by pop musicians in songs and videos, classical conductors and composers have endorsed it, and it has been heralded as 'a symbolic gadget for the nomads of modernity'. In making this claim, Iain Chambers (1990) has argued that the Walkman allows individuals to impose their own soundscape on the surrounding aural environment and, in doing so, to domesticate the external world.

In his brief celebration of these possibilities Chambers asks, rhetorically; 'Is the Walkman therefore a political act?', and answers his own question with the suggestion that this machine:

> confers a different sense on the polis. In producing a different sense of space and time, it participates in rewriting the conditions of representation: where 'representation' clearly indicates both the iconic or semiotic dimension of the everyday and potential participation in a political community (1990, p 3).

The notion that the Walkman might relate to 'participation in a political community' is somewhat obscure, to say the least. Chambers privileges a particular use of the Walkman, implying that it is somehow conducive to democratic participation due to the way it enables people to re-create their own sense of and impose their own meanings on a metropolitan environment. But the political uses of the Walkman are multiple. In February 1991 the British tabloid newspaper, the *Sunday Mirror* reported that troops who were on the 'front line' intervening in the Gulf conflict between Iraq and Kuwait were creating their own soundscapes, quite different, I imagine, to those envisaged by Chambers: 'Everyone seems to have a Walkman, and there is much discussion of what song will be played when they cross the border. Phil Collins seems to be edging it with *In The Air Tonight*' (Wills, 1991, p 6). This was undoubtedly a political act, and certainly involved participation in a political community. It is also an interesting example of a consumer technology and a specific piece of music being appropriated and redefined for use in a particular cultural context. But in viewing the use of the Walkman in such a way this example also highlights the partial perspective provided by the concept of 'appropriation' as a form of cultural politics when posited purely at the level of consumption. The uses to which consumer technologies can be put are not limitless, and greater attention needs to be paid to the way in which the music machines of production and reproduction have favoured certain experiences of music over possible alternatives.

The way in which the personal stereo enables an individual to listen to music privately in a public space does not seem to suggest a participatory experience, but sets it apart as 'the ultimate object for private listening' (Hosokawa, 1984, p 168). As an extremely private and mobile piece of musical reproduction technology, the 'politics' of the Walkman would seem to be a logical step in a continuing tendency Raymond Williams (1990) identified emerging with the communication technologies of the late nineteenth century: a shift away from communal and public technologies, such as railways and street lighting, towards forms of 'mobile privatisation'. It is one step on from the car stereo which enables bodies to be immersed in a box of sound whilst travelling along a motorway or through a city. The Walkman enables its user to take music wherever they go and exclude the external world and other human beings.

It may enable Japanese commuters to cope with crowded subway trains, but the Walkman induces a sense of solipsism. It isolates individuals from the world through music, evoking a sense of fantasy similar to that indulged in by various celebrities on the BBC Radio's *Desert Island Discs* programme, and its various imitations around the globe. Here a celebrity chooses the music they would listen to if they were isolated on a desert island (presumably with their record player and power generator, or personal stereo and a supply of batteries). As Eisenberg has observed;

The paradox of music for a desert island is right at the heart of phonography. To take the sounds of a full-fledged culture, sounds made possible by the efforts of thousands of musicians and technicians over the course of centuries, and enjoy them privately in your own good time, that's the freedom records give you. That freedom is purest when you are farthest away from society . . . the desire to be inside a record is made graphic by the desert island fantasy (1987, pp 35–36).

The Walkman allows the listener to enter a similar fantasy. To shut out society without going to a desert island.

However, the politics of the Walkman are not just about the nomads of modernity dissolving into desert island fantasies or filling their bodies with sound and viewing the city as yet another semi-detached hyper-real sound-scape. The politics of the Walkman involve issues of design, manufacture and competition for markets. Beyond the various stories of how the idea of the Walkman first came to Morita, of which the often repeated anecdote about him being struck by inspiration whilst walking the streets of New York is just one, there is an unexplored corporate history. A glimpse of this was provided by Stephen Bayley when he remarked that;

There are a lot of benign myths going around [about where Morita got the idea of the Walkman] . . . but I think the real reason is that in 1978 the radio cassette machines were separated from the tape recorder division of Sony and were put into the radio division. Japanese companies are organised into divisions which compete ferociously and the honour and the pride of the tape recorder division depended on them coming up with a new product (BBC, 1990).

The experience of consumer technology threads ever further back to political decisions made within corporations. A whole range of productive practices and decisions are implicated in the act of consumption, decisively influencing the way in which the technology might be used. The Walkman was specifically designed with a preconceived notion of its use value, to be carried on the person, fitting into the existing pockets of clothes. Once introduced into the consumer market this technological device assumed a position in relation to other artifacts and consumer goods. Its compactness, mobility and popularity has undoubtedly contributed to the declining importance of the vinyl LP, which increasingly appears cumbersome and must be played and listened to in one place. The Walkman marks a shift away from musical reproduction equipment as furniture of the home, to a portable fashion accessory of the body.

The Walkman has become synonymous with the name Sony, a name deliberately derived from the Latin word 'sonus' meaning sound, and recognised and pronounced in the same way throughout the world (Morita et al, 1987). When the consumer takes out their cassette marked with the Sony Music corporate logo, recorded by artists who are signed to Sony Music Entertainment, and plays it on their Sony Walkman, not only does the hardware meet the software. A strange tautology occurs as we listen to the sound of Sony.

Throughout the twentieth century the development and introduction of sound and visual technologies has increased the number of component parts which are required for the composition of popular music. Technologies of sound such as the microphone, magnetic tape, multi-track and digital recording have brought about a situation where music can be composed across space and time and sounds continually modified; a process involving a range of producers, engineers, re-mixers and supporting personnel. Developments in the visual media of cinema, television and video have resulted in images and iconic composition being an integral part of pop, requiring coordination and input from marketing staff, video directors, stylists and publicists. This has required ever more involvement of personnel within the music industry and it is to the work of these staff that I now turn.

3

PRIORITIES AND PREJUDICE

Artist and Repertoire
and the Acquisition of Artists

Artist and repertoire (A & R) staff are formally responsible for acquiring artists, and have usually been described as 'talent spotters' – continually engaged in seeking new acts and material. However, this is only a small part of what they do. Most of their time is devoted to working with acts who are already under contract. An A & R person can be involved in every aspect of an artist's relationship with a record company; from the initial negotiations and signing of the contract through to the rehearsal, arrangement and recording of songs, to liaising with staff employed in marketing, video production and promotion.

In the past A & R staff have often signed artists without reference to the opinions of other personnel within their record companies. However, as the costs of producing and marketing popular music have increased, and as record companies have been re-orienting themselves towards entertainment rather than just music, other divisions within the corporations have begun exerting a greater influence over the type of artists which are acquired. This book has been written at a time when some of these tensions – particularly between A & R and marketing – are becoming more sharply defined. However, as A & R staff have, historically, had the first say in proposing the type of artists and music acquired by record companies, this chapter is about the distinctive activities and beliefs which guide the work of artist and repertoire departments.

Formal Divisions and Business Affairs

All record labels, regardless of their size, identity and specific history, divide their departments or staff into the following occupations: artist and repertoire; marketing; public relations; publicity and press; radio and television promotion; sales; business affairs/finance and legal; manufacture and distribution; administration and secretarial. The organisation is coordinated by the directors of the company, with the managing director or president responsible for day-to-day policies and practices.

The work of record company departments is carried out within the general business plan of the company, which is based on the corporate strategies discussed in Chapter 1. The business affairs division (incorporating both accounting and legal staff) is involved in setting parameters to the deals that can be offered to prospective acts, and the company lawyer will often negotiate the details of a contract directly with an artist's lawyer. As Simon Frith has noted, all decisions about who to sign and record 'are basically financial and calculations have to be precisely made' (1983, p 102). However, this does not simply mean that the accounting and business affairs departments 'outweigh all the creative divisions in wielding company power' (Denisoff, 1986, p 158). Company power is not something that is exerted by an identifiable faction, such as accountants or lawyers. Record company power arises out of and is exercised through the internal and external relationships which are stretched throughout the production, mediation and consumption of popular music. Senior executives establish general policies and accountants and lawyers advocate certain business strategies, but this does not 'determine' who is signed or what is recorded. In day-to-day practice it means that staff are involved in constantly negotiating these demands as they translate the business requirements of the record company into an artistic policy.

The Artist and Repertoire Department

Unless it is a very small company the A & R department tends to be divided hierarchically and staff accorded such titles as A & R director, senior A & R manager, A & R manager and talent scout. These titles denote seniority and experience, and the work-load is often divided so that the more senior staff are responsible for the most established artists. However, the roster of artists for which individual A & R staff are responsible for is often built up in an ad-hoc way. The person who 'finds' and has the initial enthusiasm for an act will tend to form a relationship with the artist and initiate the process of negotiation for them to sign to the record company. Once the artist has been signed, this person will be responsible for overseeing the development and 'career' of that act for the A & R department. The less experienced members of staff will usually draw on the knowledge and informal guidance or be under the explicit supervision of more senior members of staff.

Successful artist and repertoire staff are some of the most highly paid personnel in the recording industry. In 1990, one A & R director quoted me the following figures as an indication of what A & R staff were earning: The 'cheapest talent scout', a school or college leaver would earn about £10,000 per annum and additionally be provided with a car and have all their expenses paid. A 'reasonably successful' A & R manager who had worked with acts for two to three years would earn approximately £40,000, and a senior A & R manager with over five years of success could earn about £100,000. The A & R director would, needless to say, earn considerably more.

In addition to these basic earnings, senior A & R staff receive cash bonuses when the recordings of their artists achieve high chart positions, and a percentage of the sales of the recordings of their artists – usually one per cent, although a small number of 'name' A & R directors are reputed to receive between two and three per cent. Not only do these figures indicate the importance placed on A & R staff, and on commercial sales, they also act as an incentive for staff to achieve success in an area in which there is considerable risk and uncertainty.

Investment, Risk and Uncertainty

Record company staff assess potential acts with a working knowledge that approximately one in eight of the artists that they sign and record will achieve the level of success required to recoup their initial investment and start to earn money for both themselves and the company. The response of the recording industry to this economic risk and commercial uncertainty has often been explained in terms of a strategy of overproduction combined with differential promotion, in which record companies attempt to cover every potential market possibility (Hirsch, 1972; Frith, 1983). A similar, but more cynical version of this is the 'mud-against-the-wall' model in which record companies rather aimlessly throw out as much product as possible in the hope that some of it will stick. Although record companies have undoubtedly employed these techniques they were more appropriate at a time when the unit costs of producing recordings was lower and the marketing involved less sophisticated. Throughout the 1980s greater levels of investment have been required to record, market and promote artists. At the beginning of the 1990s a major record company in Britain anticipated having to spend between £250,000–£330,000 over the first 12–18 months of an average deal for a new act; roughly broken down into £100,000 for advances to the artists, £150,000 for recording costs and £80,000 for basic promotional expenses.

In addition to the economic risk involved, a record company must decide whether they have enough staff with the relevant experience to accommodate a potential act. Most record labels have clearly defined the number of acts that they can accommodate at any one time. The acquisition of a new act will inevitably require the re-arrangement of rosters and re-assessment of the contracts of existing artists. It is easier for a record company to assess the economic and personal investment necessary if an act has already demonstrated its potential in some way.

Hence, the established record labels have become reluctant to seek 'raw' talent in dingy dance halls, smoky pubs or amongst the continuous stream of unsolicited recordings (demonstration tapes–'demos') that they daily receive. The major record companies have been increasingly looking for acts which have already undertaken a significant process of development, or who are able to provide a clear indication of their commercial potential. As a result of this an early 'discovery and development' role has been devolved to publishers, production companies, managers and small record companies; and these different parties actively mediate the boundaries between corporations and aspiring artists.

The Unrecorded Musicians

Very little attention has been paid to the vast number of amateur and semi-professional bands, performers and singers making music in Britain. Research by Finnegan in Milton Keynes (1989) and Cohen in Liverpool (1991) suggested that there was approximately one band for every thousand members of the population in the cities they studied. But, such estimates only include those who are sporadically visible at a local level, and do not take account of numerous singers and musicians who are creating music alone or with others in the home using cheap instruments and portable recording equipment.

Accounts of these 'hidden musicians' have tended to concentrate on the pragmatics of composing, rehearsing and performing and the degree of personal investment involved; emphasizing the way music making provides opportunities for individual and social expression and learning experiences (Bennett, 1980; Bayton, 1989; Finnegan, 1989; Fornäs, 1989). Whilst many of these musicians are playing purely for the intrinsic satisfaction derived from the experience, a vast number are composing, rehearsing, recording and performing in the hope that they will secure a recording contract. Yet, Cohen (1991), in her study of rock bands in Liverpool, is the only writer who has devoted detailed attention to the way in which 'unknown' musicians are attempting to shape what they do to suit the demands of the recording industry, and the way in which the logic of 'making it' informs local music making.

The experiences of these potential stars of tomorrow goes largely unrecorded, unless they are successful – in which case their story is retrospectively accommodated to the ascending tale of struggles, discovery and success found in popular biographies. These narratives, as Simon Frith once observed, are the 'dominant source of pop information', and provide an enduring source of inspiration to tens of thousands of aspiring recording artists, sustaining them in the belief that at some point in the near future they will be recognised by, and then signed to a major record company. Such recognition is rarely as dramatic as many biographies imply and various interested parties may become involved with an unknown act prior to the signing of a recording contract. Often a local manager is the first person to begin acting on behalf of an unknown artist.

Managers

From Larry Parnes who worked with Tommy Steele and Billy Fury in the 1950s, to Tom Watkins who managed Bros, and Maurice Starr who worked in shaping New Kids On The Block in the 1980s, managers have often been portrayed as 'starmakers and svengalis' – moulding and manipulating the music and image of their artists (Rogan, 1988). However, the majority of managers tend to operate as representatives and advisers, guiding rather than manipulating artists. The manager plans the overall career strategy of an act, defining objectives and setting standards. She, but more frequently he, attempts to motivate both the artist and the record company, and intervenes to resolve any disputes. Record companies have a number of artists on their books and the manager works behind the scenes, spending considerable time ensuring that staff in the record company are working for an act, and ironing out any potential problems. The manager is, in the words of Simon Napier-Bell who managed Marc Bolan, Wham! and Japan, 'the balance in the middle' who sways both artist and record company to see the other's point of view (Rogan, 1988).

An unsigned act who are attempting to obtain a recording contract may or may not have a manager. But most acts will usually find it necessary, or be required by record companies, to find management soon after signing. Artists without a recording contract will often sign a management agreement which contains a clause stipulating that the manager must obtain a deal within a specified time period or the agreement is terminated. As the manager usually receives between 15 to 25 per cent of the artist's earnings, this provides an incentive – if the artist does not obtain a recording contract then the manager is not going to make any money.

An experienced manager who can draw on a network of contacts can undoubtedly assist an act to obtain a contract. But, equally, there have been instances where a record company have turned down a potential signing because the manager was considered to be an unreliable or untrustworthy operator with whom senior staff did not wish to do business. Many unsigned acts who approach record companies have a manager who is often little more than an enthusiastic, hustling friend. In such a case the manager is often learning how the industry operates at the same time as the artists. One partner in a management company who had achieved commercial success with a number of artists could look back and with a smile reflect on some 'horrendous mistakes' that he had made on the way. Others however, may not recover from a lack of knowledge or errors of judgment. In the following chapters it will become clear that there are many points at which errors of judgment can be made.

The Deal: Recording Contracts

Although recording contracts became more complicated and highly specific throughout the 1980s as major record companies increasingly dealt with artists through the mediation of third parties, there is a basic character to the artist-company relationship embodied in a recording contract, upon which particular variations are inscribed.

A record company agrees to advance an artist a specified amount of money and to pay certain royalty percentage 'points' on the sales of that artist's recordings once the advanced sum (and all expenses involved in producing that artist's material) have been recouped by the company out of the artist's earnings. In many respects the company are advancing an artist a tax free loan which must be paid back if they are successful. For this the artist must deliver to the record company a specified amount of recorded material, usually albums, during the period of the contract. The contract will usually cover a period of 5 to 7 years, but will contain an 'option' clause every 12–18 months (or per album, which ever is longer). This gives the record company the right to retain or release an artist from a contract. If the company decides to retain an artist they will usually be required to pay a further advance.

A newly signed act will probably receive a royalty of between 10–14 points, and most contracts are structured in such a way that the advances and percentage royalty points payable to the artist increase each year; the implication being that the record company must have achieved a degree of success to make it commercially viable to retain an artist and pay out further advances.

In principle this is to safeguard the artist against a company which might sign and retain them on an exclusive contract without investing in them. The company are placed in a position where they are financially committed to an act, so they either work to establish that artist and generate a return on investment, or they save their money and free the artist from the contract to go elsewhere.

The days in which naive acts signed exploitative contracts have been well documented (Garfield, 1986; Rogan, 1988) and are by no means over. However, they have become less widespread as the music industry has consciously attempted to cultivate a more professional image. It has become standard practice for contracts to stipulate that the artists must have received professional legal advice before signing. As was the case with small jazz and rhythm and blues labels earlier this century some of the most exploitative contracts are offered by small, inexperienced, or just incompetent companies involved in signing poorly advised acts (Gray, 1988). Artists are now accredited with being more commercially minded and aware of what the contractual relationship with a record company entails. Artists are also surrounded by business advisers, lawyers and accountants who may engage in some quite sophisticated signing strategies. They may attempt to play the record companies off against each other by initiating the routine practice of 'bidding wars'. In addition they may attempt to withhold signing a publishing (songwriting) contract until the artist has secured a record deal.

Whilst a recording contract pays royalties on the discs and tapes sold (to put it simply), a publishing contract pays a much higher royalty rate (on less average income per song) on the rights of the material composed by the songwriter (which is often collectively a band). A separate royalty is collected every time a particular song is performed or broadcast in public. As a song will not usually be played until an artist/songwriter has a recording released, an artist with a recording contract is in a position to attract large advances and higher royalty rates from the major publishers.

The contract between record companies and artists is, therefore, one with legal obligations on both sides, in which a balance of power is negotiated between artists, who are dependent upon record companies to reach potential audiences, and record companies who are dependent upon artists for images and musical material.

Publishers and Production Companies

A number of management companies simultaneously operate as production companies, signing artists and financing the development of their music to a point where it is in a form suitable for public consumption (Lambert, 1980). This can then be released through a 'production and distribution' deal with a record label. Many managers have taken this step because they could not get an artist signed purely on the basis of presenting 'demo' recordings. The production company is therefore formed to develop the artist a stage further. This may be taken a step further again, and the company may develop into a hybrid management/production/record label, publishing the material themselves and operating through various licensing, production and marketing arrangements with larger companies (as discussed in Chapter 1).

Until the 1960s the work of music publishers involved signing songwriters and then placing their songs with singers who would use them for commercial recordings or public performances. The publisher would then receive an income from sales of the recordings and sheet music, and revenue from performance rights.

The emergence of rock music changed the relationship of publishers to popular music production. In the Tin Pan Alley tradition there was a clear cut distinction between writers and publishers on one side, and performers and record companies on the other. The success of artists such as The Beatles and Bob Dylan and the emergence of the rock aesthetic which placed great emphasis on individual expression resulted in performers increasingly writing their own songs. A considerable body of material now published is simultaneously composed and recorded by artists and bands, rather than the work of an independent songwriter.

In the past it was standard practice for songwriters to enter into agreements with 'publishing houses' based on a 50/50 split. Every royalty earned would be divided equally between the publisher and songwriter. In return, the publisher was performing an entrepreneurial role in placing songs with different singers and furthering that writer's career. However, as more and more performers began writing and recording their own material the publishers were able to 'publish' a song without having to place it with a singer or invest much energy in getting it commercially recorded and performed. Music publishers reached a point where they could derive a substantial income from publishing pre-recorded material and had to do very little work, merely administering music through agencies collecting copyright revenue.

As artists and their managers realised that publishers were doing less for their money, they either began forming their own publishing companies and thus retained the rights to the material and the bulk of income or artists began demanding that publishers reduce their cut. It became common practice for acts, particularly if they were in a strong bargaining position with recordings released and being purchased, to request publishing agreements split 85/15 in the artist's favour. As publishers operating costs and overheads can sometimes be as much as 12 per cent, this left a very small margin on which the publisher could make a profit. Hence it favoured both the successful acts who could generate a guaranteed return on investment that would cover these costs and the large corporations who could afford to acquire them.

One of the ways in which a small company can work alongside, and compete with a large company is to gamble with artists at an earlier stage of their development: get them under contract when they have not clearly demonstrated their commercial potential and when they will settle for a modest advance and lower royalty rates in return for the work that the minor company is going to do on their behalf. This is what smaller publishers, production companies and record labels increasingly attempted to do during the 1980s. The minor company can then be a third party taking an active interest in an act's progress, and intervening between the artist and the major corporation; establishing contact, presenting the act, making a deal and earning a cut, and perhaps establishing a reputation in the process.

In the following chapters I will be describing the work of specific occupational groupings such as artist and repertoire, marketing, promotion and public relations. Although I will usually be referring to departments in record companies I want to stress here that these different divisions may work across formal company boundaries, and tasks may be split between salaried employees and freelance individuals or organisations. Minor companies often work 'within' major companies, with staff attending meetings as a repertoire unit and then returning to their home base. An artist's musical arrangement and recording may be organised by a small label and the marketing then coordinated by a larger company. 'Independent' promotion and press staff may then be sub-contracted by the major label, or directly by the artist's management, to work for an act. Hence, recording industry personnel can find themselves constantly working across companies and continually making contact with and moving between different work places. One way I have tried to indicate these dialogues and movements is by referring to workers in the recording industry as 'mediators' rather than 'gatekeepers.'

Systems Analysis and Gatekeepers

The work of recording industry staff has often been described by reference to a 'filter-flow' model in which a vast quantity of products are transmitted from artistic originators through a series of industry and media gatekeepers who are continually engaged in rank ordering and filtering them to the public. Initially formulated by Paul Hirsch (1970, 1972), and derived from systems analysis of organisations, theories of news production and studies of industrial manufacturing, this uni-directional linear model implies that recording industry personnel are merely involved in selecting, sorting and ordering a vast quantity of 'raw materials' which then flow through the system – via assorted 'producers', agents and promoters – to the public.

The concept of a gatekeeper admitting or excluding products has been employed by a number of writers to characterise the work of staff in the music business, and has received widespread use in explaining how news items are selected and processed in studies of the press and television. Whilst useful for comparing the work of personnel in different media environments, the concept of the gatekeeper is limited because it implies that cultural items merely arrive at a 'gate' where they are either admitted or excluded. As Denis McQuail has argued, the eventual content of the media can arrive 'by several different routes and in different forms. It may have to be sought out, ordered in advance or its discovery systematically planned. At times it also has to be internally manufactured or constructed' (1987, p 163).

This observation is particularly relevant to the way in which the gatekeeper theory – and an analogous 'transmission model' which has been prevalent in the writings of sociologists working within the 'production of culture perspective' (Burnett, 1990; Jensen, 1984; Ryan & Peterson, 1982) – has been applied to the music industry. It results in a similar masking of the different ways in which material may be originated and the changes it may undergo 'within' the organisation. A few writers have drawn attention to these changes (Hennion, 1982, 1983; Vignolle, 1980), and one of the points I want to highlight in this book is the way in which the sounds and images of pop can have multiple points of origin and may be altered considerably as different people become involved in the acquisition, recording, marketing and promotion of artists.

Cultural Intermediaries

Recording industry personnel are therefore more than gatekeepers filtering products, and the music business bears only a superficial resemblance to a production line or 'decision chain' (Ryan & Peterson, 1982). Part of the inadequacy of these mechanical metaphors is that they imply the production of a concrete, material object. They are derived from an analysis of industrial manufacturing, rather than more recent approaches to the cultural and service industries in which attention has been focused on occupations involving presentation and representation and workers involved in providing symbolic goods and services (Bourdieu, 1986).

In contributing to the words, sounds and images of pop (which may not necessarily be consumed as a concrete material 'product' – but as sound and light waves in space) record industry personnel can be conceptualised as 'cultural intermediaries'. This concept is derived from the work of Pierre Bourdieu and refers to an emerging social grouping concerned with the production and consumption of consumer cultural imagery and information, working in such areas as marketing, advertising, design, public relations, radio and television, journalism, research, consultancy, counselling and the 'helping professions' (Featherstone, 1991). In these occupations jobs and careers have often not acquired the rigidity of the older bureaucratic professions, and recruitment is frequently via connections, shared affinities, values, and life styles rather than formal qualifications (Bourdieu, 1986).

A lack of bureaucratic rigidity is particularly noticeable in the music industry where artistic careers are dependent on changing fashions and the contingencies of the commercial market, and where the progress of personnel ranging from studio producers to public relations staff is related to the success of the acts they are associated with, rather than just their experience or qualifications. Occupational titles can often be a misleading indicator of an individual's work, and staff may be employed for their reputations, styles of working, or contacts they can bring within the scope of the organisation and accorded titles that can seem quite arbitrary. The lack of formal rigidity can also be observed in the way in which staff blur a number of conventional distinctions between such areas as work and leisure, personal taste and professional judgment; and where the distinction between artist, administrator and audience often becomes blurred as significant taste makers and consumers (such as DJs and fanzine writers) are recruited by the industry and artists are often simultaneously employees of record and production companies. Hence, the boundary between the recording industry and potential artists is not so much a gate where aspiring stars must wait to be selected and admitted, but a web of relationships stretched across a shifting soundtrack of musical, verbal and visual information.

Artist and Repertoire and Information Networks

The artist and repertoire department is the repository of knowledge about past, present and future musical trends and stylistic developments. Staff in the A & R department constantly monitor changes among established artists, the new acts that are being acquired by other companies, and attempt to follow developments amongst various audiences and subcultures. In order to deal with the fast-changing musical styles and fashions which are a particularly important characteristic of popular music in Britain, A & R staff regularly utilise a contact network covering a range of production companies, minor record labels, publishers, managers and lawyers. A complex web of information networks is employed so that what is happening across the country can be communicated to and assessed by the corporation.

A & R departments in the United States operate in a similar way. The main difference between Britain and the USA in this respect is one of geography. As a senior A & R manager who was based in America, but who had previously worked in London explained:

> In England you can sit behind your desk and do bugger all if you know a few people. If there's a hot act out there, within two to three weeks you've got to be an idiot if you don't know about it. It's such a small community. Glasgow's an hour's plane ride. Dublin's an hour's plane ride. Whereas here, it's a case of finding the real talent, out there in the great divide between New York and Los Angeles.

Despite this difference the basic method of acquiring information through networks of contacts, rather than unsolicited approaches or random searching in clubs, is very similar.

Within these networks there is a regular exchange of information, communicated by telephone and in person. The A & R staff ask these various third parties what they are doing: who are they signing, recording and developing? What trends have they identified or heard about? In turn these smaller set-ups present what they are doing to A & R staff. They might enthusiastically 'talk-up' certain artists. They may informally play recordings to staff at a major company in order to gain feedback or in an effort to generate interest in a particular act. They will probe the large company for information about the type of acts and material being sought. Minor labels continually attempt to find out which staff and artists are joining or leaving a major company, and generally glean any gossip that will enable them to assess the situation within the major corporations.

These smaller companies also have their own networks of regional contacts. These might include DJs and mixers who are responsive to trends on the dance floor and adept at identifying imports that might be worth acquiring. Studio producers and engineers working with unsigned artists might pass on information, as will people in rehearsal rooms and local clubs, magazines, fanzines and regional radio stations.

People at all points in this ever-changing web are constantly cultivating new contacts and consolidating existing relationships, and it is within these networks that interest in a particular act or recording is usually initiated. Rarely do staff from major record companies approach potential artists 'cold'. For the studio-quality tape they are about to hear, the video they are about to view or the showcase performance they are about to witness, the A & R staff have usually been prepared with prior knowledge which has been disseminated and acquired through these networks.

Talent Scouts

Record companies also recruit young staff who are receptive to immediate changes and emerging trends amongst various youth groups or within specific musical genres. This is a practice which can be traced back to the reorganisation of the music business in the 1950s when the industry began to restructure in order to deal with younger consumers in a less arbitrary manner (Gillett, 1983). In the late 1960s record companies employed house hippies to establish contact with the counter culture and underground musical community (Dilello, 1983). In the 1970s punk fanzine writers were enticed into record companies, and disc jockeys were recruited from night clubs during the dance music boom of the 1980s.

The young personnel employed by record companies often have a dual role of bringing material into the company and promoting the company's recordings in clubs or amongst particular audiences. The employment of these staff can enhance a company's image by presenting a 'hip' and knowledgeable face to prospective artists, and if working part-time as a disc jockey or journalist these staff may bring a further network of contacts within the orbit of the company. In the course of their work talent scouts become acquainted with the junior A & R staff at other companies and hence they are able to provide useful information about what is going on elsewhere.

Talent scouts spend their time visiting two or three gigs or clubs per night, and continually listening to demo tapes. They tend to have very little responsibility within A & R departments, although they may occasionally be involved in bringing an artist to a record company and might look after minor aspects of that artist's career. Talent scouts are primarily employed to keep the company in touch with musical changes and up to date with developments amongst other companies. Despite their job title they tend to bring information to the company rather than 'talent'; this they will do if they manage to stay at the company long enough to become an A & R manager.

The Decision to Acquire Artists

In some of the larger corporations the decision to acquire an artist is made according to the formal bureaucratic relationships inscribed in job titles: a form of hierarchical democracy takes place in the A & R department. The heads of A & R or managing directors of minor labels usually require staff to justify their choice of an act by having an overall 'vision' of an artist's musical and visual direction, the audience they might appeal to and how they may develop in the future. Senior management will usually require someone else in the department to share the same perspective on an act. This is a pragmatic consideration more than anything, as someone will have to take over the departmental responsibility for that artist should the A & R person leave or be taken ill. The head of the company or other directors will only be consulted if large sums of money are involved. In this situation the key decision makers are collectively the members of the artist and repertoire department and in the final instant the A & R director.

However, there are further variations between companies, according to the relationship between the artist and repertoire department and the rest of the company. Senior staff from other territories around the world will often be consulted about a potential acquisition, and opinions may be solicited from various people within the company. The most crucial relationship, however, is that between artist and repertoire and the marketing department. The work of marketing staff will be discussed in more detail in the next chapter. For the time being I will merely note the more formal contact between marketing and artist and repertoire.

In some companies the A & R department quite consciously try to maintain a distance between themselves and the rest of the organisation and operate what the head of one management company described as a 'bunker' mentality. This is a tactic which A & R staff adopt in an attempt to establish and maintain a reputation for signing according to what they consider intrinsic artistic criteria without intervention from other divisions within the company. It is an identity which A & R staff actively cultivate and communicate to influential media figures, contracted artists when working with them, and to prospective acts when trying to persuade them to sign to their company rather than a competitor. One A & R director who adopted this approach thought that a record company must 'believe' in their staff and trust them to carry out their job with a large degree of autonomy. He argued that 'you can't do A & R by committee'. But, on reflection added:

> It may well be that if it's an act that there's serious competition for, and there's quite a few record companies interested in the group, that you would have to expose the band at that early stage to the rest of the company. Because they wanted to see how your company worked and what sort of people work in your company compared to those working in another company.

This director was attempting to confine the decision about who to sign to the A & R department, for both the integrity and reputation of his staff as 'creative' personnel, and in order to avoid any compromise which may result if too many people became involved. However, when acquiring artists A & R staff are not working and making decisions, even at this early stage, totally in isolation from the rest of the company. There was, he acknowledged, discussion and feedback from various quarters whenever a prospective artist had been 'exposed' to the company.

Here is a different view of this type of situation described from the perspective of a marketing director based at the London office of what was an American entertainment group. I asked whether the marketing department would get involved in the decision-making prior to the signing of a potential act:

> Occasionally, but actually not as often as you might think, for reasons that, I must admit, I've never fully understood. And, there quite often isn't that much impetus from the artist to meet the rest of the record company, which I also find a little strange. But, there again, it's a fact of life. It's more often than not after the artist has been signed. Not long after in a lot of instances. Also, if an A & R person has

got talent to spot talent they might know that there's something good there, but they don't think anybody else will see it, and quite often other people don't see it. They're a little bit protective about their artists and the music, and a lot of them don't want you to hear anything until it's completely finished. Which is frustrating, but in some ways it's fair enough.

This director voiced reservations, shared by a number of marketing staff in different companies, about the way in which artist and repertoire staff do not take a wider view of proceedings at an early stage. But, at the same time, he acknowledged the right of A & R to 'protection' from the rest of the company when having to make decisions at this moment.

In many companies, however, there is formal contact and explicit acknowledgment that A & R and marketing staff are involved in the decision to acquire artists, and an indication that the relationship between the two has historically changed, and become closer during the 1980s. Here is the marketing director of a British based corporation who I spoke to in 1989, discussing when marketing would get involved with a new artist:

That's a situation that has changed quite dramatically over the last few years in the business as a whole. There used to be a very, very distinct separation between A & R and marketing. We now work much more closely with A & R departments, and we get involved pre-signing. So, we get involved at the stage where A & R have made their minds up they want to sign a band, then we get involved in either listening to demo tapes and/or going to live gigs and give our opinion. Now, we give our opinion in the context of believing and hoping that A & R haven't made a mistake. We're not looking to exercise a veto. We have that veto. So far in my tenure here [10 years] we haven't exercised it completely. From time to time we've said; 'Look, there's this problem, there's that problem' and that's made them think again about signing a band. So we do get involved. We're involved in their whole development process really from day one.

In the type of decision-making described here, marketing might formally have the right to veto a potential signing, but they do not exercise this right 'completely'. The internal relationship between the two record company departments is maintained with less conflict if marketing do not assert their 'right' but seek to influence A & R decisions in more subtle and informal ways.

In contrast to the formal-bureaucratic variations outlined above there are record companies in which certain individuals are known by people throughout the industry to be the key decision-makers. During the jazz era that immediately preceded the emergence of pop in the 1950s particular individuals exerted a decisive aesthetic and organisational influence (Gray, 1988); as did Chris Blackwell at Island Records, Joe Smith at Warner Brothers and Clive Davis at CBS (to name only three) during the rock era. Whilst undertaking the research for this book I found certain companies were identified where the influence of specific individuals was more important to the acquisition policy of that company than any formal organisational criteria. Companies mentioned in which key individuals played a decisive role in this way covered all levels of the industry and included RCA/BMG (a major transnational), London (a company then 49 per cent owned by the Polygram conglomerate), Chrysalis (a company then half owned by EMI) and Big Life (a small label with complex deals with a range of large corporations).

The individuals who were identified had usually been involved in the recording industry for at least fifteen years and had established a reputation for recognising the potential of artists, achieving success and working with integrity. As there are relatively few of these staff, they are frequently poached by other record companies and can negotiate contracts as complex as those of major artists. In such companies the artist and repertoire staff are still performing their job as outlined above, but within the additional constraints, or liberties, imposed as a result of the influence of these dominant individuals.

The Intuition of Acquisition

When artist and repertoire staff are asked to explain how they assess and respond to the music and artists they are approached with, they usually use such terms as 'following hunches', 'gut feeling', 'intuition' and 'instinct'.

Jon Stratton (1982a) found similar sentiments expressed when interviewing A & R staff for a study of the British recording industry in the early 1980s, and interpreted this use of non-rational subjective criteria as an evasive and mystifying tactic. This, he suggested, was part of the way in which A & R staff attempt to 'reconcile the contradictions' that arise around art and commerce under capitalism. Stratton described record companies as confronting a conflict between 'the aesthetic and capitalism', and argued that A & R staff attempt both to resolve and evade this conflict via 'a subjectivist appeal to intuition'. Although providing an indication of the type of dilemmas that A & R staff must undoubtedly experience, Stratton ultimately reduced the work of these personnel to merely resolving a formalistic conflict between art and commerce. He did not pursue the range of discriminations which might simply have become rationalised as 'intuition' in response to a question from an academic interviewer.

A subjective and intuitive response, in any context, is often obtained when people who are immersed in a particular environment are asked to explain activities that they take for granted and engage in habitually. The working theory, or practical knowledge, of recording industry staff is most clearly articulated in discussions about specific examples, rather than in generalisations. Indeed, it is frequently part of this body of practical knowledge that 'you cannot generalise about the production of popular music'. Stratton too easily sees the use of intuitive criteria as an evasive ploy.

When asked to elaborate, the personnel I spoke to were not only able to reflect on what their intuition was based on, but they revealed criteria, values and dispositions of far greater complexity and specificity than Stratton's abstract conflict between art and commerce would suggest. An example of this can be seen in the following comments made by the managing director of a publishing company, who was attempting to establish a catalogue by finding and working with artists prior to the involvement of record labels. I asked what he would be looking for in an act at a rudimentary stage and he initially responded very generally by saying; 'Excitement really . . . [pause, various false starts] . . . one tape will stand out. From here I will get very enthusiastic about a tape because it's got something that's exciting me, and it doesn't have to be because it's uptempo or noisy or whatever.' He paused, having offered this very vague and general explanation, which was similar to the subjective comments of other A & R staff who spoke of looking for a 'buzz' and for the music to move them. He then imediately launched into a rambling monologue about a particular act he was working with which brought out many of the characteristics that record companies are looking for in potential artists:

> We've got a band at the moment who are exactly in this position, where we've had any number of options and suggestions that we've put their way. We've done a record which got them some press. They're very good live, but maybe a bit puby. The name is wrong, so we're going to change the name. They're refining – they're not changing the music – but they had a very broad range of styles in the music which I thought was confusing because you really have to focus carefully. So I got them to think what their music was really about, as opposed to a set they've put together as a live band to please their audience. So, they were not a pub band, but they played in pubs and liked to get the audience entertained. Now the danger in that, as far as I could see, was that it was diluting the originality and strength of their particular music, and the name of the band was lightweight and the music was quite serious. So at the moment what we're looking to do is get a new set of songs together and maybe do some more demos. I've got them thinking about the voice; writing songs to use the voice as a focal point. Bands always forget when they go into the studio. They spend two days on a drum sound and then they rush the vocal and the mix because they've got a limited amount of time, and – fatal! What I'm listening for and what record companies are listening for is; 'What am I hearing in the top line': Where's the personality in the vocal? Where's the personality in the song? So, excitement if you like. You've got to have instinct.

This director identified a series of particular characteristics that he was concerned about such as press attention, a focused set of songs, live performance abilities and a personality in the voice. (All of these points will be covered in more detail later in this book). However, as he reached the end of his explanation he moved away from these specific criteria and once more returned to using the subjective shorthand of 'excitement' which was in turn understood instinctively.

From Intuition to the Rock Tradition

The experience of listening to music is frequently immediate, irrational and on occasions obsessive (Eisenberg, 1988). Record company staff are responding to the immediacy of music as a listener, but also assessing a potential artist in terms of global audiences and markets, and the media technologies available for communication. As Clive Davis, former head of CBS Records, explained when discussing how he had acquired an ear for identifying successful artists and songs:

> My 'ears' are really a question of disciplined, intensive immersion in contemporary music. Each time I hear a record my mind factors out the ingredients involved that might – or might not – make it jump on the charts. This is something you **feel** [original emphasis]. Something happens in your chemistry, your blood, when you hear the record – a tingling, a certain electricity, a sense that audiences will grab onto this song and take off with it (1974, p 218).

Hence, it is an 'intuitive' response which is based on immersion in a particular environment with its specific demands and cultural values. Various people involved in the decision to acquire artists for different record companies identified similar characteristics when describing what they were looking for. The main criteria that record company personnel are judging potential artists by are:

1. the live, stage performance
2. the originality and quality of the songs or material
3. the recorded performance and voice
4. their appearance and image
5. their level of personal commitment, enthusiasm and motivation
6. the achievements of the act so far

However, this list of criteria in itself says little about *how* a potential act is assessed. It does not reveal the distinctions and comparisons that are made, the type of qualities in artists and performers which are preferred above others.

Record company staff assess the above characteristics according to a set of aesthetic values and ideologically informed tastes which enable them to classify acts and accommodate them to the business demands of the industry. This provides another means of imposing on the uncertainty about which artists might be successful. Here are a few people talking about what they were looking for in potential artists. Firstly, an A & R director in his early 30s at the British office of an American owned corporation:

> Well, obviously, if you go through the ages of rock 'n' roll the biggest bands in the world have been live groups. Vastly successful because they've been great live and made great records. But, then again, rarely is a group great live when it starts off. Purely by the nature of its components. The guys are probably young and inexperienced but they may have something that's incredibly special, which may not be slick playing or slick delivery. I mean, you look at all the great rock bands over the years, they've always had a certain make up. You know, The Stones, Zeppelin, right through to U2 and The Smiths. They've always had great songs, a great front person, great guitarist and they've been a band, a unit, a tight band. They've always had similar qualities.

This director was one of a number of personnel in the major companies to compare what he was looking for to the 'greats of rock'n'roll'; this being a particular selection of Anglo-American rock bands which constitute an implicit canon, running from The Beatles, Doors and Rolling Stones in the 1960s to U2, REM and Guns 'n' Roses in the 1990s. A number of A & R staff referred to this tradition of white male rock groups when explaining what they were looking for. One who did so was a senior A & R manager in one of the long established British label divisions of another transnational conglomerate. He also explained:

> All the acts I've ever signed have been live, working acts . . . You know, I hate, I despise these created video-cum-pop-star things. They leave me stone cold. So unless I can go and see an act that can cut it as a live act and also write good songs at the same time and create a bit of a buzz in a club, which is probably nine times out of ten where you're going to see them, then I don't really want to know, personally.

Artist and repertoire staff continually use the term 'working' to refer to acts which are playing live rather than 'working' in various other ways. Despite developments in video, digital recording and telecommunications technology which have enabled artists to reach global audiences without the need of traditional touring and stage performances, staff making decisions about which artists to acquire place considerable emphasis on their live performance potentials and abilities. This tends to favour the self-contained working band over other types of artists. The same view is expressed in the following comments made by an executive who had worked in the music industry in Britain and the USA since the early 1960s and was then managing director of a well established small company, one that subsequently became part of a conglomerate group:

> What I'm looking for is the working act. The **real** [emphasised] act. The act that can get up on stage and do it. That act will give you a career. That act will sell records for years. I signed Status Quo 22 years ago; they are still making records. I signed Black Sabbath umpteen years ago; they are still making records. These are acts that are career acts . . . we are changing, I mean one has to change. The UK dance market looked like it was going to be a fashion fad, but it isn't. To that extent, two years ago I started a dance label, and I have dance specialists working for me downstairs because I don't profess to know that market. So, we are able to adapt. Now, that's not a career orientated label. I mean, those records are one-off situations and every now and again maybe you'll get an artist come out of it.

Somewhat in contrast to these comments were the views of a talent acquisition manager in his mid 20s who was based at a publishing and production label that had very recently been integrated into the operations of a major British based corporation. He strongly disagreed about the importance placed on live performance and explained;

> When I first started [about 8 years ago] it was more about going out and finding bands, being out 10 days a week. That method is becoming more and more redundant, that's my personal opinion. More and more these days I find it's as much about: I sit here with my record company hat on and with my publishing hat on and think; 'there's really a gap in the market for this type of project' . . . I don't go out to gigs, much to the disgust of some people. That's not how I find my stuff. It comes through various writers and producers. So if a writer comes in he may have some great songs, and maybe is looking for the front person. Or, maybe I have the front person who I want to launch into the market but I haven't got the songs. So you put the two together. Then maybe you need some production skills in to add to that, or maybe you just focus on one artist who maybe doesn't write their own material or produce, and pile a whole thing around that person.

The Organic and the Synthetic

The above quotes provide an indication of the way in which potential artists are classified in terms of two clusters of distinctions. I shall refer to these as the 'organic' and the 'synthetic' ideology of creativity.

The organic ideology of creativity is a naturalistic approach to artists. The record company acquire a 'band' (A & R staff continually refer to bands when talking about recording artists) that have reached a certain stage in their evolution. The seeds of success are within the band. It is the record company's job to encourage and direct; to 'nurture' this act. This naturalistic approach often extends to the marketing and publicising of artists, which is explained in terms of the company merely enhancing the identity of the act. Although A & R staff can often identify very specific markets for their artists they tend to speak of them spontaneously 'breaking'. Once this has been achieved the act will evolve and progress (which in practice means that their recordings are gradually bought by more and more people) until they are at a stage where they no longer require the input of the A & R department.

The synthetic ideology of creativity is a combinatorial approach to both acts and material. From this perspective the record company executive looks at the various parties who are approaching the company and working in the field and assesses their respective qualities whilst weighing up what trends are emerging amongst particular audiences. There might be someone who is a good vocalist but cannot write songs. Perhaps there is a writer with good songs, an outstanding musician but with poor production and vocal abilities. Maybe there are imaginative producers and mixers with impressive ideas but no real vehicle for them. There are continual permutations of artists available from a range of acts that are always forming, dividing and re-combining. In this approach it is not a case of discovering and developing 'an' act through a 'natural' process but a catalytic bringing together of various elements in a sort of chemical reaction under certain laboratory conditions.

These two clusters of distinctions, which during the 1970s frequently found expression in a rigid distinction between rock and pop (Frith, 1983; Laing, 1985b), are not simply metaphors for different methods of creating music. Incorporated into their practical working use is a conception of a potential artist's future as either a long term or short term act. This is a division that is made in response to the business requirements of the music industry.

Careers, Fashion and the Ideological Division of Artists

In order to sustain itself from day-to-day (pay the staff and general running costs), and reproduce and enlarge its market share over the long term, a record company needs a balance of continual chart hits that will bring in regular revenue and maintain a steady cash flow, and long term established career acts that will sell vast quantities of recordings on a global scale. Long term careers do not happen by themselves or simply as a result of public choice or because of artistic talent. Artistic careers must be carefully planned and built. This requires considerable investment in marketing and promotion and the use of a sophisticated infra-structure of distribution arrangements. If interest in an act is not maintained at certain key points in an artist's life then that 'career' may not be sustained, due to the potential audience not knowing that the artist's material has been released, or because recordings are not available in the shop on the day somebody wants them.

It is the global 'career' acts which provide the capital for expansion and re-investment in new acts. It is within these business requirements for imme-diate short term income and planned sustained long term high earnings that an artistic policy is built. The organic and synthetic ideologies of creativity have been inscribed into these commercial strategies so that they do not hold equal status. Acts which conform to the naturalistic, organic conventions of the live rock aesthetic tend to be prioritised for long term development; and artists creating music according to synthetic, combinatorial conventions are dealt with in a more ad-hoc and short term manner.

Simon Frith (1988b) has argued that there was a decisive shift in the global organisation of popular music during the 1980s. He characterised this shift as a transition from an approach based on ever-ascending logical steps up 'the rock pyramid', with public performance used to authenticate studio appeal (an organic approach), to a situation where transnational record companies irrationally fish for ideas, sounds, styles and performers from a talent pool, with video marketing decisively redefining conceptions of the audience (a synthetic approach). This argument, whilst usefully highlighting a historical dissolution of the previously dominant rock ethic of ascending cycles of dues-paying, deals, albums and tours, overlooks the continuities that a talent pool approach has with previous synthetic approaches to producing pop music. It also ignores the persistence, adaptation and mutation of the tradition of organic creativity within contemporary popular music.

Threads of an organic approach to creativity can be traced back to the rock ethic of the musician as an expressive artist that emerged and was established as a dominant form of musical practice during the 1960s. The synthetic method is often dismissed as contrived and manufactured by those working within the rock tradition, but is itself continuous with an approach to pop music that goes back to the 1950s New York 'hit factories' and the 1960s American soul and rhythm & blues production teams.

As the 'hegemony of rock' has given way to a proliferation of styles and forms (Chambers, 1985; Frith 1988a, 1988b), various genres of music have been selectively accommodated and categories constructed, according to organic criteria that were previously applied to rock music. Particularly relevant here is the labelling of an eclectic mixture of 'authentic' and 'ethnic' sounds as world music, and the emergence of the environment-friendly category of new age music.

Despite technological and artistic changes, the organic approach tends to predominate amongst staff in the A & R departments of British record companies, who are often quite indignant that they should be seen as 'manufacturing' acts in a contrived way. The divisions that the organic/synthetic distinction maps out have been an enduring source of tension throughout the development of post-war popular music and continually inform the decisions about which artists are acquired and subsequent choices about how an act's 'career' is conceptualised. This issue can be pursued further by looking at the social and historical background of the key decision-makers in the British recording industry and considering how this has shaped the culture of A & R departments.

British A & R Culture and the Rock Tradition

In an account of record company A & R departments based on research conducted in the middle of the 1970s, Simon Frith (1976) described how staff were drawn from a variety of backgrounds, including music writers, disc jockeys, musicians, promoters and sales staff. Between 1989 and 1992, when my own research was carried out, A & R staff were still drawn from similar backgrounds. However, the range of occupations that A & R staff are recruited from belies the characteristics and cultural values that they share in common. The majority of staff involved in acquiring artists for major record companies are white, male and have entered the industry from what might loosely be called the college-rock tradition. The director of a small management company that represented rock, pop and dance acts was one of a few people to remark on this bias:

> You can get a third division rock act a serious amount of money. If you're dealing with black dance, and I use the racial thing significantly, then quite often you're hard pushed to get any kind of treatment of the same order. . . . In the record companies individuals come from the rock tradition. Hardly ever do they come strictly from a soul, r'n'b, dance tradition. Very, very rarely. You know, they've been social secs at college. What do social secs at college deal with? They deal with bands, and they get used to that, and they come through the system and they go on. Or, they come out of bands themselves. Quite a lot of the staff in record companies were in bands. Very rarely in anything but a rock band. Now and again producers, but generally they're producing white acts, who, by and large, will be in the rock tradition. And there is a belief, a kind of belief that is really hard to break down.

These comments about the background of staff were echoed in an industry trade magazine profile which appeared following the appointment of Paul Conroy to President of The Chrysalis Group in 1989:

> Getting back to Conroy's roots in the business and some clues as to why he is so universally liked, he is one of a long line of college social secs of similar age (Conroy is just 40) who now man the middle and upper echelons of the UK music industry. For those unfamiliar with the British education system, social secretaries are a breed of students most prevalent in the Sixties and Seventies heyday of the live college circuit who devoted more time to booking bands than to their studies. Chrysalis founders Chris Wright and Terry Ellis, as well as Conroy's WEA boss Rob Dickins, got hooked on the music business in just such that way (Dalton, 1989, p 10).

During the 1960s there was an expansion in British higher education, and a change in the composition of the audience for commercial popular music. Whereas the music of the rock'n'roll era had been associated with working class teenagers, during the 1960s various elements of pop were 'appropriated' and re-christened 'rock' by a recently enfranchised grammar school student and 'hip' middle class audience (Chambers, 1985). Rock was not only a source of pleasure for these consumers, but it was imbued with libertarian and artistic allusions as the emergent middle class audience (and artists) drew on an aesthetic vocabulary inherited from an appreciation of European high culture. The 'increased legitimation of rock music' during the 1960s directly accompanied a shift in the social class background of the audiences and performers (Vulliamy, 1977).

The relationship between rock and the newly educated middle class frequently found expression in events associated with the student counter-culture, in which music was often central. One consequence of this was that a number of educated, middle class, mildly bohemian young people were attracted into and actively recruited by the music industry. In a business which has a high turnover of staff, reputations are established but are easily lost; executive careers follow artists into obscurity. Historically, those who entered the British recording industry during the late 1960s and early 1970s, and who had remained, were in higher corporate management, running an A & R department or managing a label by the 1990s. Throughout this period a 25 year tradition had been established during which staff were recruited into A & R departments from similar backgrounds or with similar working experiences, musical tastes and preferences.

Male Camaraderie and Handmaidens

A further dimension to the culture of A & R departments is added by the way in which women are little represented, and tend to be found in secretarial positions. The physical arrangement of the artist and repertoire department at one transnational record company I visited in London during 1989 provided a typical example of how female staff are found in a subordinate position in A & R departments.

The artist and repertoire area was located on one floor. There was little natural light and an intimate, slightly disorganised and perceptively tense atmosphere. The ceilings were low, posters hung from the walls, magazines and papers were strewn across tables and desks and music could be heard coming from various directions as different doors were opened. The physical arrangement of the space was such that all of the A & R men (four or five) had their own offices with doors which opened out onto an oblong shaped open plan area. The A & R director had his office at the far end of the floor, from where he could see all the other offices and the entire working environment. Standing in the doorway of his office he could survey his empire.

In the middle was an open plan area in which about five or six female secretaries or personal assistants sat at desks each facing in different directions. During the course of an hour I spent waiting for an appointment the secretaries were continually occupied; making phone calls on behalf of A & R men, typing and filing, arranging meetings and flights, making tea and coffee, buying food and drink for a meeting, stocking the fridge, smiling at and generally being friendly to visitors. The casually dressed A & R men frequently strolled from their offices into this space exhibiting an informal style of working with relationships based around a bantering male camaraderie, while they were waited on by their handmaidens.

In Touch with the Street, Man

In 1990, Dave Massey, who was working for Chrysalis Music, compared getting into A & R to 'joining the masons, difficult for everyone, nearly impossible for women'. In the course of the research for this book I spoke to one woman who had worked in artist and repertoire in Britain. At the time of our meeting she was working in the United States. Reflecting on the lack of women in A & R she said:

> I'll tell you why I think there are not many women in it. Because, number one, it's a very chauvinistic industry, it really is. Number two, the A & R lifestyle does not suit the majority of women at all. The fact of going out every night to clubs, being up all night in sleazy, dodgy clubs or whatever.

Although a number of younger staff who had entered the recording industry during the 1980s, and who were mainly involved in dance, pop and soul music, had begun to question the usefulness of seeking artists in pubs and clubs, A & R departments still tend to be dominated by staff drawn from rock culture with its emphasis on performing live in front of an audience in a 'natural' setting. In addition, and clichéd as it might sound, a number of people in record companies espouse a belief of 'being in touch with the street' and 'the kids'. These terms were used quite seriously by a number of artist and repertoire staff and senior executives who described their work to me. As this female A & R manager herself replied when I asked whether this type of approach, and the lifestyle it implied, was still necessary; 'Oh I think so. You have to be out there, in touch with the street. It's all about those kids out there'.

This emphasis on the street – no matter how romanticised, and whether it really is where most artists are found – further reinforces the male culture of artist and repertoire. Because most of 'the kids', out there, on the street and in the sleazy clubs are male. As Angela McRobbie has pointed out, with its negative moral connotations for women and the very real threat of violence 'street visibility . . . both proclaims the publicization of the group and at the same time ensures its male dominance . . . the street remains in some ways taboo for women' (1980, p 47). Hence, this approach militates against finding artists who might be 'in the home' and is part of a working practice which operates to exclude women from this area of the recording industry.

In discussing what she enjoyed about her work the A & R manager quoted above emphasised a more personal approach to the job than the male A & R staff I spoke to. Her work involved:

> dealing with people, and their lives as well; their personal problems, their fuck ups, their mental whatever, their little quirks. And my A & R forte is understanding those people and respecting that and trying to work with that and being supportive to them. Supporting their musicality, and believing in them, and being there to hold their hands when it gets rough. That's what I'm about. They'll bring me in when there's problems with artists. I'm good at understanding them . . . I do think that record companies would save themselves a bloody fortune if they had an in-house psychiatrist.

Many A & R men have been in bands themselves and give the impression of living out the rock life style by proxy, through the artists they are working with. They tend to stress the 'buzz' and excitement from the music and are often most animated when discussing the possibility of finding the 'next-big-thing'. Although just as involved in 'nurturing' artists, this was usually discussed in terms of the pragmatics of songwriting, studio production and arranging. In contrast this female A & R manager emphasised the supportive, caring and understanding side of the work, and the way in which this aspect was actively utilised by the company who 'brought her in' if there was a problem with artists. At the same time she was just as involved in criticising her act's songs, negotiating with producers and overseeing studio production.

Priorities and Prejudice

During a decisive phase in the formation of the modern popular music industry, the dominant practices within the artist and repertoire departments of the major record companies in Britain have been established by staff drawn from backgrounds within the rock tradition. These staff have been predominantly white, male and college educated. Unlike the United States, where record companies have employed specialist, predominantly black, staff to acquire and promote artists in the areas of rap, dance, soul and rhythm and blues, there has been a conspicuous absence of black people in the major labels in Britain. One of the few notable exceptions to this has been Island Records where the distinctive character of the company has developed under the influence of its founder Chris Blackwell and through a steady tradition of working with artists from the Caribbean. In most of the record labels in Britain there is only the occasional black messenger, talent scout or accountant; the vast majority of staff are white.

However, it is not simply that there have been hardly any women or black people in key decision-making positions; it is that there have been few people from a popular music tradition other than rock. This has resulted in a taken-for-granted way of working in which staff view artists that can be accommodated to the naturalistic organic conventions of the rock tradition as long term career acts, and pop, soul and dance acts as short term, fashion dependent artists. These are viewed as artists who might attain longevity or produce a career, but by chance or accident, rather than through strategic planning. As Ian Hoare (1975) once pointed out, the naturalistic ideology of rock has tended to promote a very simplified and restrictive attitude which regards much soul as a 'cheapened' and 'diluted' version of more authentic forms of music. There has been an uncritical and selective acceptance of the enduring dominance of the rock tradition over other musical styles, and the application of the taste preferences, aesthetic values and preferred working practices of this loosely aligned dominant group have set the priorities for the acquisition and future development policies of the major record companies.

This has been reproduced and maintained by existing staff and through recruitment policies. Staff tend to be selected to fit into the existing A & R culture, where there is peer group pressure to conform, which is reinforced by constant contact with other A & R staff at gigs, in studios and at music business events. There is also the risk of failing and making a mistake, which results in a tendency to sign acts which can be easily accommodated to existing conventions and routes which have proved successful in the past.

Will the naturalistic rock aesthetic break down throughout the 1990s? At the beginning of the decade some commentators were claiming that dance music had 'broken the mould' and that the emphasis on the live rock act was diminishing. However, not many British dance acts were established beyond a few records. Soul II Soul were one of the rare exceptions, which both excited and confused various recording industry personnel depending on their musical taste, and their assumptions about which types of artists could achieve widespread success with albums. It is clear that considerable investment is still being poured into conventional rock bands in an attempt to emulate the worldwide commercial success of U2, Simple Minds, Dire Straits, REM and

Guns'n'Roses – and there has been, conspicuously, no British equivalent to Madonna, Prince or Michael Jackson. As Cynthia Cherry from the Eternal record label, part of Warner Music, remarked in 1991; 'I find that for black music, a lot of companies still don't understand it. The record companies are still not behind dance in the way they are behind the big live act. If they gave dance acts the push that rock acts get, it could really break through'.

The practices, priorities and prejudices which I have outlined above inform the work of artist and repertoire departments and senior personnel responsible for acquiring artists for the major record companies in Britain. In attempting to deal with the uncertainty and risk involved in signing new artists, these staff have drawn on a set of cultural values and experiences which enable them to assess the potential of an act and predict its future development and career. However, artist and repertoire staff must work closely with other personnel in the marketing, promotion and publicity departments. As various other parties are introduced into this account the practices and priorities of the artist and repertoire departments will be seen more clearly as one set of principles and influences which are supported and upheld in certain areas, but disputed and challenged in others.

4

IMAGES, IDENTITIES AND AUDIENCES

Marketing and Artist Development

Amarketing director who I spoke to in a bright and spacious West London office opened our meeting by summing up the work of his department, describing it as 'selling records to the maximum number of people and finding the most appropriate way of doing it'. Put like this it seems straightforward. But in order to conduct the commercial activity of selling recordings, marketing staff occupy a central position within the contemporary recording industry, operating at a point where the work of artists directly meets the activities of audiences.

Marketing does not merely involve record companies transmitting products and information to potential audiences, who then rationally select from what is available (Burnett, 1991; Hirsch, 1970, 1972; Ryan & Peterson, 1982; Wallis & Malm, 1984). Marketing staff must actively construct consumers as identifiable markets. As Richard Middleton has pointed out:

> We do not choose our musical tastes freely; nor do they reflect our 'experience' in any simple way. The involvement of subjects in particular musical pleasures has to be constructed . . . subjects themselves . . . have a role to play (of recognition, assent, refusal, comparison, modification); but it is an articulatory, not a simplistically creative or responsive role. (1990, p 249)

This chapter is about the way in which record company staff 'articulate' the relationship between the identity of artists and the lived experience of consumers. It provides a context, and point of departure for my later chapters on studio and video production, radio promotion and press publicity.

Marketing and Artist and Repertoire

Unlike artist and repertoire staff, personnel involved in marketing are less likely to describe what they do by reference to intuition and organic metaphors. Instead they use such terms as 'putting together', 'constructing' and 'calculating.' From the perspective of marketing, a 'creative artist' is not expressing him or herself in some natural way, but is involved in a self-conscious and calculated activity. This was succinctly conveyed by a marketing director based at one of the labels of a major entertainment group, who said:

A real artist is going to have a lot more than a good record. Being a pop star is not just about making records. Popular culture is about media manipulation. It's about how you present yourself. It's about utilising the avenues at your disposal to create an image, a lifestyle, a point of identification for people. And a genuine artist may well have a real understanding of that. I mean, David Bowie is the master manipulator of the media.

This director, like many staff in marketing departments, was sceptical of the naturalistic approach to artists which tends to predominate amongst A & R staff. Referring to various rock acts he commented 'if you really start asking questions about what they do in terms of A & R and making those records I think you'll find they're just as manipulated . . . there's nothing natural about any record'.

What is interesting here is not whether the naturalistic explanation favoured by A & R staff is closer to the 'truth' than the calculated approach of marketing, but that staff in different departments draw on vocabularies expressing different ideologies of creativity to explain and give meaning to what they do. For A & R staff the creative process, for both artists and record company personnel, is to a large degree spontaneous, naturalist and evolutionary. For marketing staff the composition of popular music – and the work of a 'genuine artist' – is more calculated, self-conscious and manipulative.

The relationship between artist and repertoire and marketing is at the core of the music business. The work of these departments and the relationship between them decisively shapes the way in which the sounds and images of pop are put together. It is the meeting point of a number of tensions which can be found refracted throughout the industry, and represents a wider set of orientations and practices than formal departmental categories imply. As one senior director explained, A & R and marketing are:

> . . . the two disciplines within any record company. Between them is a rather vague area which is the role of artist development, which is the process of taking an artist from the point at which you sign them to the point at which they are a superstar. That unites the two disciplines.

Artist Development and Product Management

One noticeable difference between record companies in the United States and Britain is that American companies tend to have divisions with the specific title of 'artist development'. This difference, however, is merely one of terminology. As one vice president of artist development at a North American label explained when talking about why she preferred this title:

> We used to be called product managers. That used to be our exact title. Our new president thinks that's an insensitive title, and I agree. We are directors of artist development. We're here to develop artists' careers and sales potential. That's why we've changed our titles, we're a little bit more sensitive. Product is kind of distant, it's almost too cold.

In the United States there is often a minimal marketing department, an adjunct to artist development, in which staff do little more than place advertisements. In Britain the work of artist development is contained within the marketing division.

Although the relationship between the artist and record company will usually have been initiated by the A & R person, a number of other record company personnel have an immediate interest in the progress of a new act. Prior to a signing, staff from the artist and repertoire department will frequently have solicited the opinions of senior directors or label managers, and sought the views of representatives from marketing, television and radio promotion, press publicity, sales and international marketing. These dialogues may have included the formal assessment of marketing staff as discussed previously, but will usually entail informal judgments about the potential of an act to gain radio, television and press coverage and discussion of their possible international appeal.

A project team will be established, comprised of staff drawn from each of these areas, and a series of artist development meetings will be held to establish an act's musical direction, visual identity, and to discuss the media which might be approached and any associated promotional techniques to be used. These meetings provide a forum for staff in each department to contribute ideas, and result in an agreed campaign programme, usually based around the release of single records, staggered over a period of months and eventually leading to the release of a long playing album.

The product manager, or director of artist development, is a project coordinator responsible for a specific number of acts and recordings, and liaises with staff in different parts of the company, constantly monitoring the status of an act and the progress of specific campaigns. It is a position which often becomes more necessary as companies grow in size; the product manager attempts to monitor and maintain the communication between different departments and external personnel and ensure that everyone is working towards the same goal.

Product managers vary in their degree of involvement with artists. In some companies they contribute ideas for the artwork used in advertising and on record sleeves and might suggest ways of presenting the act in videos and photos. Elsewhere product managers may merely be administrators, involved in placing advertisements and monitoring and updating budgets, and ensuring that the work of various internal staff and external designers and printers runs to schedule.

The majority of marketing directors in Britain are white males in their 30s and early 40s, and their staff tend to have been recruited from what one described as a mixture of 'administrative and creative' backgrounds. Marketing departments include people with formal qualifications in business studies, ex-secretaries who have gained experience within the industry and worked their way up or who have been formally trained by the company, staff with a knowledge of sales and advertising, and personnel from art and design oriented backgrounds. These staff are required to understand the internal politics and organisation of the company, and how to gain access to potential consumers. Ideally, they are required to exhibit a flair for visual communication.

The Visual Image

Staff in record companies are often defensive when discussing the visual image of their acts, having been extensively criticised over the years by artists, fans and critics and accused of treating performers like puppets. As one marketing director commented:

> Maybe I'm paranoid but I get the impression that there are people in the outside world who think a major record company signs an artist and goes; 'Right, these are the styles, you're wearing this, you're doing this, you're doing that.' It's not like that. I wish it was that easy.

Marketing staff will often initially insist that they are merely involved in bringing out the personality and style that is inherent within a particular act or artist – 'enhancing' what is already there. However, the degree of enhancement can vary and is dependent upon the artist involved. As the marketing director just quoted explained further;

> You have artists that are very strong with visual ideas which are great, but they're few and far between, and when it's like that it's unwise to ignore it. You have artists who have got very strong visual ideas that are a complete pile of cobblers, in which case you have to try and gently dissuade them from being quite as extreme. And, you have artists who have got no idea at all, in which case you try and help them.

The degree of 'help' offered to an artist can vary, as can the degree of influence exerted by the company. In theory record companies can exert considerable control. When I asked one marketing director how much control the company had over an artist's image he responded; 'I could have total control. I pay for it, right. Now, I don't choose to do that.' Elsewhere a marketing director spoke of 'shaping the image', and another explained that the company 'have the financial resources, which the artist frequently doesn't. So there is a certain amount of leverage and control'.

In order to maintain a working relationship with an act, marketing staff attempt to exercise this influence diplomatically and through mutual discussion. However, this does not mean that marketing staff have to pretend to be the artist's 'best friend'. Describing a number of disagreements about such issues as the selection of recordings for singles, the photographs and artwork for album covers, and appearances on television shows, one director explained that 'falling out with artists' was part and parcel of maintaining a productive working relationship. He recounted the following anecdote about an artist who was signed to the label he worked for in the mid 1980s;

> There is one artist on our label . . . who made a record about four years ago and he'd been making a lot of substandard videos. Very poor videos, and he had a lot of records that weren't doing very well. The videos weren't getting shown on TV because they were shitty videos. The videos happened to be made by his flatmate. He made a record and I listened to the record and I thought; 'If we can get the right video, if we can take control of the marketing of this record, this record will go to number one'. I brought the artist in here and I said; 'Right, if you let us do this our way we will spend £75,000 on a video, we will take these risks, we will do it and we will give you a number one record'. And the artist kind of reluctantly said 'OK'. We made the video. The video went on TV. The sales of the record increased 650 per cent the day after it went on TV. The record went to number one. It was the biggest single of the year. And the artist hated the video and refused to speak to me for six months. Now, that's not that infrequent.

This quote illustrates the importance of the visual identity for presenting music to the public. It also highlights the importance of the music video as a vehicle for presenting this image, and I will be discussing the practical aspects of video production in Chapter 5. In addition, it provides a hint of the potential for conflict between the artist and company, an issue which arises at various points throughout this book and which I will deal with in more detail in Chapter 8. In the remainder of this chapter I am concerned with the general way in which an artist's identity is articulated and mediated to the public.

Genres of Music, Codes of Dress: You See What You Hear

David Howells, managing director of Peter Waterman Ltd, had a word association game he would frequently play on people when being interviewed during the 1980s. He would choose a genre of music such as punk, heavy metal, reggae or rap and ask a respondent to reply with the first thing that came into their mind. The most common response was for people to reply with a visual image rather than an artist's name or piece of music. So, for example, mention of hard rock elicited responses about spandex trousers and long flowing hair, punk received replies about safety pins, and reggae the mention of dreadlocks. Howells used this as an illustration of the way in which music and image are intricately connected:

> 99 per cent of people give answers that relate to the visual. The extraordinary thing is that you see what you hear. So if you accept that the two go together that's fine. But there are still a lot of people who say; 'the music speaks for itself.' It doesn't. There is a relationship that the public identify with.

Different genres of music have become associated with and signify different images, which in turn connote particular attitudes, values and beliefs. At the same time the visual images denote particular sounds. This is most apparent at live performances; when male hard rock fans share the long hair, leather, buckles and bodily postures of the artists they are watching and imitate the musicians on stage by playing imaginary guitars; and when rap performers and audiences share training shoes, baseball caps and styles appropriated from sportswear and cement their bond further by trading in mutual insults.

It is not just the predominantly male youth subcultural genres in which there is a shared iconography linked to the music. Similar connections are established between the artists and consumers of music associated with a range of age groups. When talking about different audiences, one publicist who represented country music artists in Britain explained that there were 'two types of country fans' and then characterised them visually as 'the older blue-jean enthusiast and the younger black-jean supporter who goes to The Town and Country Club rather than the Wembley festival'. In studies carried out in the United States James Lull found that audiences for a range of genres, including country and western, jazz and hard rock, identified themselves with a particular group or type of music through 'clothing, posters, bumper stickers, and other artefacts that express a musical preference'. These visual symbols offered 'a proud statement from the listener that this artist or genre actually represents his or her personality in some way' (1987, p 143).

Record companies initially position acts sartorially in relation to other artists and genres of music, and signify the adoption of an implicit life style and set of values denoted by these visual codes. Newly signed artists, like record company staff, are consumers of pop music themselves and will often have absorbed and adopted these conventions over the years of listening to and learning to play music. Performers will have developed their own styles of music and dress in relation to contemporary fashions, and through a familiarity with the history of popular music, and will often present themselves to the record company in these terms in the first place. So the initial presentation may well involve record companies merely 'enhancing' what is already there.

The Clichéd Conventions of the Pop Image

Soon after the signing of a recording contract a photo session is arranged and the results distributed to the trade press and media to signal the arrival of a new act. Many of these images are often highly imitative of existing styles, and initially articulate an artist's identity in terms of a series of visual clichés which translate the classification of performers into long term career acts and short term fashion dependent acts into a series of natural/artificial codes.

The most obvious photographic technique is the way in which an act are positioned in a particular context. Rock acts and 'serious' artists are often photographed on location. Following in the footsteps of Public Enemy and Lou Reed, they may be pictured on the mean streets of New York, or like Tanita Tikaram or Simple Minds they might appear on a hillside with hair blowing in the wind, wistfully staring away into an open expanse of sky. The background provides a series of connotations which reinforce the artist's musical identity.

In contrast, dance and pop acts are often pictured in a photographic studio environment which emphasises their clothes, hairstyles, make up and visual appearance. It refers to the body and the fashion of the day. There is nothing in the background to interfere or provide a wider set of connotations. Artists in teenage pop magazines such as *Smash Hits*, *Just 17* and *19* tend to appear in this kind of brightly-lit setting, whereas bands and performers in the *New Musical Express*, *Q*, and *Folk-Roots* are usually featured in a specific urban or 'natural' environment.

Segmentation, Fragmentation and the Middle-Aged Spread

The initial publicity photo is, first and foremost, a signal to the media and personnel within the recording industry that a new act exists and denotes the artist as a particular type. However, marketing staff also present acts in a very similar way to consumers. A campaign plan will involve the positioning of acts in the press, on television and radio, billboards, shops and in colleges – selected according to the geographic, demographic and cultural profile of the consumers for particular genres of music.

Dividing the total audience for popular music into musical taste categories such as 'hard rock', 'alternative', 'dance', 'teenage pop', 'world beat' etc, enables marketing staff to target consumers through specific publications, radio shows, media routes, retail stores and venues. The aim is then to build a 'base market' amongst audiences who are perceived to be the most enthusiastic consumers of particular genres.

This segmentation of consumers into different groupings is a feature of record company marketing practices which has been remarked upon by a number of critics over the years, and has been accentuated by demographic changes and media expansion over the last ten years. The proliferation of musical styles and genres in Britain during the 1980s was accompanied by a growth in printed publications. The established weekly newspaper 'inkies' of *New Musical Express, Melody Maker* and *Sounds* (which ceased trading in April 1991) were joined by a range of more glossy magazines such as specialist publications catering for fans of a particular genre (hard rock, rap, soul, teenage pop, alternative rock, dance, world beat etc), style magazines (the *Face, iD, Blitz*) and periodicals aimed at slightly older music buyers in their twenties (*Select, Vox*) and the 'thirty something' generation (*Q*). This has accentuated the different taste groupings for contemporary pop music, and made it easier for record companies to identify and target specific audiences.

This growth of publications has been facilitated by demographic changes in the constitution of the total market for pop music. From the late 1950s the record market in Britain and the United States was oriented towards 15–24 year-olds. When discussing popular music in the 1970s sociologists could focus explicitly on young people and with some justification claim that popular music was 'virtually the exclusive playground of the young' (Denisoff, 1975). However this age group has been declining as a percentage of the population. In Britain it reached a peak of 9.2 million in the middle of the 1980s and is projected to fall to 6.3 million by the end of the century – a drop of 30 per cent (Talbot, 1991). In addition, the teenagers of the 1950s and youth of the 1960s who grew up with the record buying habit are becoming an expanding market of middle-aged pop consumers.

In response to these demographic changes record companies have set up variously named 'Enterprise'(BMG), 'Strategic Marketing' (EMI), 'Catalogue Marketing' (Polygram), 'Special Projects' (MCA) and 'Operations' (CBS) divisions concerned with the 'secondary exploitation' of existing back catalogues and finding new methods of selling contemporary music to these potential consumers. One marketing director based at a major British corporation expressed the concern of a number of senior executives when he explained that:

> The biggest challenge for us as marketing people is the pure demographics of the market. The decline in the teenage population, the decline, relatively speaking, in their disposable income compared with the 1960s and 1970s and the growth of the burgeoning middle-aged, middle-class for whom there is, at the moment, not enough music and no easy marketing outlets, and who are not catered for properly by either record companies or the media.

One implication of these changes is that new artists are no longer merely aimed at 'youth'. Even if they are initially, a youth market alone cannot sustain long term artistic development. There are economic pressures to 'cross-over' and reach this expanding constituency of consumers. A strange process of recycling the old to the young, and the new to the old has been occurring. New bands in the late 1980s such as Deacon Blue and World Party were producing material bought by people in their 20s and 30s, whilst the music of artists such as Marvin Gaye was being listened to by 15 year olds. When Polydor released *The Very Best of the Righteous Brothers* in 1990 it was aimed at a wide audience, and company executive George McManus who was involved in its marketing explained that its success had less to do with nostalgia than the purchases of young consumers who had discovered 'a new band called The Righteous Brothers'. Pop has developed its own canon of 'classics' and the music which is heard now and influences performers, audiences and record industry staff is the result of multiple inter-generational tastes and experiences. Entering a record shop is becoming similar to entering a book shop, where the consumer expects to chose from a historical accumulation of recordings, rather than simply the latest hot new band (or bright young novelist). This obviously makes marketing more complicated, hence the drive to rationalise, divide and target particular segments.

The segmentation of markets into discrete genres and lifestyle groupings is the result of a dual process. At some point these divisions are clearly an expression of lived social and cultural differences (Lull, 1987). At the same time, however, these cultural divisions are reinforced by the way in which the recording industry actively divides the audience in order to construct iden-tifiable markets. Garofalo (1986) is undoubtedly right when he argues that this process limits the range of musical styles available to a given segment of the consumer market. But in stressing the way in which the record companies, as part of the capitalist cultural industries, 'conspire' to atomise and fragment social experience, Garofalo overlooks the resulting problems this poses for an industry increasingly dependent on selling large quantities of recordings to people *across* social, cultural and national boundaries. The escalating cost of producing and marketing pop music means that the aim of record companies is always to reach a broader audience and move out from a particular market segment.

The Ironies of Authenticity

Beyond the initial presentation of an artist in terms of the visual codes associated with genres of music, a range of staff involved in the entire process of artist development employ ideas about the authenticity and uniqueness of an act. There is a widespread belief that the image and the music should in some way express the character and personality of an artist. As one of the partners at a production and management company remarked: 'A lot of debates about style in the UK are actually about authenticity. It's about whether someone is authentic or inauthentic, and the music business is equally part of that image process'.

This is interesting because it seems to contradict the claims of marketing staff who espouse a calculated approach, and the assertion that there is nothing natural about the production of music or presentation of artists. I am certainly not suggesting that staff in the recording industry hold totally coherent beliefs, or that the organic and synthetic ideologies of creativity which I identified earlier are rigidly adhered to. This would merely lead to the 'fallacy of seeing axioms where there are only shared habits, of viewing statements which sum-marise such practices as if they reported constraints enforcing such practices'

(Rorty, 1991, p 26). The day-to-day work of recording industry personnel is perhaps better thought of as guided by 'habits of action' (Rorty, 1991) or 'orienting practices' (Bourdieu, 1986) rather than coherent and rigid belief systems. These enable individuals to predict and retrodict daily behaviour, but they are continually being modified as new beliefs are generated and new activities engaged in.

Notions of authenticity are not employed in the marketing of an act because staff hold romantic beliefs that the image should express the real experience and origins or innermost soul of an artist (Stratton, 1983). It is for the very practical reason that an artist has to live with their image and carry it convincingly in a range of settings. It is a persona that the artist will have to present in interviews, concerts, on television programmes and in personal appearances. As the partner at the production and management company, who I quoted above, explained further:

> The closer an image is to what an artist can actually feel comfortable with and genuinely interested in as a projection of themselves and their own ideas the more successful it'll be in our experience. The further away you get from that, that's when it gets really difficult; trying to foster an image on someone. If you go too far you've had it. They can't cope with it, and they probably look stupid anyway.

Not only does the artist have to feel comfortable with and committed to their image in some way, but the audience has to believe it. In the fan literature written to, and about, both film stars and pop performers, certain adjectives continually recur: Artists are referred to as 'sincere', 'immediate', 'spontaneous', 'real', 'direct' and 'genuine' (Dyer, 1991; Vermorel & Vermorel, 1985). Dyer has argued that authenticity is one of *the* qualities necessary to make the star phenomenon work. It legitimises both the public identity of an artist and at the same time it guarantees the authenticity of the other characteristics a star embodies such as girl-next-door, man-of-the-people, wasted-drugged-survivor, woman-in-control etc.

Consumers who have grown up with popular music, television and the conventions of advertising are well aware of the way in which artists are packaged and images put together (Willis, 1990). There is a widespread knowledge of 'hypes', and a number of marketing personnel perceived a growing sophistication amongst the audiences for pop music. It was often pointed out to me that audiences are much more discerning than academics and journalists gave them credit for. Consumers are, in the words of one talent acquisition manager; 'pretty sussed these days and they can see something that's contrived and put together'.

Yet, as Richard Dyer has remarked of a similar process of image building in the film industry: 'in the very same breath as audiences and producers alike acknowledge stars as hype, they are declaring this or that star as the genuine article' (1991, p 135). It is an irony of consumption that, as audiences, we acknowledge that our favourite artists, whether Bob Dylan, Public Enemy or Madonna are studied, calculated and hyped in various ways, but at the same time we accept them as 'real'. This was what Adorno & Horkheimer, writing in 1944, viewed as a vivid indication of the 'mass deception' perpetrated by the culture industry: 'that consumers feel compelled to buy and use its products even though they see through them' (1979, p 167).

Consumers, however, do not feel compelled to buy all of the products, and the act of purchase is informed by a number of discriminations, in which an ethic of authenticity is central. This was illustrated in the much publicised case of Milli Vanilli who had their Grammy award confiscated in 1991 when it was revealed that they did not play or sing on any of their recordings or in their public performances. This was an example of audiences seeing through the act and *not* feeling compelled to buy the products (or, perhaps, wishing that they hadn't bought them). A number of consumers in the United States filed law suits against Arista Records charging that the label had perpetrated 'consumer fraud'. Groups of fans, as plaintiffs, cited 'emotional distress', and demanded reimbursement on money spent on recordings, merchandise and concert tickets. The two band members, Rob Pilate and Fab Morvan, subsequently lost their recording contract and re-emerged making commercials for sugar free chewing gum. This is not only an indication of the way in which the sounds and images of pop are inter-related, it is an example of how an ethic of authenticity informs the consumption of popular music.

Yet another further ironic twist can occur when artists are exposed in some way. The gossip and investigative reporting which reveals artists as 'hype' – as not like the image – does not necessarily display the artist as false but provides further access to the 'real' person (Dyer, 1991). The exposure of the image further authenticates the artist: Colonel Tom Parker's manipulation of Elvis is exposed to reveal the true Elvis; the hype is peeled away from Michael Jackson to reveal that – yes, he really is bizarre in his private life; Kylie Minogue authenticates herself in magazine interviews by acknowledging that when she was young and naive she really was a 'manipulated puppet'.

Marketing a Unique Brand

Not only are artists presented so that they convey authenticity in some way, but there is a belief amongst marketing staff that a successful artist must be 'unique'. Parallels can again be found in the cinema. Dyer has pointed out that in the film industry there is a belief that the 'great stars transcend the type to which they belong and become "utterly" individual' (1979, p 111). Recording artists do not have the additional mediating characteristics of the role they are acting, but musical and visual 'roles' are demanded by different genres. If great actors and actresses can transcend one 'type' of role to become totally 'unique', in the recording industry the great artists are seen to transcend specific genres of music.

Once again this has less to do with romantic notions of individuality and genius (Stratton, 1983) than the practicalities of presenting and placing performers. One senior executive who had worked in artist publicity and corporate public relations, spoke of attempting to 'brand' artists. By this he meant that the unique quality of an act would become instantly recognisable and condensed into a specific image which could become a trademark. This director referred to the presentation of U2, who were not signed to the company he worked for, but whose marketing he spoke of with great admiration;

You try and brand the artist, in the way that U2 are branded. The most brilliant corporate branding I have ever seen, without anyone ever thinking that they were being corporately got. Brilliant. You never saw a picture of U2 if it wasn't in front of the joshua tree. Bono was out there [clenches fist]. He was an OK kind of guy because he was saying the right things. I say this as a huge U2 fan. Brilliant piece of marketing.

The visual marketing involves an attempt to articulate the authenticity and uniqueness of an artist and to communicate this through a concise image which operates as a metonym for an act's entire identity and music. The succinct branding of artists may become more important as the vinyl LP declines and the large 12 inch sleeve design is superseded by images which must communicate from small compact disc and cassette covers. It is also easier to place a branded image across a range of consumer merchandise.

Mobile Meanings and the Relations of Authenticity

Simon Frith has, on a number of occasions, drawn attention to the ideological character of notions of authenticity within the discourse of rock music, and argued that; 'what we hear as authentic is already determined by the technological and economic conditions of its production: it does not exist in any sort of ideal or innocent state' (1988b, p 130). Only hinting at the 'real' which may be lurking beneath the illusion of authenticity, Frith opts in this instance for the 'postmodern' explanation and argues that; 'authentic sounds are only recognised by their place in a system of signs' (1988b, p 91).

This has become a typical explanation of the relationship between identities and images in recent years. Moving away from merely exposing notions of authenticity as false and the resulting problem of then accounting for the 'real' that lurks behind the appearance, it is proposed that the meaning of authenticity arises in relation to other signs and meanings rather than through a connection to any concrete origins or audiences. A form of postmodern theory has been applied to pop music which, from this perspective, appears to be awash in a sea of signs:

> The star is a mobile sign which can be linked to any practice, product or language, freed from any message or set of values. The star is no longer an individual measured by their creativity, their authentic relation to their performance, or even the possibilities of an audience projecting its fantasies on to them. The star is a commodified and mobile sign, moving across the broad terrain of cultural tastes and entertainment (Grossberg, 1988, p 319).

My earlier discussion of the positioning of artists in terms of genres of music and the lived experience of consumers gave some indication of how images are *very* connected to certain meanings, experiences and audiences. The codes and conventions of popular music, particularly those of specific genres, cannot simply be mixed and matched and endlessly re-constituted. These signs are not simply connected to other signs but to very specific social conditions and life experiences.

In the following section I want to use the example of two global stars – Bruce Springsteen and Bob Marley – to suggest that in the marketing of popular music, the issue of authenticity is not so much about the way in which an act truthfully represents its 'real' origins, but about the way in which the affective relationship between artist and audience is mediated and articulated. Notions of authenticity cannot be explained as myths which conceal more real conditions, nor as mobile meanings continually emerging out of a sea of endlessly circulating signs. At some point these meanings connect human beings.

Bruce Springsteen: From Macho Motorbikin' to Mother's Boy

Bruce Springsteen has frequently been presented as an ordinary 'man-of-the-people', as an authentic representative of a genuine blue collar New Jersey lifestyle. The lyrical imagery in his songs – riding motorbikes and automobiles along the freeways, the recurring references to refineries, the general chronicling of everyday working class life – are re-presented as lived experience in magazine articles which report him to be hanging out with workers in New Jersey bar rooms and performing impromptu and spontaneously with local rock'n'roll and rhythm 'n' blues bands (Sutcliffe, 1990). This imagery is complemented by music which draws on the blues, country, folk and rock'n'roll; sounds which have a historical association with the voices of oppressed groups – black people and the white working class in the United States.

Bruce Springsteen's identity is communicated across a 'total star text' (Dyer, 1991) of musical recordings, videos, magazine interviews, concert appearances, album covers and advertisements. It was succinctly 'branded' on the release of his *Born in The USA* album in an image composed of worn worker's jeans and a crumpled baseball cap pushed into a pocket in front of the American flag. This branded image operated as a metonym for the music and imagery on the album, which was preoccupied with manual work, the experience of ageing, lost relationships and ambivalent musings on what it was to be North American.

Springsteen's own comments about what he is doing tend to echo those of record company staff who stress that there has to be something real there in the first place for it to be credible. Springsteen once remarked that he didn't know whether he 'played' characters; 'but I write in characters. . . . To make it real you have to have some enormous piece of yourself in it. For it to be just believable, credible, to create a character that is living and breathing' (Flanagan, 1987, pp 145–146).

Unlike fans who share in the articulation of these meanings and creation of the characters; who believe and dis-believe; who see-through and purchase the legend; critics often seek to carry out their own form of exposé. One such writer wrote of Springsteen's *Live* album (released in 1986): 'The small-town male American experience detailed in his songs has achieved the status of a new American mythology and, amazingly, this cultural self-image has been accepted all over the world – sales of the album already amount to five million' (Connor, 1987, p 229).

There is an arrogance to this type of statement, as the writer attempts to expose the 'myth', and is 'amazed' that Springsteen's image has been accepted and has contributed to selling the album. But the question has to be asked: who believes this myth? And how? Everyone who purchased Springsteen's albums around the world, regardless of the contexts within which they viewed and heard him? This type of unmasking of myths is often based entirely on a 'reading' of texts and images. There is frequently no reference at all to how the audience – or the artist – might relate to the myth. Does the audience merely accept it, as implied? It suffers from a similar problem of exposing notions of authenticity as false; it does not ask *how* the myth relates to concrete experience of and dialogue between artists and audiences. It assumes that the myth is transmitted, accepted and persuades consumers to purchase the commodity. But, in this instance the argument is taken further. Not only are the consumers being duped, in the same article Connor declares that; 'The collector of Bruce Springsteen's albums can never be satisfied with these forms of reproduction, for they bring about a thirst for more authentic contact with the original' (1987, p 131).

There is no acknowledgment that myths, legends and stories are what people live their lives by. It is the myths and legends shared by both Springsteen and his audience which connect them. To expose them as false, ideological illusions, or mere signs floating amongst media texts – apart from leaving the problem of what *is* then behind or under the myth (had the 'true meaning' been revealed) – does not address the nature of the relationship between artist and audience. Not only does Connor imply that consumption is induced by ideological manipulation on the part of the music industry and artist, and gullibility on the part of consumers, he then argues that poor deluded Springsteen fans can only relate to 'simulacra' or an 'aura' which has been commodified; which in turn is driving them to neurotic desires for the original. Part of the problem here is that Connor is employing a notion of the 'authentic original' derived from a European high art aesthetic. The 'authenticity' and the 'myth' of Springsteen, however, is not about origins in this sense. It is a far more complicated, mediated and messy (but perhaps more mundane) situation.

The assertion that consumers are in some way responding to substitutes for an original misses Adorno's point that the 'culture industry is defined by the fact that it does not strictly counterpose another principle to that of the aura, but rather by the fact that it conserves the decaying aura as a foggy mist' (Adorno, 1991, p 88). It is across this foggy mist – where marketing staff acknowledge that consumers are 'pretty sussed'; where artists are aware of the techniques they must employ to reach audiences; and where fans are quite capable of acknowledging the hype, the myths, the games and marketing ploys they participate in whilst still finding pleasure in the products – it is across these 'webs of beliefs and desires' (Rorty, 1991) that the 'authentic' character of Springsteen is articulated; not as a false point of origin, nor a mobile sign without a referent; but as a relationship between people. As De Certaux observed: 'The public is not so credulous. It is amazed by these celebrities and simulacra. But it is not taken in by them' (1988, p 181). As Kearney has pointed out; 'The images of all signifying systems . . . remain ultimately answerable to the face to face relation. Behind and beyond the image a face resides.' (Kearney, 1988, p 315).

Within the myth of Bruce Springsteen is a human being called Bruce Springsteen. Inside the electronically mediated voice in the stadium and on the recording, is another voice. Regardless of whether Springsteen is the sole author of the meanings which have become associated with him (and the implicit argument in this book is that he is not), and whether he really lives the stories he narrates, it is the human being Bruce Springsteen who sings and speaks of these experiences that audiences are responding to.

John Street has discussed his affection for Springsteen in his book on the politics of rock. This provides a good illustration of the way in which consumers identify with artists and balance the sense of belief and dis-belief; the knowledge of hype but the recognition that there is a human being in there somewhere. Speaking for a particular group of consumers, Street argues that Springsteen 'gives a passionate voice to our sense of injustice', and on a more personal note he reflects that:

> what I get from his songs . . . is a way of expressing the outrage that unfairness inspires, but accompanied by dignity and defiance . . . my view of Springsteen may be as misty-eyed as my feelings about Lennon, but I am convinced by how much he seems to care: about his audience, about the world outside his mansion, about his responsibilities (1986, p 224).

Feminist writer Angela McRobbie (1980) might not share John Street's misty eyes. If her eyes have gone watery it is through being out in the wind, consigned by Springsteen's discourse of urban romanticism to the 'back seat on a drafty motorbike.' McRobbie is referring to the macho freewheeling street imagery of the song *Born to Run* in a critique of male subcultural theory, and what is interesting here is that as the masculine conventions of rock have been criticised and challenged, Springsteen has sought to re-articulate his identity and relationship to the audience. Springsteen himself occasionally made comments to journalists about the way in which he had to 're-invent' himself during the 1980s, and referred explicitly to his own myth when re-articulating his masculinity directly to an audience in November 1990. Introducing an unreleased song at Shrine Auditorium in Los Angeles, Springsteen made the following rambling prologue;

> Tonight I'm going to try something different. I wrote this song quite a while ago. I never really recorded it or put it out. It's a song about my mother. It's a funny thing because I had this song and I said 'Gee, in rock'n'roll nobody sings about their mother. Why is that?' It's against all that macho posturing you have to do and stuff. So I said, 'Wait a minute, wait a minute, wait a minute.' This was a real problem, so I wanted to figure it out. So I went to see this psychiatrist. This is a true story. I told him what the problem was. I said, 'I have this song about my mother and I haven't sung it 'cause of all the macho posturing that I have to do' ('Mrs. Springsteen's Boy', *Musician*, March 1991, p 17).

Springsteen went on to tell his audience about how men are afraid of their mothers, and how this fear informs the relationship between men and women. Exposing his anxieties about his own 'macho posturing' he concluded that he was 'man enough' to sing about his own mother, and then performed the song.

Multiple Meanings and Markets: Bob Marley and the Polysemantics of Sound and Image

The aim of marketing is ultimately to establish an artist in such a way that their unique and individual musical and visual identity crosses genres, and local and regional life styles. This was achieved in the marketing of Bob Marley who was presented with a similar combination of uniqueness and authenticity: a branded, instantly recognisable, identity based on a combination of the imagery of rastafari and Ethiopianism, with the traditions of the rock rebel and global pop playboy. Marley was a powerful political and cultural symbol and at the same time merely another icon in the history of pop styles.

Bob Marley was marketed with a degree of calculation and in a sophisticated way which retained these pop and political meanings. His music was inflected with influences which enabled it to communicate to, and be appropriated by, a range of white pop and rock audiences and black soul and rhythm and blues fans. Although Marley has been characterised as yet another black artist who 'compromised' in order to reach a wider white rock audience (Wallis & Malm, 1984), this simplistic argument has been criticised by Paul Gilroy. Gilroy has pointed out that the minor adjustments in presentation and form that rendered his reggae 'assimilable across cultural borders', such as the incorporation of bluesy guitar styles and disco rhythms, were not concessions to a white audience but 'attempts to utilise the very elements most likely to appeal to the black audiences of North America' (1987, p 170). As Chris Blackwell, the head of Island who signed Marley, recalled when interviewed by Timothy White in 1991: 'He was really keen to try and sell records to black America . . . *Rastaman Vibration* was a conscious attempt to break into that market.' The market for reggae in America is comparatively small and mainly composed of radical, student and 'alternative' white audiences. Marley was attempting to reach the predominantly black 'urban' or rhythm and blues audiences. A further irony is that these commercial motivations contributed to the development of his musical identity and led him to synthesize rhythm and blues, rock and reggae in a way never achieved before.

Bob Marley provided multiple visual and musical points of reference which were accessible to various audiences across the world. But, this is not to imply that these were endless optical-rhythmic signs floating across media texts until someone gave them their own preferred meaning. The messages from Marley were finite and presented to emphasise certain particular interpretations. Working with Chris Blackwell and record company personnel at Island Records, in composing himself as a polysemantic pop icon capable of reaching various audiences for music across the world, he did not become a mere signifier without a referent. All signs pointed to a specific man – Bob Marley – and audiences responded to this, recognising that 'beyond the play of masks and mirrors, there are human beings who suffer and struggle, live and die, hope and despair' (Kearney, 1988, p 388). As one of the young men interviewed for Paul Willis's book on *Common Culture* remarked: 'A lot of people relate to Bob Marley, and I can see why, 'cause a lot of the things he sings about I've been through myself' (1990, p 70). It is at this point, where the artist and audience meet, right in the centre of the commercial marketing of recorded music, where pop has the potential to join human beings in communicating and sharing ideas, emotions and experiences.

The Rhetoric and Ethics of Authenticity

The meanings of authenticity arise out of specific relationships between human beings (no matter how electronically mediated). They are not endless but they vary according to musical genre and change over time. When the Pet Shop Boys boasted about their inability to perform 'live' and made various 'anti-rock' statements which were intended to undermine notions of spontaneity and performance, they were themselves employing different notions of authenticity. As Andrew Goodwin has pointed out; 'The Pet Shop Boys can defy some discourses of authenticity because they invoke others, such as the authorship of their own marketing images and a source of "truth" that lies in an explicit critique of "rock music" ' (1990, p 268).

The rhetoric of authenticity employed by recording industry personnel and artists, and the ethics of authenticity adopted by audiences are continually changing. As Dyer has noted; 'yesterday's markers of sincerity and authenticity are today's signs of hype and artifice' (1991, p 137). Hence, the ageing rock audience does indeed 'lose its hold on rock's secret', as Frith argues (1988b). But it is rediscovered and re-articulated by this same audience on the 'margins' or in world beat or in new age music. Each emerging genre posits its own conventions of authenticity, which at the same time exposes previous conventions (just as rock exposed the 'falsity' of the Tin Pan Alley tradition). But within these conventions is the 'authentic' relationship – the shared sense of being – which is articulated between artist and audience.

Fantasy and Dreams

Not all artists are marketed so that the audience identify with some experience of authenticity. One genre in which this does not apply is teenage and preteenage pop. The basic marketing of the teen idol has changed very little over the past thirty years. The emphasis has been on 'fun, energy, glamour and dream material' (Harron, 1988). Artists who have been marketed to preteenage audiences – from The Monkees to New Kids On The Block – have been presented in such a way as to encourage 'imaginary' identification with the consumer.

Male rock critics, often following Greil Marcus (1977), have tended to treat artists as expressing social, personal and cultural experiences in a real space and time. This has become a taken-for-granted way of approaching performers, feeding into both the marketing process in the recording industry and the reception of music by fans. However, feminist writers have often stressed the elements of fantasy and imaginary identification involved in the relationship between an artist and audience.

Sue Wise, in a personal account of the way in which she identified with Elvis Presley, noted that male writers had tended to write about Elvis as a macho folk hero, emphasising the way *they* identified with his expressions of youthful rebellion and male sexuality. Wise contrasts this with the 'warmth and affection' which she felt for Elvis as a 'dear friend' in her own 'private Elvis world' (1990). In many ways John Street's misty-eyed affection for Bruce Springsteen and belief that he cares is a similar form of imaginary identification; and, equally, Sue Wise's Elvis world is dependent on a notion of the authenticity of Presley's sincerity.

The activity of engaging and sympathising with an artist – the social-psychology and affective relations of fan-performer identification – has received very little critical attention in popular music, and comparatively little in the film industry (Stacey, 1991). Whilst fantasy is clearly an integral part of the beliefs and desires which connect artist and audience it is ultimately part of the way in which consumers appropriate and make use of music and images. The aim of marketing is to set up the point of identification in the first place. Fantasy can only follow the initial positioning of an artist in various media. And, it must be stressed that for all the opportunities provided for both artists and audiences within the marketing process, the 'point of identification' is being engineered by record companies in order to sell discs and tapes and engender a sense of loyalty which will lead consumers to purchase further recordings. However, I hope I have shown that this is not simply based on illusion and manipulation. I now want to end this chapter by briefly looking at what happens after this point of identification has been established.

Monitoring the Consumer Through Market Research

The way in which record companies identify and respond to consumers has undergone considerable change since the 1960s. The reliance on what one executive, looking back over twenty years in the industry, recalled as 'experience, gut feeling and guesswork' has been supplemented by a greater use of market research and more sophisticated methods of reaching audiences through specific well defined media routes.

Market research is mainly used to make decisions about acts with recordings already released, to assess a band or singer's popularity amongst a particular social group or in a specific geographical region. A typical survey will ask a cross-section of the record-buying public how familiar they are with an artist's music, to rate on an ascending scale how much they like it, whether they regularly purchase recordings and how they became aware of the artist. This enables the company to build up demographic profiles of the consumers of particular acts and genres of music. Marketing staff can then use this to identify the factors which are either contributing to an artist's popularity or impeding their success, and assess the potential for expanding the appeal of an act and the avenues they might use to do this.

Record companies often carry out research if there is concern about an artist's image or if a performer is considering changing his or her visual identity in any way. The views of the consumers who buy an artist's recordings, or who previously purchased them but have stopped for some reason, will often be solicited in small group discussions. These findings will often lead to quite conscious visual changes in response. For example, the views of consumers were sought when a major company were considering the proposed album cover artwork for one long standing English male solo singer (who, for sensitive executives, must remain anonymous). This was to have featured the artist with his shirt undone and chest exposed. The research found that the main purchasers were often men who bought this performer's recordings for their wives or female partners. The findings revealed a geographical division in Britain – a high percentage of men in the north said that they would be reluctant to purchase the record because the cover had connotations of homosexuality; So, the proposed cover was duly changed and the chest went back inside the shirt.

Research is frequently carried out when an artist has not released material for some time, or to establish the most suitable iconography for marketing greatest hits compilations – collections which are often purchased by a broader range of people than those who regularly buy an artist's material. Both types of research were carried out on Bryan Ferry during the 1980s. When Ferry recorded some new songs these were played to potential consumers and the response was so negative that a decision was taken to shelve these and to re-issue some of his older material, remixed with a contemporary sound. A short time later, when *The Bryan Ferry and Roxy Music Ultimate Collection* was being put together, the cover artwork – a full length black and white shot of Ferry in a classic tailored suit – was arrived at as a direct result of group discussions during which Ferry had been identified as 'sophisticated, stylish and cool' (McGinley, 1991).

This type of research is not, yet, used to assess the potential of new artists, although with greater emphasis being put on marketing this may change. When I spoke to the director of one market research company, ever eager for business, he argued that A & R staff would benefit from researching the appeal of an artist before signing them. However, this poses the problem of identifying just who might like it – who should be asked? With an established band or singer the consumers who purchased previous discs and tapes can be identified. But with a new artist it is more difficult. As I have stressed in this chapter, the reception of music is influenced by perceptions of an artist across a range of media which continually interact and build up over time. Music is not simply received as sound, but through its association with a series of images, identities and associated values, beliefs and affective desires. Marketing staff are acutely aware of this and strategically attempt to create these links – between the music and image, and between the artist and consumer. These are then monitored and re-articulated during marketing campaigns. However, as one marketing director who used research but stressed that he was always ignoring it because it either told him what he already knew or was totally lacking in any imagination, commented; 'There's no point in researching a new act because nobody's going to know who they are. If you had market-researched Boy George it would have come out that nobody's going to buy it'.

5

STUDIOS AND VIDEOS

The Production of Sound and Vision

For a newly signed artist the production of musical recordings and videos will immediately lead into the most explicitly collaborative process in the recording industry. In describing this I want to highlight the way in which the sounds and images of pop are often composed in an arbitrary and adhoc-manner rather than according to some well thought out plan. It is in the process of visual and musical production where artists and various recording industry personnel experience some of the greatest autonomy and liberty. It is in these areas where the control of entertainment corporations is often reduced to a semi-detached monitoring operation. Limits are set by imposing budget restrictions and retroactively modifying, mixing and editing the songs and videos which have been produced.

Artist and Repertoire and Musical Development

Whilst marketing staff are identifying audiences and articulating identities, the A & R person works with a newly-signed act in transforming the music into a commodity form suitable for reproduction on discs and tapes and broadcasting across various media. The way in which A & R staff do this varies. Some profess a casual approach, allowing the artist considerable autonomy and speak of merely sending artists away to 'get on with it'. In contrast, other A & R personnel are more interventionist, and adopt an autocratic role; deciding the material to be recorded, where and who the artist should work with, and may be credited as an 'executive producer' or extend their supervisory role to producing the studio session itself. However, the majority of A & R staff tend to work between these extremes.

Most A & R staff favour a facilitator role, acting as a catalyst by offering encouragement and criticism, and linking the act with various parties who may be able to assist in their musical development. As one director who had been both a musician and producer explained:

> Sometimes, if we're lucky, we don't have to bring anything to the artist. They just seem to know what to do and it works. But that isn't often the case. What you do,

really, is you try and help them bring out the best in themselves. I suppose it's a bit like the trainer of any athlete, or swimmer, or a football manager. You recognise the talent, then you help them develop it and bring it out.

A variety of techniques are utilised to 'bring out' the talent. Initially the A & R person will sit down with an act and systematically go through their material, discussing its relative merits and weaknesses, identifying where it might need improving or where the act might need assistance.

The material is analysed in terms of song structure, instrumentation, lyrics, and vocal performance, and the contribution of A & R staff varies. Some may suggest very specific musical changes, chord patterns, melodic modifications, bass lines or lyrical changes. Others may identify more general reasons why they think a song needs improving. The act will be continually encouraged to write, record and rehearse in small, inexpensive studios or using portable recording equipment and may test out their material in front of an audience.

It has sometimes been observed that contemporary pop music is more about 'the sound' than 'the song' (Kealey, 1982). Whilst a major concern of A & R personnel is to produce a 'unique' sound, considerable emphasis is put on song writing as a craft, employing techniques of structuring a song around a repeated musical theme or riff, and building it up to a distinctive and memorable refrain. The basic song structure of verse/chorus/verse/chorus/middle/chorus has been an enduring framework within all pop genres from hard rock anthems to soul ballads and can be detected in the most un-song-like sampled rap collages, where fragments of other recordings function as choruses alongside semi-spoken raps as verses.

If artists are having difficulty writing or completing songs, the A & R person may arrange for them to collaborate with, or receive guidance and assistance from more experienced songwriters. If the artist does not write their own material, or the songs are considered unsuitable, the A & R person will locate material from back catalogues or by commissioning new songs from writers or publishers.

Hence, not long after signing to a record company an act will begin modifying their material as a result of these dialogues with artist and repertoire staff. In the process of experimenting, trying out ideas and subjecting them to criticism there are inevitable disagreements and differences of opinion; between members of bands themselves and between artists and A & R staff. But there is usually give-and-take on both sides. As an A & R director explained:

> If guys have got common sense they will listen to what you've got to say and they will try out what you've got to say. If they find it works then hopefully they've got enough common sense to override their ego and say; 'You're right, it feels better this way, thank-you very much'. I'm quite happy for an artist to think through what I've told him and come back and say; 'I'm sorry but I don't feel this'. That's OK. At least if he's done it and he's tried it and worked it through that's OK.

A & R staff may occasionally disagree with what an artist wants to do, but if the artist feels strongly committed to a particular idea they will usually be allowed to proceed. Equally, an act may not initially like the suggestions of A & R staff, but may try them out and use them if they think it will help sell records. This occurred when the band Cheap Trick recorded *The Flame* which became their 'comeback hit' in 1988. Don Grierson, the A & R Director at Epic

Records who suggested that they record a version of this song, recalled that when he first brought the song to the attention of the band 'they hated it. But they did it and it became a number one song' (Baird, 1990, p 70).

When the act has three or four songs suitable for recording in a professional studio, and enough further material to make up an album (10–14 songs), the task is then to find a suitable producer.

The Marriage of Artist and Producer

The record producer extends the work of A & R, making the key decisions about how specific material should be recorded in a studio and supervising the sessions. The A & R person will have acquired a knowledge of the way different producers work and what they can achieve and will seek someone who is musically and temperamentally compatible with an act. The artists will have an idea of the type of sound they wish to produce and an opinion of the sort of producer they would like to work with. The A & R department will often have examples of producers' past work or specially produced sample reels which they will play to artists and discuss with them. A short list will be arrived at and the preferred producers will be contacted and sent recordings, and perhaps invited to see the act in performance or rehearsal. If the producer is interested in working with an act a meeting will be arranged, in order for the different parties to discuss how they envisage a recording session proceeding.

Artist and repertoire staff attempt to find a producer who will be actively involved in the selection and arrangement of material and who can assist an act in specific ways. As one director explained when discussing newly signed rock bands:

> Specific types of producers are good for specific types of music. Some are excellent in some areas, but totally irrelevant for others. I look and see what a band has and what it needs in its early development years. First of all I have an idea of what sort of record the band should make and how it should sound. I look to see what the group have and what the group are actually missing. Then it's my intention to get a producer in that would be able to help them in the areas that they're not particularly good at. It may be in the playing area, it may be in the song structure area, it may be in the arrangement of the songs. It may be that they don't require those things so you don't need to get a producer in whose forte is song structures and arrangements, so you get a more engineer-based producer in.

In locating a producer A & R staff do not necessary confine themselves to their own country. British acts often wish to work with American producers and record in the United States. This can be for musical reasons, or because it is felt that the music is more suited to an American audience, and that a particular producer would provide a useful point of reference when introducing the act in the United States.

Alternatively the act may wish to record in a particular location in order to use specific facilities or studio personnel. When the Eurythmics were working on their first album *In The Garden* under the influence of German bands such as Kraftwerk and DAF, they chose to record with Conny Plank at his studio in Cologne. This also gave them the opportunity to make use of contributions from Holgar Czukay and Jaki Liebezeit, two members of the avant garde rock band Can (O'Brien, 1991).

Budgets and the Producer's Stake

An important consideration at this stage is the recording budget, which is calculated in relation to the type of artist, and the anticipated sales of their first recordings. In addition to producers' fees the budget includes the cost of hiring the studio and equipment, payments to engineers and musicians, and accommodation and travelling expenses. For a newly-signed artist the first recording sessions will often be restricted by budget considerations and may be limited to using local producers.

There is some debate and disagreement amongst various producers, record company staff and studio owners as to the advantages of large recording budgets and expensive studios. Some staff feel that using an established 'name' producer can benefit an act musically and can also get them noticed. However, others point out that this often generates too many expectations and can lead to the resulting work being judged more critically by key opinion formers within the industry and media. A number of A & R staff felt that good albums could be recorded cheaply, and that extra budgets often led to complacency and self-indulgence. In 1988 the first Fairground Attraction album was made for £38,000 and in the same year The Wonder Stuff recorded their first album for £28,000. These figures were often contrasted to recordings made by established artists, such as the Tears for Fears album *The Seeds of Love* released in 1989 which cost a reported £1 million, took three years to record, involved four producers and nine studios, and was neither commercially nor critically well received (Sutcliffe, 1989b).

In the UK, producers are contracted by record companies for specific projects. The producer will initially undertake to record a limited number of tracks with the option to proceed to the completion of an album. The producer receives a cash advance on commencement of recording and the payment of a further sum on successful completion and delivery of the finished tapes. Depending on their past work and reputation, a producer can receive between one and four royalty percentage points on the sales of recordings. This percentage will be paid out of the artist's royalty earnings. In most cases involving newly-signed artists the record company will have negotiated a 'total talent royalty' which will be paid in a contract. A new act is likely to receive 12 per cent, so if they use a producer who charges two royalty points, the act will receive 10 points. Thus, if it is a five piece group, the producer's royalties on sales of an album will be equal to each band member.

Established artists may have re-negotiated an arrangement whereby the record company pays the producer a separate royalty to that of the artist up to a set limit (perhaps three per cent). After this any further points must then be paid out of the artist's royalties. In the USA deals are conducted directly between artist and producer. The record company usually pays the artist a 'recording fund', and out of this the artist decides how much they want to use for themselves and how much they want to pay a producer. All of these arrangements directly acknowledge that the artist is 'giving' some of their 'creative' royalty points to the producer. Hence, the producer's musical significance and contribution is inscribed in these financial arrangements.

The Recording Environment

Studios are chosen for their atmosphere and technical facilities, and producers tend to develop a preference for a particular environment where they have completed successful work in the past. However, it is important that artists are also comfortable in the studio and one of the producer's tasks is to create the conditions which are most conducive to the working style of a particular act.

The initial environment is the studio itself. The interior and the location of a studio can influence the atmosphere at a recording session and have subtle but profound effects on the music produced. The studio interior may be small, dark and intimate with low ceilings and no natural daylight. Alternatively it could be a cavernous, well-lit room in a converted church or barn. The location can range from the middle of a city, such as Air Studios in central London looking down onto the hustle and bustle of Oxford Circus, or it may be in a converted manor house in the English countryside with luxury accommodation and an accompanying swimming pool.

The techniques employed by the producer in shaping the recording context can range from subtle psychological and social skills involved in creating a dialogue and repartee between those involved (Stokes, 1977), to physically creating a particular environment. This occurred when Daniel Lanois produced the album *Yellow Moon* for the Neville Brothers in 1989. Rather than take them into 'an alien environment' he built a studio around the band by converting a New Orleans apartment into a recording studio. An ambience was created by burning incense and hanging Spanish moss and alligator heads on the walls. The result was a relaxed, but intense, atmospheric and soulful album. Clearly this is an elaborate example of what record producer Tony Visconti once described as 'creating an atmosphere in which an artist can work', but it has been an increasing possibility as recording equipment has become more lightweight and mobile.

Engineers, Technicians and Musicians

While the producer works as director of proceedings, the engineer is involved in technically finding the combinations of settings to create the sounds required. Although the importance of producers is acknowledged throughout the music industry, assessments of the significance of engineers varies. Certain engineers are recognised for their contributions, and some 'name' engineers such as Hugh Padgham may work in a co-producer capacity with artists who are supervising the production of their own work – as he has done with Phil Collins and Sting. Their importance is also noticeable in the way in which a number of producers have formed working relationships with particular engineers and work together as a team. However, whilst carrying out my research for this book I often came across a rather more negative assessment in which engineers were dismissively referred to as 'knob twiddlers.' One artist's manager felt that as long as a producer was competently doing their job then the engineer would simply 'get on with it and be paid the daily rate for engineering that record'.

The engineer is assisted by the tape operator. This person, usually a male school leaver, may eventually become an engineer, perhaps a producer or go on to work in an A & R department. The tape operator is starting at the bottom performing the most basic duties, such as setting levels, marking tape, setting up equipment, making the tea and getting the sandwiches.

A further contribution the producer makes to a recording is to act as a link between the artist and session musicians. The producer will have worked with a number of musicians in the past and will be able to utilise a contact network. Although session musicians are represented by agents and managers, a large amount of their work is gained through personal connections. As British session drummer Geoff Dugmore remarked in 1988: 'It's very cliquey and most of the work comes by word of mouth. There's an inner circle of about two dozen at the top, then an outer circle of about fifty on the next rung.' Session musicians may be called in to add specific sounds and embellishments to a particular track, in which case they may be contacted at very short notice. Or, they may be employed for their adaptability and may be required throughout a session. Dependent upon networks of contacts and having to work irregular hours at short notice, the working life of a session musician can be an erratic and insecure existence.

The development of digital studio technology has led to an increasing role for programmers and required session musicians to develop additional skills in this area. Much of what is referred to as 'programming' involves the use of existing software packages and is done outside of the studio during pre-production work. A programmer may then be on hand for the first few days of recording or called in later to make any necessary modifications. Some of the most respected programmers are keyboard players who use programming as an extension of their existing musical ability and arranging skills. But assistance may also be sought from self-confessed technical 'boffins' such as Chris Newman who, whilst not playing keyboards, has acted as a musician's accomplice, and was involved in 'making up the sounds' which were required by The Pet Shop Boys during the late 1980s.

Like keyboard players, drummers have also had to develop programming skills, particularly as digital technology has created a situation where a 'real' drummer can be made to sound like a machine, and computerised drums to emulate the 'imperfections' of a real drummer (Goodwin, 1990). These technical changes affected the work of June Miles-Kingston, who has been a professional musician since 1976, and found that she was increasingly being called in for sessions to add drums to a recording by synchronising her playing to a metronomic 'click track', and eventually having to use drum machines. Out of necessity she took up programming to support her existing skills and in order to keep obtaining work (Horkins, 1989). This is an example of the way in which technology has changed the character of musical skills, as discussed in Chapter 2.

Another Male World

Unlike June Miles-Kingston, women have usually been found in studios taking the bookings and in reception, but excluded from the recording process in the studio itself. In January 1988 *Studio Week* published a comprehensive list of Britain's pop and rock producers and engineers; it consisted of 222 men and one woman. The following year another trade magazine, *Studio*, reported that there were only 12 female tape operators and engineers working in the recording industry in Britain. In recent years a few female engineers have begun to be recognised for their work – rather than the oddity of them being in a male profession – most notably Arabella Rodriguez who engineered for Soul II Soul, Angela Piva who engineered Color Me Badd's *I Want to Sex You Up*, and Raine Shine who has engineered for Vangelis. The opportunities for women, however, are severely restricted by the 'masculine culture' which dominates most recording studios (Bayton, 1989). As Steward & Garratt observed in the early 1980s:

> In most studios there is a general air of all-lads-together-camaraderie. Even the equipment colludes: if a wrong instruction is fed into a solid state logic computer desk, it won't give a simple 'error' message. Instead, the screen flashes increasingly coarse abuse. 'These are genuine insults', crows the SL4000E mixer manual 'If you don't like them don't use them'. It may sound petty or puritanical to complain about a machine being programmed to say 'Go screw yourself with a poker' (and that's one of the softer insults). But this is the latest in studio technology, and the fact that it was added tells us a lot about the attitudes of its makers and users (1984, p 76).

Since this was written the manufacture of cheap computerised drum machines, keyboards and multi-track recording equipment has enabled music of high sound quality to be produced more easily in the home, and this partly created the conditions for the emergence of much of the dance and house music of the 1980s. A number of commentators have argued that these new technologies may provide the potential for a more flexible, do-it-yourself approach to music making, with sounds produced outside of the conventional studios with their male culture and dependence on professional producers and engineers. These technologies have the potential to challenge the way in which the production of pop has been gendered.

However, it has tended to be boys rather than girls who have responded to the opportunities provided by new electronic instruments and recording equipment. Angela McRobbie has viewed these new technologies with an air of pessimism, arguing that they are reinforcing existing divisions:

> The move towards pre-packaged effects relying on drum machines and all sorts of computerised hardware, had disastrous consequences for girls. The resulting music was a set of sounds created in boy's bedrooms and the only girls who got involved were the few girlfriends patient enough to sit around and wait to be offered a tiny role doing occasional vocals . . . this new computer technology kept the girls firmly at bay. (1988, p 24).

It is not just the technology which is keeping the girls at bay. Detailed research by Sara Cohen (1991) into the culture of unsigned rock bands in Liverpool found that male musicians at grass roots level exhibited a fear and hostility to any idea that women should be involved in the studio and at rehearsals and performances. As Mavis Bayton wrote following her own experience of playing in an all woman group; 'Women musicians are joked about, patronised, leered at, insulted and verbally abused, threatened with violence, and physically attacked on occasions' (1989, p 24). Such observations were illustrated in a trade magazine interview with Robin Hilton. Whilst engineering during a tour by The Thompson Twins she continually had to put up with provocation and her equipment being deliberately sabotaged by other members of the road crew. The intimidation culminated one night when she was, in her own words 'rumbled by a very drunk crew which resulted in a badly bruised back' (Moss, 1990). Hence, the existing conventions of artist and repertoire departments, the male ethos of the studio and the use of technology has provided a formidable barrier to women musicians and female recording industry personnel being received into these areas.

Studio Production Practices

The professional status and working practices of producers and engineers has changed throughout the twentieth century, as recording techniques have been re-organised in response to the technological changes discussed in Chapter 2. Describing these changes, Edward Kealey (1979) identified three 'modes of collaboration' which have characterised the work of 'sound mixers' during the latter part of the twentieth century: the craft union mode, the entrepreneurial mode and the art mode.

The craft mode guided recording immediately after the Second World War, when studio practice was governed by a utilitarian preoccupation with capturing the sounds of performance. This required technical expertise in order to position microphones and artists in the correct acoustic environment, and at the same time involved unionisation of the work force and considerable corporate investment in studios and expensive immobile technologies.

During the 1950s, following the introduction of recording tape and plastic microgroove discs the opportunities arose for recording on cheaper, less cumbersome equipment. This enabled a freelance 'entrepreneurial' type of producer without conventional training to record. These producers, such as Sam Phillips who recorded Elvis Presley, were less concerned with received notions of technical correctness, and began to experiment using tape editing, multiple sound recording, distortion and slap back echo effects.

'Sound mixers' began to be recognised for their contribution to the recording process and during the 1950s the occupation of 'producer' emerged as a distinctive activity, separate from that of the sound engineer and A & R staff. Whilst the engineer was still performing technical craft skills, the producer was directing and supervising the recording sessions. Producers such as Leiber and Stoller at Atlantic in America, and George Martin at EMI in Britain began exerting pressure on their respective record companies and subsequently received credits on the packaging of records and royalty payments for their work (Tobler & Grundy, 1982; Gillett, 1988).

By the middle of the 1960s the studio producer had become an 'artist', employing multi-track technology and stereo sound to use recording as a form of composition in itself, rather than simply as a means of documenting a performance. As production changed to an 'art' it became less common for producers to be technical personnel and a number of musicians, songwriter/arrangers, A & R personnel and artists' managers began to move into production.

As the 'art mode' of collaboration began to dominate the production of popular music, an analogy was often drawn between record producers and film directors. A pop version of 'auteur theory' – the producer as creative author – was employed to describe people ranging from Phil Spector and his dense, reverberating 'wall-of-sound' techniques in the early 1960s, George Martin's classical and surreal influenced productions of The Beatles and the sampled musicollages of DJs like Paul Oakenfeld producing dance music during the late 1980s.

However, the way a producer works and their contribution to a session can vary enormously depending on the act and the type of music being recorded. Although Kealey identified the 'three modes of collaboration' as dominant during particular periods, elements of each can be found in contemporary recording practices.

A producer may adopt a naturalistic 'craft' approach when working with bands who have been signed to a record label with a repertoire of complete, rehearsed songs. The initial material may have been composed via a process of extended improvisation and 'jamming' around a musical or lyrical idea or basic song introduced by a band member – as described in accounts of U2 (Dunphy, 1988) and unsigned bands in Liverpool (Cohen, 1991). For an act who compose in this way the aim in the studio is often to record the best possible arrangement and in the words of one producer, to 'extract a performance out of the band'.

This approach to recording, informed by both the craft mode and the naturalistic ideology of rock with its emphasis on feel, atmosphere and spontaneity, was adopted during the recording of the first album by David Bowie's band Tin Machine in 1989. Bowie himself characterised the project as a self conscious attempt to 'return' to a more spontaneous type of recording, and as producer Tim Palmer recalled:

> I wanted to capture the band as they were at that particular moment. There are very few overdubs on it. It was very much a case of set the sound up and keep the tape rolling all the time . . . As it turned out, most of the vocals were done live in one take . . . it was a performance album, and everyone was allowed to perform (Smith, 1989, p 44).

In contrast to this method is a more 'entrepreneurial' approach. Entrepreneurial activity has been characterised as the 'novel combination of the available means of production' (Peterson & Berger, 1971, p 98), and the production-writing teams at Motown often worked in this way during the early 1960s. One writer observed that the producers at Motown would 'ruthlessly cannibalise old songs for spare parts; verbal phrases, thematic ideas, musical figures, accompaniments, even saxophone solos are shuffled together and re-worked from disc to disc; every song is a collage' (George, 1985, p 118). A number of artists, including John Lennon and Bob Dylan, have often commented on how they have used existing chord patterns, lyrical motifs, riffs and melodies as an initial point of departure when composing songs (Wenner,

1973; Flanagan, 1987). More recently the explicit use and recombination of existing elements was referred to by soul singer Sydney Youngblood, when describing how he was being produced by Claus Zundell in Ibiza during 1989:

> When we write our stuff, we all go down to Ibiza and hang out in this place, The Pasha Garden, which is a big outside club down by the beach. We listen to all the stuff they're playing and say we can do it better. So we go back up to Claus' place and sit around a micro cassette machine and sing the thing out. I'll be sitting banging out the rhythm on the chair, someone will be singing the bass line, someone the melody and someone else the harmony . . . We're taking popular grooves and using them in our music so people can relate. When we come home I work on the lyrics, me and Souly work on the melody, and me, Claus and Serious work on the music. We all go round to NT Gang's place and with a Portastudio and MC500 work on the arrangements so that when we go into a studio we get it right first time. It's a system that works all the time and we don't have to argue about anything. (Grant, 1989, p 60).

Here the 'entrepreneurial mode' meets the 'art mode' in a collective-synthetic approach to popular music, a technique which characterised the production of some of the most imaginative and commercially successful dance music of the late 1980s and early 1990s recorded by acts such as De La Soul, PM Dawn and Deee-Lite. When the KLF released their album *The White Room* in 1991 the record sleeve proudly displayed their sources. The songs on the album were composed from a combination of performed vocals, the sampled voices of The MC5, Stevie Wonder and Wanda D, the use of synthesizers and drum machines, the sampled trumpet of King Tubby, crowd noises from recordings by The Doors and U2 and a 'real' Gibson 330 semi-acoustic guitar. The music was the result of a process of sound collage, the producer as 'artist' rather than the capturing of one specific performance – but threads of a 'craft', 'entrepreneurial' and 'art' mode can be detected in the way in which the album had been 'produced, performed and programmed'.

The production of popular music involves a continual 'dialogue with the past' (Lipsitz, 1990), not only in how artists use and combine elements of previous musical styles, but in the way in which the production practices themselves contain residues of previous 'modes' of producing and composing popular music. Producers provide a repertoire of techniques, incorporating the possibilities provided by new technologies with the more conventional production skills of song arranging and capturing a musician's performance. One of the most important performances is that of the vocalist.

The Personality in the Voice

The voice is the part of a recording which most directly addresses the listener. It is the singer who, through intonation, phrasing, and para-linguistic vocal utterances, most directly communicates the emotion of a particular song. It is the voice which encodes the identity and history of a performer and which conveys a singer's authenticity (Hennion, 1983).

Roland Barthes (1990) used the metaphor of the 'grain of the voice' to refer to the aspect of the singing voice which communicates 'the presence of the physical body'. Barthes made a distinction between the conventions of singing and rules of a genre (the 'pheno-song'), and the particular way in which a voice works and signifies meaning – not 'what it says, but the voluptuousness of its sound-signifiers' (the 'geno-song'). Barthes noted that vocal pedagogy, in the classical European tradition, has emphasised the pheno-song – the techniques of respiration, disciplines of breathing, functionality and clarity – rather than 'the grain'.

What is immediately apparent in popular music is the way in which A & R staff, producers, artists, critics and fans have been far more concerned with the 'grain' of the vocalist; the unique and idiosyncratic way in which an individual voice communicates, rather than in correct technique. All genres have their conventions, whether the sentimental country whine, the fey mournful plead of alternative rock, the snarling macho sneer of hard rock, the street wise assertiveness of rap or the soft sincerity of the singer-songwriter. But A & R staff in record companies are always looking for the individual and distinctive grain, the quality that rises above the simple genre conventions. As Hennion found in his study of popular music production in France; 'Having a "voice" in pop music terms does not mean possessing a vocal technique or systematically mastering one's vocal capacities. Instead a voice is an indication of one's personality' (1983, p 182).

Considerable effort can go into recording the voice which most explicitly expresses a performer's personality, and singers have employed a variety of techniques in the past ranging from the consumption of drugs and alcohol, singing in a studio toilet, to using electronic effects to create a particular vocal sound. The recording of the voice can proceed by recording a number of vocals on different tracks and then selecting the best one or by combining parts of different takes. Alternatively the vocalist may concentrate on each lyrical phrase in isolation before moving on to the next.

Journalist Bob Greene provided an insight into the effort involved in capturing a singer's voice in an account of the recording of Alice Cooper's *Muscle of Love* album at the Record Plant in New York during 1974. At the beginning of the recording session Greene noted that the singer's voice 'wasn't even close to the normal Alice Cooper sound'. Having subsequently sat through hours of recordings and re-recordings, barely detecting any difference in the quality of the various performances, Greene asked producer Jack Richardson why so much time and effort was being spent on this one element. The producer's comments illustrate the point I have been making here. Richardson stressed that he was not:

> looking for the traditional flawless voice. With Alice, it's almost the opposite. You remember the other day, when I told him to stop trying to sound like Jack Jones? I wasn't being facetious, you know. With Alice I'm looking for a very rough, raw, primitive sound. . . . We want to give the impression that Alice just walked into the studio and laid down a mean, raunchy rock and roll track, and then walked out. But that takes a lot of time, to create that impression (Greene, 1974, p 71).

Hence it is the voice which most explicitly articulates the singer's (and the act's) unique identity; and at the same time it is the voice which signifies aurally the singer's physical presence within the music.

The Surveillance of Studio Production and the Quest for the Right Mix

In the above discussion I have highlighted the way in which artists and producers may enjoy a large degree of liberty and have considerable scope for personal expression and experimentation when composing and recording music in the studio. However, artist and repertoire staff have usually got their ear to the door, conducting a covert surveillance operation, listening to judge whether the sounds coming out of the studio will be suitable for radio play, media exposure and public consumption.

The first judgment will be made after the initial two or three songs have been recorded. The company will assess the compatibility of the producer and artist and quality of the material before deciding to commit themselves financially to recording an entire album. If everything has gone well the record company will give the go-ahead to proceed, and the artist and producer will usually be left to get on with it. A & R staff may occasionally drop into the studio, but this is actively discouraged by producers, and A & R staff themselves often acknowledge that interruptions and interventions can disrupt concentration and confuse things.

However, there may be initial reservations. The director of a management company who represented a number of producers explained a typical scenario:

> Often the first two tracks haven't worked and the record company thinks; '[sigh] It's not one hundred per cent. Let's do a couple more tracks with somebody else and see how that goes.' Then, maybe they are not quite right either, but they think; 'We'll save the mixing until the end'. And then, maybe they find Mister Right and he delivers five tracks which are absolutely fantastic. So then they get him to go back to the early tracks, the ones that the other producers have done, and maybe he changes a couple of things here and there, puts a new lead vocal on it, mixes it and then, bang! You've got your album. And you've got two tracks produced by Mr A although they've been mixed by C. Two tracks produced by B but again mixed by C. And the rest of the album produced and mixed by C, and they finally end up with a producer they can work with and who they get good results with.

Apart from revealing the way in which producers are assumed to be men, this quote illustrates the way in which the production of an album can proceed in an ad-hoc manner, almost by trial-and-error, with different individuals being involved along the way. Whilst A & R staff are often reluctant to work in such a piecemeal fashion, as costs mount up it is often the cheapest way to proceed without incurring additional expenses by starting again.

Once the sessions in the studio are complete copies of a final mix will be submitted to the record company. At this point there can be three possible responses to what has been recorded: One reaction might be 'Brilliant'. Little needs to be said about this, except that it is very unusual. At the other extreme is a response bluntly summed up by one A & R director as: 'Absolute crap! We're not going to release this!' Whilst this does tend to be rare, instances are occasionally cited with relish by record company staff – but always about artists contracted to other record companies. Often the album will not have reached the completion stage before this type of opinion is voiced, but it may still be a considerable way into the recording. If the production of an album has arrived at this point it is highly likely that there is conflict and poor communication between the various personnel involved – an issue I shall be pursuing later. Here I am concerned with the most common response to the completion of recording: 'Good, but certain changes are needed'.

These changes often involve minor modifications and remixing. A short break is frequently necessary to re-assess what has been done, and after a few days away a fresh pair of ears may soon hear that certain sounds are not right. The drums may sound 'flat' or 'dull', the bass may need replacing or re-recording, additional solos or vocals may be required, the balance between the different instruments and voices may need adjusting. During the mixing a producer (or re-mixer) usually works alone at the desk modifying sounds, balancing the relationship between them and selecting different combinations from the recorded tracks. The permutations are endless and the recording can be altered considerably and dramatically re-worked to continually create new and different experiences of the same song (Tankel, 1990).

When A & R personnel, along with marketing and promotion staff, are assessing the finished recording and deciding whether to undertake further production work or employ a re-mixer, they are listening for distinctive individual tracks which can be released as singles to promote the album and gain radio exposure. Record company staff may decide that no amount of modification and re-mixing is going to provide these and they will then undertake further recording explicitly to produce radio-friendly material.

The decision to use one producer to record material for singles and another to make the bulk of an album is a calculation which can be made in advance of recording, as well as at the end of a session when listening to the completed work. Certain producers acquire reputations for being able to turn songs into singles at particular moments or for writing tracks which can be used by artists as singles. Whether this reputation is based on the actual sounds they produce, or whether it is derived from the propensity of their 'name' to signify to the media that this is important – a potential hit – and thus help it gain exposure is never really clear. There are undoubtedly strong elements of the latter at play in these situations.

These producers inevitably charge high rates for their services, and here A & R decisions are very noticeably informed by financial considerations. As a director based at the London office of one of the labels of a European conglomerate explained:

> You'll say; 'Right we'll go and use this expensive producer to make the singles, and then we'll use this little guy down here – because he isn't so expensive – to do the rest of the record.' There are producers who are very expensive, and you'd go to them and say; 'Could you produce me three hit singles.' And they'll go 'fine, sure' because maybe they've got a project to do for someone in two months time and they've got a six week period to do this . . . So, say you've spent £60,000 doing three tracks with somebody who's that expensive, but they're all the singles. Then you think; 'Well, I don't really want to spend more than £100,000 on this album.' So you have to go; 'Right I've got £40,000 left, who can I get to make eight tracks for £40,000?' So you go to a cheaper studio with a cheaper producer. A lot of it is money oriented. It's not quite as bad as padding the album out; I know that's what it sounds like.

So, whether by design or default the final musical recording which appears on an album will have had contributions from artist & repertoire staff, producers, engineers, musicians and mixers, and will often have been composed in an ad-hoc way with considerable trial and error, experimentation and modification in the process. In the next chapter I shall describe in more detail how the radio networks influence the type of music recorded and released. Before doing this I want to outline a similar collaborative process of production which occurs in the making of videos.

The Production of Video

The video made by Queen in 1975 to accompany *Bohemian Rhapsody* is generally regarded as the first conscious use of music video to promote a pop single. In the years following its release record companies began producing videos in order to promote established artists around the world and occasionally to overcome the logistics of touring. It was the launch of Music Television (MTV), however, the first 24 hour round the clock service of pop music relayed through the cable television network in the United States which provided the momentum for the establishment of music video as an integral part of the pop process.

Emerging out of a complex history of corporate wheeler–dealing, experimentation in programme formats, and extensive market research, MTV was launched on 1 August 1981 and rapidly expanded its operations in the United States during the early 1980s (Denisoff, 1988). In August 1987 MTV began broadcasting in western Europe, and moved into eastern Europe by setting up a service in Hungary in March 1989. Through its company Viacom, MTV established networks in Japan, Latin America and Australia, and in August 1991, on its 10th anniversary, MTV claimed to be broadcasting in 41 countries and reaching 204 million homes.

Not long after MTV started broadcasting, music video was identified as the 'embodiment' of postmodernism (Kaplan, 1987), and a wave of intellectual analysis followed which drew on semiotics and film theory. Like much of the analysis of pop music during the 1950s and 1960s, which focused on song lyrics abstracted from any musical context, this type of theorising treated the images in great detail but had little to say about their relationship to the music. Videos were routinely divided into 'narrative' and 'non-narrative', a distinction which completely ignored the way in which music itself has a narrative structure built around melodic tensions, releases and repeated phrases – a structure which frequently binds together images which lack a narrative according to the conventions of visual analysis alone (Cubitt, 1991; Lewis, 1989).

In addition to ignoring the music, this type of analysis had little to say about the connections between video and the music industry, and the way in which meanings had been composed within specific conditions of production. Whilst audiences might be able to interpret videos in various ways, these images and meanings have not merely been erupting 'orgasmically' out of the screen, as some writers seem to imply (Fiske, 1986). As Andrew Goodwin observed, 'the presence of promotional strategies goes curiously unnoticed in postmodern textual analysis, as if industry and texts were quite unrelated' (1987, p 48). It is this relationship, between industry and texts, that I want to focus on here by outlining some of the ways in which the relations of production and promotion have shaped the meanings which have been made available in music videos.

Video in the Record Industry: Corporate Confusion

Simon Frith has argued that the view of video in the music business is 'straight-forward': the rise of video is an indication of a shift in the organisation of corporate entertainment. The value of the visuals is ultimately dependent upon the quality of the soundtrack and as an art form music video is insignificant. Whilst it can be a useful promotional tool and hence 'good for business . . . No one would pretend that there's much more to them aesthetically than a flow of mediocrity' (1988a, p 205).

Whilst Frith's comments were intended to counter the celebratory tone of much postmodern visual analysis, this caricature is itself somewhat simplistic. To refer to the view of video in the record industry as straight-forward is to smooth over a whole range of issues and problems arising around video production at this time. To dismiss the content of music videos in such sweeping terms as 'a flow of mediocrity' is to demean the imaginative work of a range of video directors, artists and record company personnel and to obscure the potentials which music video has introduced into musical practices.

Whilst I was carrying out the research for this book between 1989 and 1992, it became apparent that the music industry was still coming to terms with video. The enthusiasm and occasional extravagance which had resulted in a series of mini-epics during the early 1980s had given way to a period of uncertainty and reflection. Recording industry personnel were voicing a number of reservations about the lack of new ideas in what were becoming routinely produced videos, and questions were being asked about the effec-tiveness of video as a promotional tool. The view of video within the recording industry, in Britain in particular, was far from straightforward. A range of opinion and differing degrees of enthusiasm were affecting the way in which videos were being commissioned and produced. There seemed to be three broad positions:

Firstly, there were companies who had embraced video totally and who were recruiting specialist staff with a knowledge of film to commission and make them, and who were in many ways leading in this area within the industry. The enthusiasm for video in such a company was captured in the following eulogy from a marketing director speaking in early 1990:

> I would make a comparison of a record company in the late 1980s and early 1990s as being like a Hollywood studio in the 1940s that made musicals. We're actually about making music and then putting it to pictures. It's exactly the same function which is selling music via the screen. And I think record companies are beginning to fulfil that kind of function . . . I think it becomes intrinsic to people's lifestyles. I think it's going to be more so in the 1990s. I mean, I think it's fantastic myself.

Somewhat in contrast to this were companies in which staff were confused by, or openly antagonistic towards video. There appeared to be no coherent policy, the company had not formed a department or appointed specialist staff, and seemed to be stumbling along in an ad-hoc manner from project to project. One director, based at a different label in the same corporate grouping as the director quoted above and speaking in the middle of 1990, angrily declared:

I hate videos. I just think they're so expensive and, certainly for this country, I think they're completely useless. I think they're blown out of all proportion. There's no new ideas coming through that don't cost a million quid. It annoys me that you can spend as much money making a video for three minutes as you can making a whole album.

Midway between these opposing views there were companies in which staff seemed to be reluctantly producing videos with reservations about their cost, the problems involved in making them and their effectiveness as a promotional medium. When I brought the subject of video up with one marketing director he sighed and wearily remarked that; 'Yes, it can be effective, but it gets very complicated. You get a lot of political factors. Everyone and their uncle wants to get involved and have a say'.

Video is a comparatively recent media form and the production practices within the industry have not developed into the loose arrangement of occupations, routines and conventions which characterise music production. There was still considerable confusion about who was responsible for doing what, a blurring of boundaries and a lack of fixed working practices. In addition, videos are far more expensive to produce than pop singles, and often cost more than albums. During the 1980s the majority of music videos were made for anything between £10,000 and £100,000, with a few major artists such as Queen and Michael Jackson spending considerably more. In early 1991 a typical budget for one video for an average act was £30,000, based on two days shooting; one on location and one in a studio. For a new artist the cost is usually met by the record company at the time, with 50 per cent recouped later from the artist's eventual earnings.

Making the Video: Directors, Stylists and Actors

Making a video is similar to producing a musical recording, with the director's work analogous to that of the record producer. A video director is chosen for their reputation, style of filming and because they can deliver a video within a particular budget. A director's reputation may simply be based on delivering successful videos in the past, but like record producers they are usually employed to contribute in specific ways to an artist's identity. For example, David Bernard was asked to work with Climie Fisher in 1990 and explained that he was chosen to 'weird-up the act a bit' and 'make them a little bit more 1990s.' Jean-Baptiste Mondino has made videos for Madonna, Prince and David Bowie and, drawing on fashion photography and old American movies, is perceived to 'lavish his stars with classic otherworldly glamour', whilst retaining their human characteristics. Sophie Muller, a 1983 graduate of film studies at the Royal College of Art, was employed by the Eurythmics for her 'wry, offbeat and deadpan' approach and developed a reputation for being able to deliver fast-paced three minute dramas and for introducing 'subtle twists' into standard performance videos (O'Brien, 1991; Bode, 1990).

Discussions about the content of a proposed video will be held between the artist, director and marketing staff in a similar way to how A & R staff liaise with studio producers. It is often at this point that the most critical assessment is made of an artist's image. Unlike a photo session, a video cannot just be torn up and re-shot if it doesn't look right. Assistance is therefore sought from stylists who can be called in to work with a range of different artists. For 'serious' musicians like Mike Oldfield or Level 42 the stylist might recommend subtle modifications and compose a naturalistic and casual image. For other acts a stylist might be called in to glamorise artists and to undertake what one publicist described as 'a complete transformation.'

The stylist may make suggestions and contributions over a long period during which they build up a relationship with a particular artist, such as that between Annie Lennox and Carol Semaine. Carol, a textile design graduate, and Sheila Sedgwick, the press officer at RCA, assisted Annie over a period of time during the early stages of The Eurythmics, working by trial and error, searching through bargain basements and theatrical outfitters and trying various designer styles (O'Brien, 1991).

Alternatively, the stylist may be called in at very short notice to compose an image for an artist who has had a sudden hit record. As the managing director of a record company producing teenage pop and dance music remarked: 'Most young people take 3–5 years to find a style: Our problem is that we have 3–5 minutes.' These few minutes can be spent desperately searching for an image by looking through magazines and old films, or may simply involve taking the artist shopping.

One problem which video directors face is that artists have often been acquired by record companies for their musical material and looks, but not necessarily for their ability to perform in front of a camera. Film and video maker Julian Temple publicly expressed his frustration about this in the 1980s, complaining that it was very rare 'to find a pop star like Ray Davies, who has the requisite skill and sense of humour about himself to be an actor' (1983, p72). Record company staff attempt to resolve this by preparing artists in advance. They may rehearse the band or singer making pilot videos in small studios, or arrange for performers to receive guidance from acting schools and work with choreographers. For a video which needs to be made quickly however, there is often little time to prepare for it and the available budget may restrict the amount of advance work that can be undertaken.

The video is, therefore, made to suit a number of aims and within a number of limitations. It must project the identity of an act, suit the music of a particular track, and must be made quickly with due consideration for the dramatic skills of the artists involved. The artist's ability to act and present themselves visually may lead the director to resort to predictable, unimaginative performance based videos rather than intricate theatrical conceptual pieces. Alternatively the inabilities, which only become apparent during shooting, will have to be resolved immediately. The structure of a video may arise as it is cobbled together on the set and in the editing room, rather than as a result of a carefully constructed narrative. The limited time available may result in less communication between artist and director beforehand and this may lead to confusion, compromises and series of spontaneous and ad-hoc decisions during shooting. These issues decisively shape the 'meanings' available in the video, but remain unacknowledged in the analysis of the texts alone. As video director Lynn Kippax Jnr remarked when asked about the meaning of certain references in a video he made for The Pretenders: 'There's a difference between the reality of production and the reality of the viewer. What may look to the viewer like a statement may be, in production, the way a mistake is covered up or a technical problem is solved' (Lewis, 1989, p 84).

The Effect of Promotional Outlets on the Production of Videos

Although collections of music videos have been sold directly to consumers and generated revenue for both artists and corporations, the effectiveness of an individual video has usually been judged in terms of its use for promoting a specific recording. Here the limited opportunities for exposure, and character of media promotional outlets influences the content of videos and the way in which they are commissioned and recorded.

In Britain, during a typical week in 1990, there were 146 opportunities to place a video. The majority of these were routinely used for current Top 40 tracks and oldies, and only about twenty four spots were available for new videos. The most airtime, twice as much as any other show at 41 minutes, was on the ITV *Chart Show* which was broadcast on Saturday morning children's television, and then repeated in the early hours of Monday morning. The producer of this show estimated that the programme was approached with about 50 new videos per week, out of which he selected five or six (Webb, 1991). During the same period opportunities in the United States were just as limited, with the main outlet for placing new and 'alternative' videos being MTV's *120 Minutes* which was broadcast between midnight and 2 am on a Sunday morning.

Due to these limited opportunities there has been an increasing reluctance to produce a video for a new act without first gauging the response of various media and radio to the single. The experience of producing a lot of videos that were not broadcast in the 1980s has resulted in a more reactive, wait-and-see approach, particularly in Britain where this was accentuated by the recession of the early 1990s. As David Steele, a marketing manager at Virgin, remarked in 1991; 'In a lot of cases we are waiting until we are virtually sure that a track's going to happen before we go ahead with a video.'

In the United States it has become almost obligatory to make a video to accompany the first single release from any new artist. This is to signal to the industry, and in particular the decision-makers involved in radio programming, that the company is serious about and committed to an act. However, there is still a certain amount of caution in putting out videos to accompany the early releases from an artist, and staff are continually weighing up whether to use their budgets on videos or re-direct funds towards touring and other promotional activities.

A video for a well known artist with previous releases is more likely to gain exposure than a video made to accompany the release of a recording from a new artist. The video for an established artist will therefore receive a greater budget and can be planned, scripted and made in advance to coincide with the release of a musical recording. For a new artist the wait-and-see approach means that if a single begins to receive airplay and starts selling there is inevitably a rather chaotic few days when a video is planned, written and produced in a very short period of time, adding to the production problems already discussed.

In addition to the limitations imposed by budgets, the time available and an artist's acting abilities, the way in which videos are produced has been decisively shaped by the demands of the major promotional outlets in the UK and USA. Videos are made to be suitable for viewing throughout the world, and the company tries to take into account the requirements of various territories so that they will not be involved in editing them for different countries. Due to the commercial importance of the North American market the video must be suitable for showing in the United States, where the major outlet is MTV. Although less significant in terms of sales, the UK is an important region for establishing an artist's credentials within the industry and a strategic point of access to the media and consumers of continental Europe.

The requirements of the video outlets in Britain and the USA influences the making of a video in two distinct ways: editing and content. One vice president of artist development based in Los Angeles explained that: 'MTV is incredibly important. But they are very aware of their own power . . . MTV is adamant about fast editing; because they say that a video has to stand repeated viewing and that a video has to have fast editing. Now, I know that is not something that Europeans like so much.'

Thus, the fast editing which became a feature of videos during the 1980s was more to do with the requirements of the programmers of MTV than any 'creative' decisions. Video is primarily a form of television programming in which the emphasis is on entertainment and maintaining interest rather than presenting music. This, in the opinion of one marketing director is 'why you see a lot of bright bouncy videos. That does distort the process.'

The process is further distorted by the way in which the main outlets for broadcasting videos on UK terrestrial television have been children's shows. As a result there have been stringent restrictions on smoking, any hint of sex and on the portrayal of violence; constraints which do not necessarily apply to other European territories but have to be taken into account when making the video.

Another issue which the analysis of visual narratives misses is that videos are rarely broadcast in their entirety. In 1990 the average video slot on British terrestrial television during a typical week was 73 seconds (Webb, 1991). Yet, the majority of videos are made to accompany songs of between three and four minutes. This means that the video narrative will often never open or close for the majority of the television audience, and as a result videos tended to be composed with this in mind. John Waller, a marketing director at Polydor, when interviewed during 1991 explained that the character of video outlets in the UK at this time was forcing record companies to produce videos composed around repetitive visual refrains which could be digested in small chunks and which were suitable for a young audience. However, it is worth noting that there has been considerable discussion, research and lobbying from record companies with a view to producing more adult-oriented music programmes. So there may well be changes in these restrictions, particularly as satellite and cable systems increase the outlets for video throughout the 1990s.

Potentials and Possibilities

Whether or not music videos are judged to have any aesthetic worth depends on the particular values and ideology of creativity being employed to assess them at any one time, but there is every indication that video makers are becoming increasingly recognised for their contribution and developing particular relationships with artists as producers have done. Directors may be invisible to the public, as most record producers are, but they are becoming increasingly important in mediating between performers and audiences, and articulating an artist's identity.

The directors of music videos have often been drawn from backgrounds in film, photography, album sleeve design or advertising. The presence of this latter category has tended to reinforce the often repeated opinion that video is organised according to the conventions of advertising. However, there are subtle but decisive differences in the production of adverts and videos. Far greater budgets are available for shooting adverts, they are not constrained (nor inspired) by the visual abilities of musicians and the soundtrack, and they usually take up a much smaller segment of time. A number of directors involved in making music videos are actually using video direction as a step towards making adverts so it is perhaps not surprising that, in building up a portfolio, the director should use advertising conventions and clichés. However, video has also provided opportunities for directors who are committed to using the imaginative opportunities provided by the medium itself.

One such director is John Maybury, an experimental film maker and artist, who initially had a 'phobia' about music video until realising the opportunity it provided to gain greater exposure for his work and reach a wider audience. Once considered Britain's 'hippest' young underground film director, Maybury was soon being critically acclaimed for his music videos for artists such as Boy George, and for his multi-layered, multigraphic style. He often used images from his experimental projects in his videos, and then incorporated elements from his music videos into his avant garde film work. Maybury considered that the form gave him a lot of scope to work: 'I suddenly realised that some of the snobbery I attached to making videos was actually a bit misguided . . . the only compromise I had to contend with was that I was handed this soundtrack I had to use and that I had to have this person in the centre of the screen' (Bode, 1990, p 15).

Music video is still at an early stage of development. Many of its potentials remain unexplored and it is still eyed with suspicion by many contemporary artists, fans and critics who view video as something that has been added-on to and is corrupting the purity of the experience of music. Responses have been similar, but by no means as dramatic, as the reaction to the introduction of sound into the movies: silent movies had been an 'art form unto themselves' declared director King Vidor. 'Adding sound to movies would be like putting lipstick on the Venus de Milo', said actress Mary Pickford (Berg, 1989, p 173). Pop stars have not shot themselves because they could not act – as actors did when finding out that they had the 'wrong voice' for the screen – but responses to video have been similar in attacking the way it has contaminated the pure experience of music.

As a new generation grows up with music video, it is likely that artists will emerge who are working with music and images together. This approach has already been adopted as a philosophy by director Tim Pope who has built up a relationship with The Cure and directed some very idiosyncratic videos which have become an integral part of the band's identity. Pope sees a great potential in video that has largely gone unrealised:

> The marriage of images and sound is a great form, but a lot of videos are simply a soundtrack with images that squat on top with no correlation between the two. I try to bind them until it's hard to tell which came first, the video or the song (Millington, 1991, p 9).

Just as sound recording technologies changed the nature of composing and performing, enabling artists to develop a 'recording consciousness' (Bennett, 1980) so the growth of video may lead to a more holistic audio-visual consciousness. As I stressed in the last chapter, music is rarely heard purely as sound, there are always images denoted by particular sounds. The integration of sound recording and video into computerised multimedia systems will undoubtedly increase the opportunities to compose music and visuals as mutually enhancing, produced simultaneously and adding to the experience of each, rather than detracting from one another.

6

PROMOTIONAL WAR GAMES

Pop Radio
In Britain and North America

The radio stations of North America and Britain provide one of the most important promotional outlets for popular music, setting agendas for record companies and radio stations throughout the world, and exert a further influence on the type of music recorded and the way in which artists are acquired, developed and presented.

Although video and television appearances have become important promotional mediums, it has largely been radio play which has encouraged retailers to stock recordings and consumers to purchase them. As one marketing director remarked, when interviewed for a music business survey carried out in Britain during 1990; 'If you're going for a Top 10 record, if you're going to appeal to the broadest number of people that might conceivably buy your record, I think airplay is critical: it's absolutely vital.'

Radio promotion requires a strategic approach and the adoption of a range of tactics. It is often discussed with a number of war-like metaphors: Promotion staff are described as being in the 'front line' involved in 'targeting' specific individuals and stations, and enter radio stations 'armed' with recordings and knowledge. Record companies provide their promotion and sales staff with information packs of press cuttings, stories and release details. When I visited Capitol Records in Los Angeles in September 1990 these packs were titled 'Ammunition'. Sales teams in both the USA and Britain are routinely referred to as 'strike forces'. One American executive referred to radio promotion as 'a complicated battle', and when discussing how she was involved in trying to 'break' records across the radio system one vice president of artist development based in the United States remarked; 'It's almost like a war game. You're moving your troops around trying to get another area to play it.'

On the promotional battlefield, where record companies are competing for limited amounts of airtime, it is often the new artists and releases that die before even being heard by the public. The promotional life of a single record is brief. In Britain a record can be 'plugged' for three to four weeks by which time, if it has not been programmed or has received little airplay, its chances of commercial success are reduced. In the United States record companies can promote singles over a longer period of time – sometimes up to six months.

But in North America companies face logistic problems due to the size of the country and the segmented nature of the radio system.

Radio promotion is one area in the music business where there are distinct differences between Britain and North America. Radio promotion in Britain has mainly been directed towards one national non-commercial station (Radio 1) which plays an eclectic range of musical styles. In the United States radio promotion is aimed at a complex of commercial stations which broadcast 'narrowcast' music very clearly defined according to various 'formats'. In the UK the individual tastes and opinions of disc jockeys and programme producers can be influential, and is utilised by record companies when attempting to get a record placed. In the United States getting a record played is far more dependent on presenting records and artists according to the commercial considerations of the radio station. It seems particularly relevant to make these contrasts at a time when the re-regulation of broadcasting in Britain is gradually leading to an expansion of local radio and creating the conditions for the emergence of further national stations which may come to challenge Radio 1's historical dominance of pop broadcasting.

Radio Promotion in the USA

American radio stations are defined by the type of music they play and the size and scope of their listener profile. Whilst providing an outlet for the recordings of record companies their income is derived from delivering very specifically defined audiences to advertisers. As Jody Berland has observed: 'Music-programming is not the main commodity produced by radio, but is rather the means to the production of radio's real commodity – the audience – to be sold to advertisers in exchange for revenue to the broadcaster' (1990, p 183). As a consequence, the total potential audience between 18 and 49 years old have been divided into 'demographically, psychographically, and sociologically fine-tuned targets, each served by a specific contemporary radio format' (Barnes, 1988, p 10).

From the record companies' perspective the most important and influential stations are those defined as CHR (Contemporary Hit Radio) stations. These stations play music which over the years has come to be referred to as 'Top 40'. This is a format which was first introduced in the early 1950s and has been used, with various refinements, ever since. It is based on playing repetitively, and in well coordinated rotation, the most popular hits of the day. These stations are divided into three categories within the industry; P1, P2 and P3, as defined by the influential trade paper *Radio and Records* (a very similar system of platinum, gold and silver is used by *Billboard*).

A station categorised as Parallel 1 has a weekly cumulative audience in excess of 1,000,000 and is usually located in a major urban area such as New York City, Los Angeles, Washington, Miami or Chicago. A Parallel 2 station tends to be based in a smaller urban area which has an audience of between 200,000 and 1,000,000, and stations classified as Parallel 3 tend to be found in smaller towns or rural areas which have audiences of under 200,000.

The P1 stations must be reached to maximise exposure and gain high chart positions. The charts are based on a complicated system of points for airplay which are weighted according to the type of station playing the record, with further adjustments made for retail sales depending on the position of a track in the charts.

In addition to the CHR stations there are a number of other station formats. The most important for selling contemporary pop music are currently:

AC (Adult Contemporary): This format developed out of the MOR (Middle of the Road) category and plays a combination of soft rock and music from singer-songwriters. Combining contemporary hits with oldies it is aimed at an audience aged between 25 and 54 years old.

Urban: The urban format has almost become a euphemism for black radio and is a direct descendent of the previous 'rhythm and blues' and 'race' categories. In the late 1980s and early 1990s urban stations were broadcasting a large amount of rap and dance music featuring artists such as MC Hammer, Prince and L.L. Cool J.

AOR (Album Oriented Rock): This format developed from the 'progressive rock' radio of the late 1960s when 'serious' artists were distinguished according to their albums rather than single records. The music played is predominantly that of white hard rock guitar bands such as The Allman Brothers, Slaughter, Aerosmith and Led Zeppelin.

NAC (New Age Contemporary): This format was introduced following experiments in programming in California, and broadcasts a mellow combination of instrumental, atmospheric 'environmental', world beat, jazz and some soft rock.

Alternative/Postmodern: Largely confined to college radio stations, this format became an important outlet for exposing new artists throughout the 1980s. Previously run by enthusiasts and only casually approached by record companies, college radio has been subject to record company targeting and lost a lot of its maverick image. These stations tend to broadcast alternative guitar rock, and music from various rock-dance hybrids such as The Talking Heads and Living Colour.

In addition to these categories there are country music stations. This is the oldest format category in North America, but these tend not to be used for promoting pop and rock artists. Although reaching a wide audience, the production of country music tends to operate out of Nashville, at a distance from the contemporary pop sounds coming out of the New York–Los Angeles axis.

The formats, and the artists and radio stations which are included in a particular category, change over time according to research, and as a result of the emergence of new styles and genres. The most recent – the new age or wave format – partly replaced the easy listening category, and postmodern appeared as a new, fashionable label for alternative, but also in response to the fusions of black dance and white rock in the late 1980s. It seems likely that a world beat format may emerge out of the gap between these categories.

There is not the space here for a detailed discussion of how this system of radio stations emerged or how it operates. It has come about as a result of the combined influence of advertisers, radio stations and their consultants, and record companies. In a country in which ten thousand commercial radio stations compete for about seven per cent of North America's $110 billion media advertising budget, each station attempts to find a niche and presents itself as a consistent and reliable outlet (Barnes, 1988). This system enables radio stations to have a clearly defined identity which is attractive to advertisers, and at the same time it makes it logically easier for record companies to market music across North America.

Promotional Strategies

The dependence on such a complex radio system makes promotion a complicated process requiring considerable coordination and investment. As Barnes (1988) observed, the effort required to convince hundreds of diverse and widespread stations to broadcast a recording at approximately the same time, so that it will gain enough airplay points to enter the charts, 'regularly traumatises record labels'.

Record companies attempt to deal with this by adopting two simultaneous strategies. Firstly, artists, or specific recordings, are defined in terms of a particular radio format. Relevant stations are then targeted, with the aim of 'crossing over' from one format to another and eventually gaining airplay on CHR and across the various formats. Secondly, a track may be started in an area of the country where a particular type of music is more popular. It is rare for a single to be released regionally, but the focus of promotion and retail sales activity will take account of geographical variations in musical consumption throughout the country. Just as marketing staff in the UK work with various heuristic models of audiences for particular types of music, in the USA sales and promotion staff utilise a working knowledge of regional variations in musical taste. For example, alternative rock and dance records will often be targeted at major urban areas such as New York, Los Angeles, Boston, Minneapolis and San Francisco. Hard rock is popular in California and in Dallas and the south west, and the mid west is considered to be an area for traditional rock and roll and Top 40 pop. Rap is popular in New York, Miami and Los Angeles, although there are variations in the language of rap styles which often make it difficult to cross this genre over from the west coast to the east coast and vice versa.

It was when discussing the logistics of attempting to gain airplay across this complex of formatted radio stations and regional variations in taste, that the vice president of artist development quoted earlier used the analogy of a war game. She added that it was an ongoing struggle:

> to get another area to play it. So, for example, you start in LA with something and then you spin it off a little bit into the south, and then you're trying to get it across the country. Or, you're trying New York and you've got this big hole in the middle. You finally get New York, but by this time the people in LA have been playing it for two months and they'll say 'No, I want another track.'

A further tactic which record companies may adopt is to record and produce a number of mixes of the same song and promote them to different formatted stations. This may extend to promoting multiple tracks simultaneously to different radio formats. As the vice president of artist development just quoted explained further:

> You'll have an artist who has got different sorts of tracks on the album. Once you've launched the record and launched the artist and tried to get one track focused in on everybody – if that doesn't really work, or even if it does – you can actually go to different formats with a different track, and do a promotional single. For instance, if there's an artist that's got a dance mix on something you can go with a dance mix to dance radio at the same time as going with an alternative track to the alternative radio. And you can actually have three or four different tracks being worked in different formats. Because different people listen to these formats, it's not as if you're confusing the issue. And you can sell albums off the back of it.

The Decline of the Single Record

The practice of releasing different tracks purely as promotional singles for radio use, in order to persuade consumers to purchase an album, highlights a historical change in the recording industry's approach to the single. In the United States the single has become a device for marketing an album. Between 1979 and 1990 sales of vinyl singles declined by 86 per cent from 195.5 million units to 27.6 million. Even allowing for the additional growth in sales of compact disc and cassette singles the total sales of singles declined by 41 per cent during the 1980s (RIAA, 1991). When an album is released a limited number of cassette and CD singles are manufactured and made available for consumers, and vinyl singles are often produced for use in existing juke boxes. But singles are usually released simultaneously with, and to draw attention to, an album.

In Britain the decline of the single has been less dramatic. Total sales fell by 21 per cent from 77.8 million units in 1980 to 61.1 million in 1989 (BPI, 1991), and sales of cassette and CD singles have been very low. Vinyl singles have been used as more than just a promotional tool and one or two singles have usually been issued prior to the release of an album.

However, there are indications that record labels in Britain are following the United States and beginning to view the single primarily as a marketing device. As Maurice Oberstein, then Chairman of Polygram UK, explained when interviewed for British television in early 1991:

> The single has always been the leader into the music of the artist. It's an easy introduction from an album to get the artist known. And I don't think that's changed much. The thing that's changed is the sales have gone down. It's a much less valuable vehicle for us. We used to sell millions and make a profit. Now we sell hundreds of thousands and think of it as a promotional tool (Channel 4 TV, 1991).

The cost of producing and releasing singles has escalated due to the proliferation of hardware formats (CD, vinyl 7 inch, vinyl 12 inch, cassette, picture disc etc) and the pressure to produce the obligatory video to accompany it. Small companies who often work to very tight budgets and manufacture a limited number of formats have claimed that the large corporations have responded to the single's declining profitability by actively 'talking it down' and encouraging the broadcasting of album tracks. David Howells, one of the directors of PWL Ltd, the British company which produced over 100 chart singles in the late 1980s, was one executive who considered the single to be more than a promotional device, arguing that; 'If you go back to the old method of mass production and concentrate on the seven inch, then you make good profits.'

Few companies however, are in a position to carve out a niche by 'going back' to an old method, and perhaps more importantly, singles alone do not allow a company to build an artist's identity in the manner described in Chapter 4. As Peter Waterman, Howell's colleague at PWL commented when interviewed in the same programme as Oberstein:

> The record industry as such would rather there not be such a thing as a single because it's an animal that's very difficult to predict. The artist is of little importance to the public when it comes to singles. They either like the record or they don't like it. And they don't buy it just because it's so and so or it's this or it's that (Channel 4, 1991).

Despite these arguments from entrepreneurs who are dependent upon the continued existence of a market for singles, the sales of single recordings have been declining worldwide. As cassette machines and programmable CD players have provided more flexible and mobile ways of consuming music, the single will probably continue to become a promotional tool rather than an essential consumer purchase.

Programmers and Independent Promoters

At American radio stations it is the music programme directors who decide which tracks are to be broadcast. Their first concern is inevitably whether a particular recording is compatible with the station's format. After this the programme director considers the 'support' a recording is receiving from the record company.

The first indication of support is the 'story' the record company is using to promote the artist. This may concern the sales success of the artist in the USA or around the world, might be details of outstanding tours and personal appearances, or it could simply be newsworthy anecdotes. The most persuasive story, however, is the one about other radio stations programming a particular recording.

A P1 station will often not be prepared to programme a record unless it is receiving airplay on a number of P2 stations and a substantial number of P3 stations. Alternatively, the station may wait to see if the single is receiving play on another format such as Adult Contemporary or Urban before playing it. Music programme directors use various consultants to advise them on trends in programming, and refer to a number of privately run 'tip sheet' magazines which provide detailed information about releases, radio plays across the country and listener responses. Once a record is included on a playlist the radio station monitors its progress through 'passive' research when the public call or fax into a radio station with requests, and by using 'active' research when listeners are contacted by the station, consultant or a research agency.

The radio station also assesses the potential of a recording by examining the amount of investment the record company is giving to a particular track or artist. Here, a prominent indicator is the record company's use of an independent promoter. Although used initially to relieve some of the workload from record companies, independent promoters have become very powerful organisations which mediate between the record company and the radio station. From the record company's perspective the rationale for using independent promoters is that they can focus and devote effort to specific projects. From the radio station's perspective they indicate that a company is serious about a particular track, and spending money on it. However, independent promoters have developed into a powerful force in their own right and this is one area in the North American music business where anecdotes about corruption and inducements to play records ('payola') have recurred throughout the history of pop. Rick Sklar, a radio programmer at various New York stations since the 1950s, described in his memoirs how staff in record companies 'detested payoffs for airplay' but noted that:

> the pressure to "break" a record – to get it started – was always present. So were the independent promotion men – the promoters who are in business for themselves and who, by taking on individual records or assignments from the record labels, are a step removed from the corporate environment and its restraints. Some of these independent promoters function mostly as money conduits. Certain cities are controlled by the independents. They get the ball rolling and break a new release by simply sharing their fee (in cash or cocaine) with a few key programme directors (1984, pp 148–149).

By the late 1980s a loose alliance of independent promoters had evolved, nicknamed 'The Network', who exerted considerable influence over the records played (Dannen, 1990). However, they were rarely involved in gaining exposure for mediocre records which would not normally be played. More than anything else, independent promoters maintain the dominance of the existing major companies and artists who can afford their services. They have become an institutionalised link in the system, employed by all of the major record companies for the way in which they can facilitate or block the broadcasting of recordings.

In 1979 CBS experienced a vivid illustration of this when they released Pink Floyd's single *Another Brick in the Wall*. Eighty per cent of America's Top 40 radio stations across the country added it to their playlists. But in Los Angeles, where the band had just played five nights at the sports arena and attracted considerable media attention, none of the four main stations in the city was playing the record. Dick Asher, the Deputy President of CBS, for reasons of economy and because there was so much interest in the act, had decided that it was not necessary to employ independent promoters in Los Angeles. But, mysteriously – and despite its obvious popularity – it was not receiving airplay. When the band's management heard that the record was not being played they demanded that the company employ independent promoters. CBS immediately held a morning meeting and reinstated independent promotion on the single. By the afternoon it was being played on radio stations across the city. As Frederic Dannen observes in his book *Hit Men*, from which this example is taken; 'The Network's power came not from its ability to make a hit record but to prevent one . . . the network was the means to deprive small labels of access to the Top 40 airwaves and increase the market share of the large labels' (1990, p 16).

Whether or not the major companies were using independent promoters in such a machiavellian way to dominate the airwaves, Dannen presents a convincing case. Certainly, with all the major companies using them, independent promoters operate as a reliable way of gaining entry to the airwaves and of maintaining a company's profile and competitive edge.

The Impact of Radio Format Categories on Artist Development

The ultimate aim of radio promotion in the USA is to achieve a 'cross over' hit – to move out from urban, new age or adult contemporary and gain nationwide exposure on Top 40 radio. With so many records to promote there is often not the time or budget available to attempt this and the vast majority of records remain stuck in their rigid formatted groove.

In addition, the segmented character of the radio system permeates the entire record company operation, with staff working in small concentrated areas. Promotion departments are subdivided into specialists who deal with the different radio formats. In a large number of companies this is rationalised through to the artist development and A & R divisions where different staff or sub-divisions deal with different categories of music. This makes it difficult for an artist to cross over *within* the record company itself – let alone on the radio stations. One senior executive at the New York headquarters of a major recording group remarked that these format derived divisions raised:

> the whole question of; 'Is there any communication between any of these divisions?' We have one company that has an alternative department. And they're very proud that they're now out there getting the early shot on projects. The problem is; how do you get it from the alternative department into the mainstream of the company? And the answer is; very rarely can you do that. It's like the kiss of death.

Hence, artists can become 'ghettoised' into particular formats and the corresponding company departmental divisions, rarely moving out of them.

Not only does the format system affect the potential of particular artists to reach audiences other than those defined in this way, it also has a direct impact on the type of performers and bands who are signed. Although artist and repertoire staff usually have a large degree of formal autonomy to sign who they choose, in practice they need the support of the radio promotion staff who will be handling the recordings of any artist they acquire. A & R staff often find acts they wish to sign, but are immediately confronted with the promotional staff who want to know what format the artist fits into. As a senior A & R manager at a label office in Los Angeles explained:

> There was a band . . . that I found really interesting. They were like a seventies progressive English band. Very musical, very out there, eight minute songs, but extremely interesting. My problem was; I really liked this band, I loved this band, I was going down to our promotions people and they were saying: 'But, what is it? It's not alternative. It's not rock. Where does it fit?' And, ultimately I didn't sign them because I didn't have the support.

The formatted radio system decisively demarcates and defines the market for popular music in the United States. One senior executive at an American corporation who was also involved in representing an artist provided another example of the way in which this system of format categories constrains the opportunities for new artists:

> I'm working with an artist, and the idea was to basically take the sounds and instrumentation of NAC, you know environmental, world beat, orchestra sounds, and marry them with really strong pop AC ballads. I've been running around trying to sell this act. Great reviews, great songs, television commitments, she's been on the *Today Show*. I figure I'm showing record companies an unsigned act with great songs, great voice. Here's my promotion plan, here's my marketing plan. And I zip it out, Adelaide Arts Festival, Montreux Jazz Festival. I figure I'm not going to have any trouble. And, the reaction I'm getting is; 'Musically this is wonderful, but where does this fall?' Which is crazy. Because none of us are just one thing. We all have spectrums of taste . . . I've had presidents of companies saying to me; 'Well, musically this is quite brilliant, she's got a great voice. But, it's not exactly where the market is.'

Lenny Kravitz is an artist who initially had difficulty getting a recording contract because his music and image did not fit these rigid formats. Kravitz was producing music drawing on an eclectic range of influences from black rhythm and blues artists and white pop and rock acts. Although impressed by his music, record company staff were concerned about the way in which his black identity was being expressed in both his image and music. As Kravitz remarked in a magazine interview:

> The companies all said the music wasn't black enough, 'cos it didn't sound like Cameo or Prince. Oh the way A & R is run in America! man it's so stupid. There's one office full of white people and they're pop and rock. And there's another office full of black guys and they're into soul or hip hop or whatever's going down on black radio. I got so sick of being told, get a drum machine or put a curl in your hair – cos it was short and spiked back then – and then we'll sign you. (Sandall, 1991, p 52).

The format categories operate at their most pernicious and restrictive in the organisational division which separates black and white artists and staff. Freddee Towles, the lead singer with the Los Angeles-based band Euclid Drive was experiencing similar problems to Kravitz in 1991. Frustrated and angry, he described how staff in record companies liked the group's music, but were 'completely perplexed when confronted with a black rock singer fronting a white band'.

This division is a vivid illustration of the disjuncture between the rigid categories of commercial marketing which treat ethnicity as a discrete and finite entity, drawing 'sharp lines among black, white and brown music and audiences'; and the lived experience of audiences and artists for whom ethnicity is 'plastic and open ended', a continual dynamic process involving 'bifocality, juxtaposition of multiple realities and inter-referentiality' (Lipsitz, 1990, p 152).

The system of format categories also restricts the opportunities for overseas acts to be promoted in the United States. During my visits to record companies, staff spoke of the difficulties involved in promoting what they variously referred to as 'south London rap', 'very English rock' and 'Euro-pop'. Hence, artists in Britain and other territories – for whom North America is an important potential source of income – often find it necessary to modify both their musical and visual identity in order to meet the demands of these format categories.

The system of format categories directly informs the type of acts which are signed by American record labels and the artists which are acquired or licensed from other territories. It also directly affects the way acts are developed and presented to the public. The level of investment required to pay for independent promotion, and the cost of coordinating and servicing this complex system favours the major companies and established artists. This tends to marginalise minor labels, and more alternative or newly-signed artists into particular regions or specific formats where they reach a limited audience. If an artist does not fit any of the existing formats they will find it difficult to gain radio exposure in the USA, and may find it hard to obtain or retain a recording contract.

Radio Promotion in Britain

Music radio in Britain has for many years been dominated by one national non-commercial station playing an eclectic range of popular music. Radio 1 first began broadcasting in 1967, following restructuring within the BBC, and by the early 1990s was reaching 17–18 million listeners a week and four million at its day time peak. Alongside Radio 1, just over 100 Independent Local Radio (ILR) stations were broadcasting, the vast majority featuring a combination of Top 40/contemporary chart hits, middle-of-the-road/easy listening, classic hits and oldies (although a few 'incremental stations' were transmitting to more specific audiences for jazz, dance and r'n'b.); and about 50 BBC local radio stations were broadcasting 'grown up' pop music aimed at an audience of 30 and over. Research conducted on behalf of the recording industry (Lambert, 1990), and my interviews with a range of record company personnel, suggested that Radio 1 led the regions, playing records earlier and providing more opportunities for new artists. Staff in record companies, whilst having their favourite anecdote about Radio l's resistance to specific acts and genres, devote most of their promotional effort to this station. As Barnard (1989) has noted, although resented for its power virtually to make or break a record, Radio 1's near monopoly of pop radio has, over the years, greatly simplified the promotion process.

Radio 1 plays a wider range of music and operates a less rigid playlist system than American commercial radio. Informed by an enduring distinction within the BBC between 'entertainment' and 'stimulation' Radio 1 has, since its inception, played softer, more Top 40 material suitable for workplace and family home listening during the day and introduced more free form and specialist programming in the evenings.

The programming of records by radio stations in North America is based on a number of commercial considerations, with the main musical criteria being whether a track suits the station's format. The musical taste of particular individuals has little to do with what is selected. Indeed, records are frequently programmed by radio stations without being heard. Radio promotion in Britain also entails providing records which suit the individual programme styles on Radio 1 and the character of specific regional commercial stations. However, the idiosyncrasies and tastes of particular producers and disc jockeys can have far more influence on what is broadcast.

Building a Profile

Promotion staff in Britain usually become involved with an act immediately after they are signed, and begin 'building a profile' within the radio media in preparation for the release of material. This involves identifying those radio personnel, whether DJs or more frequently the producers of their programmes, who will be most receptive to a particular artist. By contacting radio station personnel in the early stages of a group or singer's development a record company can gauge the likely response of the radio media to a particular act, and gain feedback on what might be the most suitable single tracks. One head of promotion at the British office of an American entertainment group explained that it was important to make contact with radio personnel early because:

> you'll know who your supporters are going to be straight away. Rather than shunting it out and hoping. For instance, if you've got a live act more in the rock area you know that on the fringe you've got maybe John Peel. You've got Bob Harris, you've got Richard Skinner. You've got the *Saturday Sequence*. I'm just talking Radio 1 here, but it works individually throughout the stations, with Radio 1 being the standard bearer.

Promotional staff approach disc jockeys or producers with recordings and information, and may invite radio station personnel to performances, or introduce them to artists. Record company personnel will often try to involve a particular radio personality in an artist's discovery and development. As one head of promotion who had been in the industry for seventeen years and spent most of her time working in promotion for two major corporations explained:

> There's probably 200–250 media people, essentially it's a small amount of people. And, basically, our job is to match the artists to the right people. I mean, somebody like Mark Goodier [a DJ] at Radio 1 is very good at wanting to break new bands. So, I might think the [X-band] are right for him. So, I might take him a tape and say; 'Look, do you want to be part of the build?' He might go 'great!' and then he will champion them throughout. But we put them in touch. It's a slight myth that things just get discovered. When you hear a DJ on air going; 'I was at a gig last night', nine times out of ten he wasn't. Or; 'this tape was sent to me and I thought they were great and I thought I'd give them a session'. We gave it to him. It's rare that it's not connected.

The disc jockeys themselves wish to establish their own reputations, which they seek to enhance by being associated with the 'discovery' of new artists. Very often an act are initially presented to the public through a session recorded for Radio 1. This is then broadcast as an exclusive recording from a new 'unknown' act, without any reference to the record company involved.

This tactic blurs the conventional boundary between the record company and the radio station, actively involving broadcasters in the 'discovery' and development of an act. Whether or not a particular radio personality is actively 'co-opted' (Hirsch, 1972) in this way, promotion staff spend considerable time informing producers and DJs about new artists. The aim is to identify those individuals who will be favourably predisposed towards a particular act. These contacts can then be used to increase awareness and to create a sense of anticipation about an act within a radio station. One head of promotion, based at the London office of an American entertainment group, mentioned the profile building of one celtic inspired rock act which the company had initiated nine months prior to the release of any recordings. The campaign had resulted in Radio 1 staff anticipating the release of the act's material to the extent that they were asking the record company when it was coming. As this executive recalled: 'We had three or four people telling us; "We must have this record now". And during the first week we had 14 plays on daytime radio'.

It is not just DJs and producers who are approached by record company promotion staff. The secretaries and messengers who work in the offices may also be given merchandise and recordings, and invited to performances. These staff are an integral part of the culture at radio stations, where a large amount of discussion, gossip and opinion about records and artists accompanies daily work. Office staff frequently play music in the building and talk about the artists they have seen the night before, and this can influence both disc jockeys, producers, and the playlist organisers.

Plugging Records

The promotional strategy of profile building, and the marketing campaign in general, will have been preparing the environment for the 'plugging' of specific records. Over the years pluggers have employed some elaborate, idiosyncratic and extravagant stunts in order to draw the attention of disc jockeys, producers and radio programmers to particular records. Examples include Judd Lander streaking through Soho Square playing a pair of bagpipes to promote Chilli Willi and the Red Hot Peppers for Charisma Records, and the time when Taryn Hill promoted a record by Hank Williams Junior by dressing up in country and western clothes, wearing six guns and a stetson hat and riding up to radio stations on a horse.

However, these and many other legendary stunts have tended to become less common. Not only have radio station personnel become somewhat immune to these practices, but both radio stations and record companies have tried to present a more professional face to the world. In addition radio stations have increased the use of faxes and computers and have demanded efficient information rather than gimmicks.

Pluggers are required to arrange weekly appointments with Radio 1 producers at which they will be seen for very brief ten to fifteen minute meetings. Hence, they have a very limited amount of time to promote the recordings from their company. As a result the plugger must be selective. One head of promotion based at a major corporation described how she would plug a Radio 1 producer:

> You have to be, I would say, very honest. Because if I came to you tomorrow and I gave you my current list of singles and I went; 'That was on the Eurovision song contest, it's fantastic. This came number 29, it is brilliant. This is number 1 in Holland, it's fantastic.' By about the sixth single you'd just switch off. Now what I would probably say is, and I'll give you an example [picks up a pile of singles]: 'These are four records from the Eurovision song contest. None of them won. They're all a piece of shit.' Now, at that point – and we're on tape – I could get

fired – but I wouldn't, because everybody in this building would think it's a piece of shit . . . So, I would be realistic and on that basis establish that I'm not wasting your time and I'm not wasting my time. If you're going to waste his time on four records that he's never going to play you've had it. Then you'd move onto something, what I'd call in between. Like this record. They *are* playing it, but they are not playing it very much. So you do your sell: 'Do you know it's gone to number three in America? Did you know it's number 22 in the chart here? Did you know he's coming back on tour?' Now, whether I thought that was a brilliant record or not is irrelevant, I could sell it. But only sell it to the right person.

Eric Rothenbuhler found a similar tactic being adopted in a study of radio programming carried out in the United States. He observed that promoters 'offer an explicit rank ordering . . . they can tell programmers not to worry about a particular album, saying such things as "nobody else knows what to do with it" or "there probably won't be a tour" (1987, p 89).

The plugger regularly visits the same radio personnel and must maintain his or her credibility with disc jockeys and producers. The personnel at radio stations may take more notice of a plugger who has established a reputation for being straightforward and who has not attempted to fob them off with unsuitable recordings in the past. But, the response of the radio producer will vary according to how well they know the plugger. The tactics of promotional staff in turn vary according to the personality of the radio personnel, and the particular situation at the time. As one experienced radio plugger said; 'Some producers will let you sit down and plug them, others just don't want it. It's like; "Leave the pile over there, so what's happening at [ZXY] records, any gossip?"' Record company pluggers are continually assessing the personalities of the producers and DJs they are visiting, monitoring the internal politics and personal relations at the radio stations and adopting a range of ad-hoc tactics in response. As one head of promotion remarked: 'You have to gauge people. If you gauge them wrong you'll never survive'.

Dead on the Promotional Battlefield

Promotion departments in Britain are often populated by staff, working side by side, who promote to both television and radio. A very similar technique, based on profile building and plugging specific products via personal contact, is adopted in approaching both media. The relationship between the pluggers and media personnel is usually built up over a number of years, and can involve what one member of a noisy and chaotic promotions office described as 'the mutual doing of favours'. These favours might simply entail furnishing information and recordings, or they might involve providing a band or artist for a television or radio appearance at short notice when someone has dropped out. However, the record company staff can extend these reciprocal relations by offering access to prestigious events. The acceptance of such a proposition can then put media personnel under certain obligations. Tony Wilson, who has promoted records for his Manchester-based Factory label, and been plugged when presenting a TV show for Granada Television during the 1970s, described in the following anecdote how he had realised the obligations which the plugger – producer relationship can involve:

A good friend of mine who worked for a record company offered me tickets for a David Bowie concert at Wembley which had been sold out months before. I said thanks and he brought me and a friend down to London – paid the train fare, put us up in a good hotel and gave us a limo for the night. Then a couple of weeks later he came to me with a certain act. They weren't right for the programme, but I put them on. I wouldn't have if I hadn't accepted those favours. Let the industry move in and you're dead meat. (Sutcliffe, 1989a, p 47)

Whether or not DJs and programmers end up as dead meat on the promotional battlefield, corrupted and with their integrity in tatters, it is often the new, developing artists who suffer most. The excitement and enthusiasm which often accompanies the signing of a recording contract and production of musical material, and the momentum which is often being built up in the early stages of a marketing campaign, can be brought to an abrupt halt if the artist cannot gain airplay.

As so many records are released and as there are always a limited amount of spots available for airplay, promotion is very competitive and it is often hard to gain exposure for an artist no one has heard of. However, there have been far more opportunities for new artists on British national radio than on the formatted stations of North America. This is largely because Radio 1 has been less commercially driven to appeal to specific advertisers and can therefore take more risks in programming. It is also because BBC radio has historically attempted to represent a broad range of interests, and due to the way in which different personnel select the music for programmes broadcast throughout the week. However, if recordings are not receiving airplay, record companies can use alternative promotional activities as a means of bringing an artist to the attention of the public, and in order to persuade radio stations to programme a recording – most important here is the work of the press officer.

7

MEDIA MATCHMAKERS

Press Publicity and Performance –
Stores and Dance Floors

I n a perceptive and entertaining account of the achievements and predica-
ments of women in pop Sue Steward and Sheryl Garratt wryly remark that:
'In the big, happy record company family, a woman's place is in the press
department' (1984, p 68). When I repeated this observation to one male head
of press who I interviewed at a major company in 1989 he replied that it was
'probably not a coincidence either, because most journalists are men'. The
implication was that female publicity officers are employed to perform traditional roles servicing the needs of male journalists, and had been recruited into
a 'sexualised' occupation, similar to that found in a range of industries, which
involves 'institutionalised flirting relations between women boundary staff and
men customers' (Hearn & Parkin, 1989, p 59).

The work of publicity officers in the recording industry, however, involves
more than just a traditional service role. Public relations staff play an integral
part in the process of artist development. The press officer contributes to
the way in which artists present themselves verbally and visually, is centrally
involved in negotiating the balance of power between record companies and a
range of publications, and plays an important part in the articulation and
mediation of an artist's identity.

Much of the work I will be describing in this chapter involves the employment of skills which have traditionally been associated with women rather
than men; looking after sensitive artists, maintaining personal relationships,
providing support, and acting as a matchmaker by bringing people with similar
dispositions together. However, most of the practices I have described in this
book so far – 'nurturing' artists, acting as a facilitator and catalyst, offering
encouragement, acquiring knowledge through personal contact – would seem
to be more suited to a 'feminine' sensibility than what have conventionally
been perceived as 'masculine' traits. Beyond the liberal rhetoric of the pop
world, is an industry which has justifiably been described as 'one of the last
bastions of male chauvinism' (Moss, 1990), where fear and prejudice – rather
than the requisite skills for the work – have kept women out of some of the
most important decision-making jobs.

Three Positions in Public Relations

Since the 1960s there has been a growth in the number of freelance publicity set-ups working within the music business. These small companies, often run by one or two individuals with considerable experience of the recording industry, are often subcontracted specific tasks when a record company is overworked or when a particular artist requires special attention. Alternatively, they may handle the entire publicity for an artist who is constantly in the public eye, in which case they may work directly with the artist's management.

In recent years the work of publicising artists has been augmented by an emerging role for staff involved in 'corporate public relations'. This is part of a trend in management and business generally, where there has been an increasing concern with how a company maintains its 'corporate culture' and communicates its identity to the outside world. Corporate public relations staff are involved in monitoring morale and facilitating communication between different occupational groups within their record company, and engaged in representing the organisation to a range of external business, political and educational institutions. They have little direct involvement in the day-to-day work of publicising artists.

Although public relations is often considered a woman's place, corporate PR and freelance public relations companies (which are often hybrid plugging/promotion/publicity concerns) tend to be made up of a mixed male and female staff. It is within the record company publicity departments where women tend to predominate.

Press Relations and Holding the Artist's Hand

For a newly signed act with a limited marketing budget, the printed media provide a relatively inexpensive outlet in which to begin building a profile. Press coverage is often the first signal to personnel within the recording industry itself that a new artist exists, and can decisively affect the way an act is perceived and received by the media and consumers.

The work of the publicity department is similar to that of promotion staff, in that it involves matching artists with particular publications and individuals. It entails locating journalists and editors whose musical taste or publication profile may predispose them to an act, and then persuading them that there is something worth writing about. It is a job which revolves around personal contact and continual socialising. Publicists must have reliable contacts throughout the printed media, be aware of their personal idiosyncrasies, and maintain the trust and cooperation of these individuals. As one publicist remarked:

> It's who you know, not what you know. What you know is actually irrelevant if you don't know anybody on the who you know list. And what you know comes with who you know. The two things build up. I've been doing this for 14 years and I've worked in four record companies and I know people back from 13 or 14 years.

The relationships with journalists, and with personnel throughout the music industry, are built up over time and maintained through constant contact. As the publicist just quoted explained further: 'You know them. You lunch them, you dine them, you eat with them, you have tea with them, you drink with them'.

In addition to maintaining 'press relations', the publicity officer must respond to the needs of the various acts who are signed to the label or handled by the company. This can involve preparing artists for interviews, photo sessions and performances; giving them morning calls, making sure they turn up where and when they are supposed to; booking them into hotels and health clubs; arranging transport and generally being at their beck and call. When Lee Ellen Newman was head of press at WEA Records she once spent three days looking for a special kind of face cream for Cher. At one point she found herself looking through the *Yellow Pages* directory at mid-day on a Sunday desperately trying to find somewhere that was open which stocked the special cream (Giles, 1989a).

A number of people I spoke to in record companies made passing comments about the way in which artists can be demanding and 'expect the world to revolve around them'. Bob Greene, a journalist who travelled as a performing member of the Alice Cooper band during the 1970s, wrote of the way in which the band were cocooned from the world and constantly pampered. Members of the entourage were running around day and night in order to find a band member's favourite liqueur, replace lost clothes, or locate a particular food somebody wanted. He quoted Alice Cooper as saying:

> I don't even know how to write a cheque. I've always been sheltered from anything like that . . . I can't even open a door for myself. I walk in a room and just put my arms out, and the coat's on, and I don't even have to button it. Everybody does everything for me all the time. (1974, p 317).

Although this type of life style is most frequently associated with established artists, many younger and inexperienced acts often expect people in record companies to run around for them. It is usually public relations staff who find themselves doing this. As Penny Valentine remarked, when looking back at her time as a press officer: 'You had to "nanny people" . . . it was just like running a bloody kindergarten, except that the people you were dealing with weren't as nice as kids' (Steward & Garratt, 1984, p 68).

It is this aspect of the work which makes it a job considered to be more suitable for women than men. As one head of press explained when talking about the staff in her department:

> I've got two girls. I did have a boy, but he was difficult and punched somebody out one day in a fit of temper and I had to fire him. Now, that isn't typical, but boys get very frustrated in PR because they want to be something else. And, there's a slight servile attitude in PR. You've got to make the teas for the artists, you've got to do this, you've got to do that. And girls are much better at that than boys.

It is in this area of public relations work where women are required to adopt overtly gendered tactics, exhibiting a subservience and sympathetically responding to the needs of others (Hearn & Parkin, 1989). However, one of the most important tasks of public relations staff is to act as a 'matchmaker': that is, to assess the mutual compatibility of artists and journalists and then bring them together in order to gain the most suitable publicity.

Music Journalists

Rock journalists have been described by Simon Frith, a journalist himself for a number of years, as 'professional rock fans' (1983). The same is true of journalists writing about other genres of music such as soul, rap, roots/folk and new age. But they are more than just fans. Journalists operate as opinion formers and interpreters for various audiences. Although often viewed as part of the audience – responding as consumers – music journalists are important cultural intermediaries, forming a link between artists and record buyers. Their writings play an important part in articulating an artist's identity.

Frith (1978) has traced the development of the music press in Britain and has charted the way in which the style of journalism has changed from an approach in the 1950s which provided little historical or social perspective and had no developed critical positions, to a less frivolous, theoretically informed and analytical style of writing in the 1970s. Serious rock and pop journalism developed in the late 1960s under the influence of the 'underground' press, and in the 1980s a 'cultural journalism' emerged which was informed by theories of semiotics and youth subcultures in such magazines as the *Face*, *Blitz* and *iD* (McRobbie, 1989). In addition, quality national newspapers such as the *Guardian*, *Telegraph* and *Observer*, and publications such as *New Statesman* and *Society*, began paying critical attention to rock and pop music.

Although popular music publications have become more critical and analytical, they are still dependent upon record companies for their material. Record company press releases and campaigns have taken account of these changing conventions. It has always been a practice in public relations to write press releases in such a way that they can, with little modification, be used as copy by publications, and this has continued to apply – from the 1950s breathy prose of advertising (Frith, 1978) to the intellectual name dropping and knowing irony with which Frankie Goes To Hollywood were promoted in the 1980s.

The music publications used by record companies to build artist profiles and gain exposure for new acts tend to be those dominated by male staff, and which have a predominantly male readership – such as *New Musical Express*, *Melody Maker* and *Q Magazine*. Publications which have a higher female readership and employ more women as journalists tend to be in the teenage pop area, such as *Smash Hits*, or general teenage magazines like *Just 17* and *19* which treat music in a less analytical and more anecdotal manner, and are more concerned with fashion, health and social relationships.

Far fewer women than men apply to work as journalists on popular music publications – a phenomenon which led a writer for London's *City Limits* magazine to suggest wryly that the male obsession with pop is an anally retentive masculine characteristic which ranks alongside train spotting, stamp collecting and cricket scoring as a gender idiosyncrasy (Giles, 1989b). As rock journalist Simon Reynolds commented, when asked to describe how he saw himself and his peers:

It's men . . . mostly . . . from a certain kind of class background – on the whole, lower-middle class to middle class – but they seem to come from a certain hinterland in British culture which is very unstable and rootless. There's a certain religious fervour about it. I'm sure that people who are rock critics, if they'd been born in the Middle Ages, would have become monks or priests, and have been fervently discussing all those archaic things like how many angels you can get on the head of a pin. (Giles, 1989b, p 17).

There is no doubt that many male journalists are obsessive about music, and it is this enthusiasm which publicists seek to tap into. When I spoke to one head of press she had recently been involved in the promotion of an American singer and explained that she arranged for a particular journalist from *Melody Maker* to interview this artist because he was 'in love' and 'absolutely besotted' with her. Perhaps it was Chris Roberts who 'reviewed' a week of concerts by Deborah Harry at a small club in London during 1989 in the following terms:

I am a fanatic . . . this week is a magnificent celebration of The Pop Star . . . Outside, people offer ludicrous sums of money for tickets. Inside, we worship. At the end of each night everyone leaves dazed, babbling, radiant . . . it sinks in that the motions of those tiny face muscles are more transcendental and unique than any camera could tell . . . (*Melody Maker*, October 14th 1989, p 22).

However, women and girls can be just as obsessive about pop stars (Vermorel & Vermorel, 1985; Steward & Garratt, 1984). Whilst gender might influence the type of coverage given to artists in subtle ways, the lack of women journalists is probably more the result of the general marginalisation of women in the music industry than any male or female characteristics.

Locating Journalists

Journalists are initially approached because of their enthusiasm for particular artists and styles of music. When working with a new act the publicity officer contacts a specific writer (rather than an editor) and gives them a copy of an early studio recording and a biography.

The biography will probably be put together by the press officer and provides details about the act's past, how they were 'discovered', and includes any human interest information or newsworthy anecdotes. The aim is to introduce the identity of the act to journalists in such a way that the writer will want to find out more by talking to the group or singer concerned.

When an artist becomes more established a particular journalist will often be asked to write the biography. The journalist is selected for their writing skills and enthusiasm, but this is also a way of involving a critic in the process of artist development – it signals to the media that there is an act worthy of attention, and it is another example of the way in which personnel in the recording industry seek to enhance their reputations by association with artists. A journalist may be yet another person who can claim to have 'discovered' an artist.

However, a biography alone is not going to make a music critic want to talk to an artist if they don't like the music. So the initial contact is very dependent on matching a particular act to the musical taste of a journalist. Having provided a journalist with a recording the publicist contacts them again after a few days to find out their response, and to see if they would be interested in writing about the artist.

In a similar way to promotion staff, the press officer is attempting to sensitise a journalistic community to an act. At this stage she is trying to build an awareness within the media rather than communicate directly to the public. By the time the artist's material is ready for release the press officer will know who likes a particular act and who might write the most interesting and influential feature or review.

Having located and gained the attention of particular journalists, publicity staff then make further judgments regarding the respect and influence which the journalist has amongst peers, and assess their relationship with the editor of the publication they are working for. Some journalists are in a better position to influence editorial policy than other writers. One head of press remarked that certain journalists are 'hated by their editors', and in such cases the editor may consciously obstruct or inhibit what is written and when and where it appears.

Here again knowledge of this type of situation is being built up by the press officer through constant socialising. As this head of press explained when I asked him how he knew about the relationships between journalists and their editors:

> It's gossip really. You know, how do you find out what sort of music people like? It's a vague sort of feeling you have. If you go out with people you might listen to people's conversations. You might be going out with the editor who's slagging off somebody, and you make a mental note of it. It's a small world. It's quite insular.

Hence, writers are selected for the way in which they can re-present an act in their particular publication. Journalists have different styles of writing and a range of pre-occupations. Some bring a 'hip' style to the presentation of an act, whether Charles Shaar Murray's cool combination of beat writing and black slang, or the blissed-out metaphorical meanderings of Simon Reynolds. Others adopt a more provocative approach when interviewing or writing about acts – a strand running from Lester Bang's confrontational interviews during the 1970s, Julie Burchill's barbed cynicism in the 1980s and to Steven Wells blend of ranting socialist rhetoric and personal abuse in the 1990s. Less controversial and more predictable is the measured and researched style characteristic of publications such as *Q* and the 'quality' press.

Features, Reviews and Gossip

The most important type of press coverage is the two or three page feature article which heralds the release of an album. This is usually based around an interview, and often supported with a cover photograph. The press officer attempts to gain as much coverage in as many relevant publications as possible, and tries to synchronise publication to coincide with the week in which a particular recording is released. Considerable thought and preparation goes into this. Different publications have different lead times; monthly magazines may need an interview and advanced copies of recordings three months prior to release, whereas weekly publications may only require material two to three weeks in advance.

The feature article is usually composed of photos, an interview and an accompanying contextual description. To be effective it must be internally consistent and in harmony with the coverage the act is receiving in other media. The setting within which an act is positioned in a feature article articulates an artist's identity in a similar way to the use of photographs discussed earlier. So, for example, Sting – the urbane intellectual – was interviewed by a journalist from the *New Musical Express* in April 1991 and spoke about politics, the environment, sexuality and the meaning of existence. The text was accompanied by pictures of the artist sitting in New York's Central Park reading a copy of the *New York Times*.

The artist and journalist may have met prior to an interview and discussed the way in which they want to approach a feature. If they have not met – or if the act has little experience of giving interviews – the press officer will often prepare artists in advance. The publicist may rehearse an artist by using 'role play' techniques or may arrange for a journalist friend to work with an act and make them aware of the type of questions they are likely to be asked and assist them in preparing answers. Artist development and publicity staff are mainly concerned that the artist is going to appear interesting and be worth reading about. One head of press explained that 'journalists deal in quotes' and said that it didn't matter how much excitement there was at gigs, or about records, 'they can't last press-wise if they can't really think of anything to say . . . So, you just keep reminding them to think up some quotes'.

'Thinking up quotes' may involve deliberately contriving controversial and provocative statements, fabricating or exaggerating incidents and anecdotes, or may involve a careful attempt to avoid controversy – depending on the artist's image and audience being approached. Just as the necessity of making a video puts pressure on artists to present themselves visually, so the need for press exposure requires artists to be able to express themselves verbally and have something interesting to say. As I have emphasised throughout this book, to be a musician or singer is not enough, an artist must be able to communicate across multiple media.

The degree to which publicists actively arrange for journalists to conduct interviews and reviews in specific locations varies. It can range from merely organising the transportation of writers from London to Cambridgeshire in order to attend a Julian Cope gig, to flying critics half way around the world to speak to an artist in a specific location. A journalist might be flown out to interview an artist on a particular point of a tour or as a band are finishing recording, or for a specific promotional event – with the record company then paying the expenses, accommodation and travel of the journalist. One head of press recalled a successful trip in which she had arranged for a journalist and a photographer from a London-based national music paper to attend a concert in Scotland:

I took the *NME* up to Glasgow. They wanted to do a whole page live review and talk to X and Y afterwards. And it was fantastic. I took Terry Staunton and Kevin Cummings, and Kevin did some photos at the gig and we did some backstage afterwards. And we all sat down and had a couple of bottles of wine and something to eat and Terry talked to X and she gave him some T-shirts and they were all loving each other. And then Terry and I went back to the hotel and got drunk because it all went very well.

In this example the publicist and journalist have both achieved their goals and celebrate together. The review of the live performance will provide interesting and entertaining copy for the publication, and the favourable publicity can help sell tickets for further shows and contribute to the promotion of recordings.

An increasing amount of space in the music press – particularly amongst publications established in the mid to late 1980s directed at an older record buyer in their twenties and thirties, such as *Q*, *Vox* and *Select* – has been devoted to critical reviews of albums. These can, in the words of one head of publicity, 'sell records, open doors and put bums on seats'. A good critical response is also useful in establishing an artist's credibility amongst other journalists and personnel in radio and television who monitor and take note of what is being reported in the music press. It is often a favourable critical review which persuades a radio programmer to begin broadcasting a recording.

Publicity staff usually attempt to engineer a favourable review by getting an advance recording of an album to the journalist who they think will be able to provide the most positive and interesting angle. This has become a common practice in the music industry, as it has in the book publishing industry. One head of press explained that it was:

> What everybody does . . . you give somebody in the paper the tape upfront and he'll go to the review editor and say 'I'd like to review this album'. And the reviews editor will say 'great' because it saves him having to find somebody to review it. It makes his life easier if somebody's willing and happy to do it, because it's one less for him to have to do that week.

A further type of coverage which artists may receive in the music press are anecdotes and gossip in the news pages. Although this can introduce an act to the media and consumers, it is usually used as a way of keeping an artist's name in the public eye at a particular time, and to reinforce their identity. The publicist may telephone the news desk of a publication, or give tit-bits of information to a journalist over a drink, or might simply release an anecdote anonymously. One step further on from small items of gossip in the music press are the tales of scandal and controversy found in the British tabloid press.

Courting the Tabloids

Throughout the 1980s the British tabloid press devoted an increasing amount of space to the activities of recording artists, not only on their daily pop pages but in news stories and front cover articles. The tabloid press reaches a large readership, and in addition it is a medium which disc jockeys draw on when looking for anecdotes to punctuate their radio programmes. PR staff are aware that publicity can be amplified considerably by sending it through this route: A story about a pop star which appears in a morning newspaper can be talked about all over the country by the end of the day (Tremlett, 1990).

However publicists have a number of reservations about this type of coverage. The relationship with the national tabloid press is different to that between record companies and music publications. The writers do not share a similar musical world like pop journalists and publicists, and may have quite different agendas. Tabloid journalists are less concerned about recordings and performances and more interested in money, sex, death, drugs and corruption. In addition, the amount of influence the publicity officer can exert is more limited. The national press do not depend on the music industry for their copy as heavily as the pop press do. The quality of the final copy is therefore less easy to predict. Even if an interview with a journalist has gone smoothly, an article may be changed by senior editors and given a completely different emphasis by the use of headlines and unflattering photographs.

One head of press who had worked in record company publicity for twelve years, and who had one of her artists treated in what she considered a deceitful and vindictive manner, echoed the feelings of many press officers when she spoke of trying to avoid the tabloid newspapers. The most common complaint concerns the way in which they distort, exaggerate, misquote and conduct 'vendettas' against particular artists. There have been some notorious examples of this over the years, such as the well publicised libelling of Elton John by the *Sun* and the 'stalking' of Boy George which culminated in a front page story in the same newspaper proclaiming that 'Junkie George Has 8 Weeks To Live'.

It is in this area that press officers are emphatic that the adage of 'all publicity is good publicity' does not apply. It can damage both the record sales and reputations of artists, and can affect them personally. The artist may also hold the press officer responsible for an unflattering tabloid story and this can sour the relationship between the artist and record company or freelance publicist.

If a tabloid story can be harmful to personal reputations and relations between the record company and artist, it may also be an unsuitable way of presenting an act – particularly if a record company wishes to market an artist as a long term serious proposition. It can signal that an act is superficial and ephemeral. As one head of publicity remarked, in 1989, when an act signed to another label were receiving considerable attention in the tabloid press:

> People can court the tabloids to a certain extent, but they tend to drop you and move on to somebody else. Say you get a new pop band like Big Fun through the tabloid newspapers. Then you are running up a flag that says they've got two years at the most. But, if you've got a band that you feel could get bigger and bigger and bigger over quite a long period of time you wouldn't go down that road right away. You'd be more careful and cautious.

Hence different journalists and specific forms of press publicity – the critical review, the feature, the tabloid glamour story – are selected and used for the way in which they articulate an artist's identity and connote for a particular audience the life-style and music of that artist. Certain forms of publicity are better for some artists than others and as a singer or band become more successful the press officer begins to exert a greater level of control over where an artist appears in print.

From Quantity to Quality Control

When working with a new artist the publicist's priority is to get as much coverage as possible. At this stage success is often measured in column inches. Although attempting to present artists in the most favourable way and match the band or singer to the most suitable journalist, the publicity officer may often have to make do with anyone who is showing the slightest interest.

However, at a certain point the press officer's job changes from directing details of an act at anyone who might be remotely interested, to attempting tactically to control the quality of this information and where it appears. The artist may have been experimenting with visual styles and will probably have arrived at a more definite sense of the identity they want to present. As an act start reaching a wider audience the press officer will seek to exert a greater influence over which publications write about an act, and what is reported in print.

When orchestrating publicity for established artists, the press officer meets any unknown journalist before an interview to ascertain whether the ideas and personality of the writer are compatible with those of the artist. One publicist explained that she spent time 'interrogating' music critics prior to a potential article on a major artist. If she considered them to be unsuitable then she would negotiate with editors to have a different journalist assigned to the story. This publicist explained that she would: 'go back to the features editor or the editor of the paper and say: "I really want to do the interview with you, but can you find another writer". And if they want to do the feature bad enough they'll find another writer.'

This pressure from the publicity officer can result in a power struggle emerging between the record company and publication over the representation of an act, particularly if a journalist feels that they are merely being used to further the specific interests of an artist and their label. A similar tension occurs in a range of media settings due to the way in which the publicity process can make journalists uneasy about their roles and provoke them into reasserting the significance of their own contributions (Blumler, 1990). A journalist can do this in a general way by writing at a distance from the events being described or by questioning the validity of what they are reporting. The writer can also assert their autonomy by reporting things which have been said off-the-record or by relaying events which contradict the image of the act. In addition a journalist may misrepresent the artist by being selective with quotes, can be bluntly sarcastic or simply resort to personal abuse.

The publicist may perceive these tactics as deliberate attempts to damage an artist's career or reputation. One head of press explicitly drew attention to the dynamic of power underlying these type of situations, remarking; 'It's a power struggle, sometimes. A big artist will help to sell front covers and maybe the press don't like to feel that is a fact. Maybe they think; "Alright, you sell our paper, but we just want you to know that without us you're nothing."' However, instances of outright vindictiveness are not common in the music press, and probably compensated by the numerous examples when a journalist is in awe of the person they are interviewing and writing a feature about (just see some of the interviews which have been conducted with artists such as Bob Dylan and David Bowie over the years).

The publicist hopes to receive favourable coverage for the artist by selecting the journalist in the first place and arranging features, interviews and reviews in such a way that the critic does not feel the need to assert their autonomy. However, if a writer has produced a particularly derogatory story then the publicity officer can effectively sanction journalists by denying them access to artists in the future. One head of publicity explained that if one of her artists was the subject of an unfair article; 'You live with it and say "that person never gets an interview with that artist or any other artist again" '. For all their attempts to distance themselves and maintain their autonomy from the publicity process, the journalists and publications are dependent upon the record companies for their material and for access to artists. However, journalists also wish to maintain this relationship in order to pursue wider career aims within the recording industry.

The Record Company and the Music Press: Symbiosis and Osmosis

The relationship between the music press and record companies has sometimes been characterised as one of symbiosis; dependent upon one another for their daily livelihood, the press officer and journalist mutually make each other's lives easier. However, there is an additional dimension to this relationship which might be characterised as osmosis: many journalists are ex-members of rock groups, play in bands themselves or are managing unsigned artists. In such instances the press officer provides a point of access into the music industry for these journalists, and contact has often been made between an unsigned act and the A & R department of a record company through the mediation of the press officer.

Over the years a number of journalists have entered the music industry. Simon Frith (1978) remarked on this in his study of rock in the late 1970s. He noted that, in both Britain and North America, there was continuous mobility between rock journalism and rock publicity, with the record company press departments recruiting from the music papers and music papers employing ex-publicists.

Whilst there are degrees of mutual mobility between the publicity office and the music press, the movement is usually one way. It tends to be the journalists who move into the recording industry. It is rare for a female publicity officer to become a music journalist, and when the male journalists do enter the industry it is often as performers, producers and A & R staff – more male dominated areas – rather than as press officers. One female head of press, when talking about this, also spoke of the way in which working in press and public relations provided restricted opportunities for occupational mobility, commenting: 'I must admit, doing press as I do, going on one particular track, it's difficult to cross over into A & R or something else. Not many people tend to do it'. This raises the wider question of the position of women in the recording industry, an issue which has occurred at various points since my discussion of the male character of artist and repertoire departments in Chapter 3, and which I'll make some summary remarks about before moving on to discuss other promotional strategies.

Women in the Music Industry: Blending in to the Boys Club?

It should be clear from the discussion so far that the work of publicity staff involves more than an institutionalised flirting relationship or simply servicing the needs of journalists and artists, and that public relations staff actively contribute to the process of artist development. It is also worth noting that despite some of the overtly gendered dimensions to the job, public relations has not always been a 'woman's place' in the recording industry. It is a space in which women have actively established a presence over time. When Michael Wale (1972) was describing the work of publicists in his account of the 'pop process' in the 1970s, women were noticeably absent. Although mentioning a number of specific and generic 'PR and promotion men', he only referred to one woman – Pat Pretty who worked for EMI and A & M. As Berni Kilmartin, head of press at Chrysalis, and with over 18 years experience in the British music industry remarked when I spoke to her in 1991: 'There were only three of us in the PR area at one point. It's now predominantly women.'

There is also some indication that the rigid confinement of women to record company publicity departments is breaking down. Throughout the 1980s women have been increasingly represented in international marketing, product management, promotion, market research and in video production. However, there is little research available to substantiate this. An analysis of *Billboard*'s 'executive turntable' between 1966 and 1986 and questionnaires administered to a limited number of women executives in the American music industry reported that there had been an increase in the number of women entering the business, and that the types of jobs which women were moving into were becoming more varied (Parsons, 1988). Changes have been similar in Britain, with the most notable growth of female staff being in marketing and sales positions. However, women have tended to be product managers or members of sales teams rather than senior decision-making staff.

Although moving into a broader range of occupations within the music industry, women are generally having to conform to and fit in with the established conventions and existing ways of working. One female executive I spoke to at a corporate group in Britain felt that the pressures were such that women were obliged to 'acquiesce to the general ideology'. As in many areas of work, women are forced to adopt the strategy of blending into the existing organisational culture (Sheppard, 1989).

The recording industry is relatively new, developing in its modern form since the Second World War and has been decisively shaped by the rock culture of the 1960s and 1970s. As I stressed earlier, and have noted throughout this book, jobs are not rigidly defined by bureaucratic criteria, and working practices have been established over a relatively short period of time. Women who are employed in non-secretarial positions in the British music industry in the 1990s tend to have worked their way up from being administrators or personal assistants, or have been drawn into the industry following chance meetings with people already employed in the business. In contrast, male staff, with a background in rock or dance-club culture, have usually been actively recruited. Women I spoke to in both the United States and Britain frequently spoke of the way in which higher management and key decision-making jobs were dominated by an 'old boys network' or 'boys club' – a milieu in which women were not welcome. One product manager at a large corporation gave an indication of the prospects, and the formidable barriers, when she commented:

> I think it's getting better. [pause]. How can I say that? I've basically worked my way up and I know that I'm intelligent enough to work my way up. And also I get on very well with people and I just know who you should get on with, and in that respect it's good for a woman. I know that [the record company] have got their own female director upstairs. And I think it's just like your token director, I really do . . . I've never felt that I'm female and I shouldn't get on. In the same way, you are made much more aware of the politics in the company and what goes on. I am obviously aware that there are certain jobs that they just want for males and certain jobs that it doesn't matter about.

Artist Development and the Male Musical Tradition

The lack of women's voices in key decision making positions has undoubtedly influenced the type of acts which have been signed and the way in which artists have been prioritised, developed and presented. Most of the decisions about artists over the last thirty years have been made by men, and whilst there is no detailed research available on these decision-making processes, its consequences have been vividly illustrated by the portrayal of women in contemporary popular music. As many feminist writers have shown, the representation of women in texts (written, visual and musical) not only expresses wider social relationships, but also produces the ideas and beliefs which people draw on when living their lives.

Over the years a number of writers have drawn attention to the negative and sexist way in which women have been represented in song lyrics, videos and in the bohemian sex-drugs-and-rock'n'roll life style found celebrated in numerous biographies. At the beginning of the 1970s Marion Meade (1972) peered behind the 'hip camouflage' of rock at the way in which women were portrayed as subordinate in the lyrics, images and a life-style which drew selectively on the machismo elements of the blues and country traditions for inspiration. Rock was a man's world. Women were excluded or marginalised as musicians. A woman's place on the road was between the sheets or doing the catering in the kitchen.

A few years later Angela McRobbie and Simon Frith (1978) developed some of these themes, arguing that rock had become synonymous with a male defined sexuality and was reinforcing traditional definitions of masculinity and femininity. Focusing mainly on 'cock rock', they emphasised the way in which rock performers were aggressive, dominating, boastful and constantly sought to remind the audience of their prowess and control. Symbolically the electric guitar was used as a phallus, axe and gun, and rock was dominated by male bodies on display, plunging shirts and tight trousers; a visual emphasis on chest hair and genitals. As rock became musically heavier and more self-consciously stylised it became a world populated by 'men with screaming axes and screeching genitals' (Steward and Garratt, 1984). In contrast, female performers were restricted to less active roles and either found themselves as singers, a sexualised focal point, their careers assisted if they wore slit skirts or revealed some cleavage, or encouraged to adopt the more whimsical approach of 'girl groups' and singer-songwriters with their air of 'fragile introspection, innocent optimism and romantic yearnings' (Greig, 1989).

However, this picture is far from static. The punk episode temporarily offered a greater variety of voices and visions to female performers, and during the 1980s the dominance of rock gave way to a proliferation of genres and styles, and saw the emergence of a number of dynamic female artists such as Annie Lennox, Madonna and Sinéad O'Connor who refused the existing rock and pop conventions and dichotomies. In their music and images these three major global artists have asserted that a woman's place in popular music is neither on the margins nor according to rock sexual stereotypes or introspective whimsy. Whether the appointments of the first women managing directors of British record labels (Lisa Anderson at BMG and Diana Graham at Arista) at the turn of the decade signals tokenism, or indicates a wider change in divisions within the British recording industry remains to be seen. Women are still vastly under-represented, and as the artistic conventions and macho ideologies of rock have informed record company policies and decision-making for a number of years, it is hardly surprising that when women began to be represented in the recording industry it was in publicity and public relations work.

Sales and Retail Promotion

The calculations of marketing staff, the persuasions of the pluggers and the matchmaking of the press officers are all part of a concerted and coordinated attempt on the part of record companies to convince key media personnel to broadcast recordings and videos, and ultimately to persuade the customer to go out and purchase their piece of the artist. A further link between the artist and the consumer is, therefore, the record retailer. If a particular recording is not available in a store it doesn't matter how good the marketing campaign is or how interesting the publicity, the recording is probably not going to be purchased.

Record labels have often promoted new artists by approaching 'hip' retailers and small record shops run by enthusiasts in areas where there has been a strong following for particular types of music, and where the character of the owner and the identity of the store provide a focus for the more devoted record buyers interested in new sounds. A 'fan-base' for a new artist or recording can then be established via word-of-mouth and the playing of music in these shops. This can then be used to generate further interest amongst larger stores, and the radio and media networks.

However, these opportunities have become increasingly limited due to the expansion of large retail chains which have absorbed many of the smaller idiosyncratic outlets run by aficionados and replaced them with standardised stores stocking a limited repertoire of the most popular material. In 1991 the British Phonographic Industry reported that the number of retail outlets in the UK was at its lowest level for many years, and noted that the decline in the number of outlets had mainly been at the expense of independent specialists (BPI, 1991). Throughout the 1980s, record retailing in Britain became dominated by a few high street stores such as Woolworths, WH Smith and

Boots and record chains like HMV and Our Price/Virgin. In a similar way record retailing in the United States became dominated by large corporate chains such as Tower Records, Music Land (Sam Goody) and K-Mart – companies which have been expanding their operations across Europe and in Japan.

When approached by record company sales staff a retailer wants to know that someone is going to come into their store and buy a particular recording. The sales person must convince the buyer that it is not going to take up valuable space gathering dust. Like radio programmers the retailer considers the amount of investment being put into an artist, the level of publicity being generated and the amount of radio and television exposure that a recording is receiving. In the past, record companies have tried to influence retailers by offering various inducements, and this is the area in the British music business where tales of corruption circulate – mainly because the record charts have been based on the monitoring of purchases in a limited number of 'chart return shops'. Record companies have attempted to influence retailers by providing items of merchandise or by supplying free copies of records which the store then makes a total profit on. Pinned to the wall, in the office of one company where I conducted an interview, was a memo from the BPI which mildly reprimanded the company for including free concert tickets with a particular artist's records when they were delivered to retailers. The company were asked to discontinue this practice, and advised that incentives to retailers should not have a market value. Another, often mentioned tactic involves record companies, or managers of artists, arranging for records to be bought from these shops. I was told of one critically acclaimed minor label which used to hold regular informal meetings on a Monday morning at which staff would be required to produce receipts for the recordings they had purchased over the weekend.

Whether or not greater surveillance by industry organisations has eliminated such practices remains to be seen, but the use of tighter stock control procedures and computerised methods of buying and selling recordings has reduced their effectiveness. Instead of promoting to individual stores, record company sales staff have been increasingly dealing with buyers who purchase for large chains using computerised point-of-sale stock control systems – a method which has become well established in the United States. As the vice president of sales at an American office of a British owned corporation explained:

> American music retailers have consolidated down to just a few big accounts that
> control a great deal of the retail outlets across America. You're only dealing with
> one guy who buys for all those stores. He's a pretty powerful buyer who now has
> a very sophisticated form of information at his disposal. A computer sits on his
> desk, he pulls up a lot of the past information. And the computer makes a pretty
> compelling argument. It just sits there and looks at you and says 'This is what we
> sold on the last one' Erh, hmmm, don't know.

The monitoring of retail purchases through the direct input of bar codes, accompanied by the computerised tracking of digital CD signals on radio stations, has provided record companies with up to the hour information which enables them to make direct comparisons between sales and airplay.

Throughout the day they can monitor broadcasts in different areas and can accurately tell what a particular recording is selling across the country at any given moment. This can then be instantly communicated via fax, mobile phone and portable computers along webs of 'sales intelligence' to regional staff working the smaller stores across a geographical region.

Although enabling record companies to target retailers more effectively, these systems tend to favour artists who are already successful or 'building', rather than the more unpredictable new act for which there is no scientific data. In order to reduce the risk involved in deciding which recordings to stock, the limited resources of both the record companies and the retailers tend to be spent on those products with the most obvious sales potential. As the conglomeration and homogenisation of retail outlets has led to a decline in the small, idiosyncratic record shop run by a music enthusiast, the priorities of radio stations, record companies and retailers – all increasingly using similar computerised systems of information gathering – have tended to mutually reinforce one another. However, public performances and club promotion provide yet another means of bringing artists to the attention of radio programmers and retailers.

Live Promotion

Despite recurring pronouncements about the death of live music, public performances – albeit with changing conventions of what constitutes a 'live' event – are still popular and can be a very effective promotional medium. It is the concert promoter – sometimes working through a booking agent but increasingly dealing directly with artists, managers and record companies – who is responsible for the organisation of live events and tours. The promoter has the task of hiring venues, arranging stages, sorting out public address systems and lighting, employing caterers and security personnel, advertising the show and coordinating the sale of tickets. Although gaining something of a bad reputation in the past for being aggressive wheeler-dealers, making excessive profits, and occasionally running off with the takings, concert promoters have become more 'professional'. In an attempt to improve their image, and to monitor their own occupation, they took the step of forming their own body, the Concert Promoters Association (CPA) in 1986 under the chairmanship of Harvey Goldsmith.

Concert promotion for all but the most successful acts (who are often in a position to subsidise the expense of putting on shows through corporate sponsorship deals) can be a risky business. The vast majority of tours are not undertaken to earn money directly and many have to be financially supported by record companies against an artist's future earnings. Whilst an important motive behind tours and public performances is the desire to promote specific recordings directly to potential consumers, live events also play a part in persuading the media to programme an artist's recordings.

For a new and developing act touring can be used to attract a following, and construct a 'base market', who will purchase recordings and hence bring the artist to the attention of the press, and television and radio programmers. This route is mainly used when promoting rock oriented acts, in which playing live has become part of the conventions of the genre and in which the music may sometimes be considered unsuitable for daytime radio programming.

A visible consumer response to an act which has established a live reputation can persuade radio stations to playlist a record. In 1991 A & M Records adopted this approach when promoting The Milltown Brothers by using what has become a standard practice of paying for them to be the 'support' act on a short tour with The La's. In this instance the fee charged for 'buying on' to the tour was £6,500 for 16 dates. The La's were attracting a similar type of audience and were then the subject of considerable attention within the rock press and record industry. The Milltown Brothers managed to attract media coverage and generated a favourable audience response when they performed. Their manager Tim Paton considered that this live promotion was a vital part of the marketing which assisted in bringing both their single and album into the Top 40 chart (Robinson, 1991).

The Milltown Brothers attracted considerable media attention, and this example highlights one of the main aims of live promotion, which is to motivate and involve both media and record company personnel. As the manager of a Scottish band who had initially established their reputation through constant touring throughout the 1980s explained:

> There's a lot more product out there than there are bands touring. I think it's important at this level, not necessarily for the punters, but one, for the record company, so that the record company get into the band. Because if they're good live it makes a hell of a difference. For the German company to come down and see the band and talk to them, vibe them up about it . . . and two, for the media. More than thinking 'we're going to break this album', it's important to get everybody who's going to be involved in trying to promote that act to see them, like them and get on with them and think they've got more of a personal involvement.

Hence, for newly signed artists and for acts with new material to promote, public performances offer a way of generating audience interest, motivating staff within record companies and generating enthusiasm amongst various media. It is not simply a way of generating income, nor merely a means of promoting recordings direct to consumers, but it is a way of influencing various cultural mediators. It is a way of gaining supporters who will either programme a band's recordings on radio, write about them in the rock press, give them a television spot, or simply return to the day-to day work of selling and promoting in the record company itself with a greater enthusiasm and sense of involvement.

Club Promotion

Although record companies have tended to use dance clubs and discotheques to promote specific single tracks, rather than build artists' careers, a number of acts have emerged from club cultures over the years. Artists such as Grace Jones, Grandmaster Flash, and Soul II Soul all established reputations by making personal appearances and having their music played in clubs during the 1980s. Clubs playing recorded music for dancing have provided a number of opportunities for rap, soul and pop acts who do not perform according to rock conventions.

Club promotion is used, like radio plugging and press publicity, to target specific opinion formers. It also provides record companies with an opportunity to research the potential appeal of a particular track prior to an official release. In a similar way to the live promotion of rock acts, the aim of club promotion is to create a demand for an artist amongst a small group of enthusiasts and then use this to bring an act to the attention of media programmers or to generate enough sales for a particular recording to enter the charts.

In the late 1980s a number of disc jockeys in Britain such as Danny Rampling, Mark Moore, Dave Dorell, Paul Oakenfeld and Ben Leibrand began to exert a decisive influence over the type of music played in clubs. Record companies recognised this influence and began specifically targeting key taste makers with the aim of influencing the DJs and dancers who followed them. As one head of promotion commented: 'There's about 200 people, DJs around the country. There's also a sort of mafiosi in clubland, in terms of DJs – not in terms of heavies. And there's about 15 to 20 people, and they really do influence roughly about another 200 DJs.'

Record companies adopted what became a standard procedure for promoting records to clubs; the record was released with only a 'white label' which contained merely the name of the artist and the title of the track. With its lack of formal information and anonymous aura of mystique, white label records initially signified a rare import, the reproduction of an obsolete or obscure recording, or an illegally produced remix of an existing track. However, white labels very soon became the obligatory medium for promoting to the clubs. Promotion staff I spoke to acknowledged that the majority of DJs generally knew which record company had released a recording and who the artist was. However, the white label still signified exclusivity, and indicated that the record was not just a general release. Record companies utilise the exclusive appeal of these recordings to generate interest in a particular track on dance floors, amongst influential DJs and amongst media publications associated with dance music, and create a demand which can be brought to the notice of the press, radio and television media.

Club promotion also enables record companies to market research the potential of a track. In the late 1980s when a vast number of dance records were being released due to the low costs of recording and manufacturing them, record companies were tending to press up an initial 500 copies of a track and distribute these to key DJs and retail outlets. This provided an opportunity to assess the potential consumer response to a specific track. If the record was unpopular, then the record company didn't need to incur the expense of releasing it nationally. The company could also assess whether it was worth re-recording or remixing a track in any way, and often employed specialist club promoters for guidance about the type of mixes preferred by the audiences in different clubs and geographical territories. Club promotion staff also feedback information to artist development and product planning meetings within the record company, and can double as an artist and repertoire source at the same time as plugging records. In this way promotional activities have become an integral part of the process of artist development, enabling the record company to monitor the reactions of key opinion formers and consumers and modify recordings in response.

All the promotional activities I have been describing are used together throughout a marketing campaign as part of a strategic attempt to generate interest in an artist and their particular recordings. The different promotional media – radio, television, press publicity, public performance, retailing and dance clubs – implicate various cultural intermediaries and audiences in the articulation of an artist's musical identity, and can directly inform the type of music recorded and the way in which artists are presented, spiralling around the decision to acquire an artist in the first place.

8

BETWEEN SUCCESS AND FAILURE

Collaboration and Conflict in the Recording Industry

In describing how a range of recording industry personnel contribute to the sounds and images of pop and mediate between artists and their potential audience, I have been following a similar course to writers who have emphasized the 'collaborative' character of contemporary cultural production. I now want to turn to the way in which this collaborative process collapses.

In my earlier discussion of the acquisition of artists I noted that senior record company executives require staff to work with artists according to a 'shared vision'. This is similar to what Ryan & Peterson (1982) identified as a 'product image'; an overriding set of musical, visual and commercial objectives which enable personnel working in different areas to coordinate their activities. Record company staff often use the analogy of a jigsaw to describe how the various component parts involved in producing the sounds and images and marketing particular artists are brought together. This is a useful metaphor because it emphasises the way in which the whole can be put together from various parts and in various sequences, and how the 'total star text' should – in theory – be greater than the parts, organised around this shared vision. This analogy also re-emphasises my point that contemporary popular music does not follow a simple uni-directional movement from artistic producers to consumers, but arises out of the continual dialogues between the performers, corporate bodies, media and audiences. In this way there can be multiple points of origin of the sounds and images which become associated with particular artists.

However, the shared visions – of commercial success and critical recognition – which drive the process of artist development are haunted by the prospect of economic failure. The practices I have been describing; artist & repertoire staff using networks of contacts, marketing staff positioning acts in relation to existing genres, promotion staff co-opting radio disc jockeys into the profile building of an act, and publicists utilising journalists as 'fans with typewriters' – all of these are quite deliberate 'coping strategies' (Hirsch, 1972), continual attempts to reduce the possibility of commercial failure. If the jigsaw analogy refers to the way in which the process of artist development should work if successful, in this chapter I am concerned with how the jigsaw fails to come together, or falls apart.

There are two broad sets of tensions which disrupt the process of artist development. Firstly, disputes which emerge due to the affective and personal relationship between artists and record company staff. Secondly, schisms which arise between formal occupational divisions within the corporation. Informing these conflicts is an awareness of the rewards of success and the forfeits for failure. I shall, therefore, open this chapter by considering how record companies assess the progress of an act and give some indication of what 'success' and 'failure' means for the artists involved.

Assessing Success and Dropping the Failures

The most explicit assessment of an artist's progress is made when the 'option' on the recording contract comes up for renewal and the record company has to decide whether to retain an act, pay further cash advances and invest in recording new material. It is at this moment that the criteria of success and failure are most clearly articulated.

The formal decision is usually made jointly by the director of artist and repertoire, the head of business affairs and the head of the company. Each will have been briefed and presented with reports from different parts of the organisation, and the most obvious indicators which inform their decision are the sales of discs and tapes. However, sales figures are considered alongside any critical acclaim or notable media attention which has been received, any 'fan base' or following which has been established, and the judgments of various personnel as to how the act will continue to progress in the future. As an artist and repertoire director who had been in the industry for nearly twenty years explained:

> No one likes dropping a group after one record because that's an admission of failure early on. But if you feel that you've given it a really good shot and it hasn't happened at all, and you've got nowhere, then you have to question whether it's going to be any better next time around. What you are constantly encouraged by is seeing certain positive reactions in certain key areas. Not necessarily in sales, although obviously in the end that's what counts. But when you get a sense that people are warming to the group. Because it can take several years to break certain kinds of acts, so you've got to show a bit of patience.

When deciding whether to be patient with an act senior executives will compare the amount of capital which has been invested in an artist with the revenue which has been recouped from the sales of and rights to their recordings. There is no standard or average break even figure which can be applied across the board in these decisions because contracts are specifically structured to suit particular artists, genres of music and potential audiences. In the late 1980s staff in one well established British-owned corporation considered that they had 'broken' a new artist when they had sold 100,000 albums in the UK. This figure was used as an objective measure of an act's success as it would imply that the act had achieved radio play, gained press and television coverage and had produced hit singles. At the same time this would suggest that there was a 'real demand' for the act.

However, if an act have accepted a large advance on signing a contract the company's expectations will, out of necessity, be higher. For example, in 1990 record companies were often having to make an initial investment of at least £330,000 merely to release the first album from a 'hot' new rock band (based on an advance of £100,000, studio fees of £150,000 and promotional costs of at least £80,000). To recoup this type of investment one managing director estimated that the company would have to sell 600,000 albums. Whilst sales of 100,000 would be considered 'very respectable' for a first album and would certainly indicate that the act was 'breaking', the company would be acutely aware that, by the time they had released a second album their investment could have increased to £750,000, with perhaps only £60,000–£100,000 of this recouped. Needless to say, record companies are very secretive about the extent to which their artist are un-recouped. But if a company has a roster of developing acts these sums can soon accumulate. Accounts released for the UK division of BMG records in June 1990 showed that the company was £7.2 million in debt due to 'advances paid to artists in respect of future royalties together with recording costs recoverable from future royalties'. Inevitably there is pressure from senior executives within the corporation and share-holders to recoup these debts. The company may therefore promote the act quickly in order to get an immediate return, or regardless of an artist's progress they may be 'dropped' because the company simply cannot withstand a further escalation in the debt, and do not wish to gamble further on their future success.

In contrast there are artists signed to major companies who achieve more modest sales, perhaps 40,000 per album, but who have found a niche appealing to an identifiable audience. For such acts, the advances and budgets can be accommodated to this so that the company makes a steady, if unspectacular, profit. However, here again, the escalating cost of marketing, promotion and running large corporations puts pressure on staff either to widen the act's appeal – attempting this may lose their current audience and stand the risk of not finding another – or abandon them and release capital to go in quest of the next global star.

Apart from these straightforward financial decisions, the company assesses the quality of the music being produced and looks for signs that the act is going to continue producing new material. A company may be 'patient' with an act for a number of years if there are indications that it is continually 'building' and likely to break to a wide audience. But throughout this period debts will have been accumulating and pressure to recoup increasing. The dilemma involved in trying to predict if an artist is eventually going to deliver *the* hit album and balance this against the cost of retaining them under contract, was captured in the following remarks which were made by the managing director of an established label just before it was acquired by a conglomerate in 1989:

> I'm in a position now with an act that has been with the company five years and has dug a bit of a financial hole in the company. However, it's one of those horrible decisions. Commercially I should drop them. That's what my accountant says anyway. But I have this terrible feeling that it's their next album that's going to do it. Now, if I let them go and they go to Warner's or somewhere and have this hit that I think they're about to get, what a wally I look on the street. It's a hell of a fucking dilemma.

As this quote indicates, staff are also considering their own credibility in these situations. If an artist is released from a contract and goes elsewhere and then becomes successful, not only will the economic rewards for the years of patience accrue to a competitor, the reputation of senior staff – and of the label – for identifying and retaining talent will be damaged.

When attempting to attract new acts, established stars and highly respected personnel, the large companies can usually match each other's cash offers and any idiosyncratic contract clauses which may be requested. So a crucial factor becomes the way in which that company is perceived within the industry. This is most clearly visible in the established artists which are signed to a company, the way in which the company have handled the music and careers of these acts, and the ability of the company to establish new artists. In addition to providing access to recording facilities, marketing prowess and commercial clout, record companies are offering potential artists a reputation and tradition, a particular working environment and the prestigious association of being on the same label as other stars or critically acclaimed artists. Hence, there are occasions when acts – who on paper may not be commercially successful – may be retained or acquired by a label because they enhance a company's profile within the industry and contribute to their ability to attract both artists, staff and investment.

Hence, when assessing an artist's progress, record company staff are weighing up a number of factors, of which the 'bottom line' is the artist's potential to bring a return on investment. If the act has not achieved the anticipated level of success, but staff consider that it still has potential, then the contract may be renegotiated and budgets, advances and marketing costs accommodated to suit lower initial expectations. The artist must then decide whether to accept this or chance their luck elsewhere. However, this decision has its own dilemmas.

Leaving the Label

When an act leaves a record company at the end of an option period (rather than when their full contract expires) it is a signal to the industry, the media and other artists that this particular performer or band has 'failed' in some way. Although the artists are – in theory – free to find another record company, in practice it is often very difficult.

The first reason for this is economic. The artist has already demonstrated that they are a financial risk. Senior staff at other labels will be aware of the level of investment involved and the degree to which the act is un-recouped. If it has not worked once, who is brave enough to risk further investment and a second attempt?

The second reason is that a new company will probably have to reposition an act in the market place and re-articulate their identity to potential consumers. This may involve having to 're-invent' both the music and the image, and crucially it will entail changing the perception and expectations of key opinion formers and media personnel. As I discussed earlier, a large part of the marketing and promotion process involves generating a sense of anticipation prior to the release of material. If expectations are too high, or if there is a widely held belief that the act has 'not delivered the goods', then key personnel in the music press and at radio stations may be sceptical about any further claims made on behalf of the act. This is particularly so when a new group or solo performer has been paraded before the media as the latest big thing. As an A & R director who had been in the business for over fifteen years, explained:

> In my opinion, and I've seen it happen to us and other people a lot . . . when some company waves a flag and says; 'We've signed The Hair and Toenails above all competition' there's a big, big expectation of the first record release. And if it isn't a hit – and it's asking a lot for the first record of any group to be a hit – then their whole career is dismissed. I've seen it happen time and time again. You put one record out, the radio and the press say; 'OK, we'll give it one shot, we'll give it the benefit of the doubt once. They're going to hype it, the group's been hyped by the record company, we'll believe them for this one record and we'll go along with it.' But if it doesn't happen that one time around they say; 'well fuck them, look what happened to them, all that money and all that publicity.' And, I've seen groups' careers over. Finished after one single.

On a more personal level, the dropping of an act can be a severe psychological blow to the artists, their management and to record company personnel. A & R staff have compared the dropping of an act with 'being sacked' and 'divorce' and whilst it may often come as no surprise it can, in the words of one A & R manager, be 'a painful process for all involved.' Many bands split up as a result of the disagreements, recriminations, debts and soul searching that can occur at this point. Although Polydor A & R man Glenn Skinner once remarked that being dropped was 'the true test of an artist', the history of post-war pop suggests that few artists pick themselves up and return with stronger material after such an experience (Bullough, 1991; Tremlett, 1990).

Pop Paupers and the Rock Aristocracy

When Phil Collins composed his lament about homeless people in 1990 he was singing as a member of a privileged musical elite, viewing the poor on the streets of the world's cities from his position in 'paradise'. But he could have been singing about the musicians who did not make it to paradise, such as Danny Kirwan who left Fleetwood Mac to pursue a solo career and ended up homeless, living in St. Mungo's Hostel in Covent Garden (Tremlett, 1990).

Like Kirwan, the majority of artists who are signed by record companies enjoy a very brief period of success; they are famous for fifteen minutes, to repeat Andy Warhol's much used aphorism. Often their temporary fame is closer to three and a half minutes. A large number do not achieve any form of success whatsoever, either critical or commercial. When I was talking to one A & R manager in 1989 about artists who are signed and who do not achieve success he remarked that another label had just 'dumped about thirty acts. Most you've probably never heard of. Some I've never even heard of!'

Little has been written about what happens to recording artists when the spotlight has gone. Occasionally a 'where are they now?' article appears in the music press, but these usually feature acts who were once successful and whose members are often still playing music; perhaps as session musicians, engineers, jingle writers or community artists. A number of morbidly celebrated ex-stars have experienced alcoholism and drug addiction, or ended up in mental institutions. Quite a few continue to regurgitate their moment of glory by playing pubs, clubs and cabaret circuits around the world. Some who achieved minor success end up working in the music industry itself, often in A & R departments. But a vast majority simply return to their day jobs in offices, banks, factories, warehouses, equipment stores and record shops.

In contrast to failed musicians such as Danny Kirwan who end up homeless with nowhere to live, are stars who have so many homes around the world that it becomes difficult to ascertain just where they *do* live. As one lawyer quipped during attempts to ascertain Mick Jagger's residential status when Bianca was suing for divorce; 'Where is he a resident? On a jet plane circling the world?' (Tremlett, 1990, p 90).

When success does come – for the global superstars which all record companies hope they are developing – it brings phenomenal financial rewards, status, mobility and power. Behind the humanitarian concern, alms giving and philanthropy of recent years is an industry divided around massive inequalities of earnings. At one extreme are the struggling bands, perhaps with a publishing or management contract, on a small retainer or supported through welfare payments, paying out of their own pockets for the privilege of performing in a small club in Los Angeles or London. At the other extreme are stars such as Paul McCartney, whose two concerts at Giants Stadium in New Jersey on 9 and 11 of July 1990 grossed $3,415,165.

Successful pop stars earn very large sums of money and possess considerable wealth (see Appendix 1). Yet, as Alberoni has observed, stars are not usually 'perceived as a privileged class; their very existence is not regarded as a clear and brutal witness to social injustice' (Alberoni, 1972, p 87). Stars are not generally seen to use their privileged position to wield power. In the 1950s the sociologist C. Wright Mills (1953) described the 'professional celebrities of the mass media' as ephemeral figures without power of any stable sort, and in an article first published in 1962 Alberoni (1972) characterised stars as a 'powerless elite' who had no access to 'real' political power. Richard Dyer (1979), when writing about film stars, has criticised this type of approach and argued that stars *do* wield power, but it is of an ideological nature. It is exerted implicitly when individuals uphold and communicate specific values, and explicitly when celebrities support particular political issues and causes.

However, pop stars do not just wield ideological power. They can use their considerable material assets to directly influence the production and consumption of popular music; through their ownership of companies, labels, song catalogues and studio recording facilities; by directly or indirectly admitting or excluding lesser known performers from certain prestigious events and tours; and by using their commercial clout to influence record company acquisition policies. Much of this influence may well be ephemeral, but it can have longer lasting and far reaching consequences. The success of a particular type of rock star during an important phase in the development of the contemporary recording industry has decisively influenced the direction and strategies of record labels throughout the world.

The pop stars who came to prominence during the rock boom of the 1960s have now enjoyed twenty to thirty years of uninterrupted commercial success and constitute a 'rock aristocracy'. They have quite consciously engaged in activities to consolidate their position and overcome their temporality. Firstly, they have used their economic wealth to invest in land, property and businesses. At the beginning of the 1990s Ian Anderson, singer and composer with Jethro Tull, owned a 15,000 acre estate on the Isle of Skye, a salmon farm and cannery employing over sixty people, and businesses trading in rifles, guns and antique firearms. Roger Daltrey, singer with The Who, had interests in cattle, a trout farm and a sheet metal company. Carl Palmer, of ELP – whose affairs are run from Switzerland, like many other successful artists – possessed a banana farm in the Canary Islands. UB40 owned and were commercially developing the island of Toast off the coast of Jamaica. Paul McCartney had acquired homes and land throughout the world, many strategically positioned close to airstrips for the use of his private jet (Tremlett, 1990; Cosgrove, 1988). This is just a glimpse of the rock aristocracy, described by Tremlett as an 'inner circle of less than 100 people worldwide' constantly moving between multiple homes and protected by private security. These rock aristocrats have also become significant business investors, as George Tremlett noted, following his research into their earnings: 'One of the stranger features of their finances, as revealed by the files at Companies House, is that few borrow money from banks. Instead, they lend *to* banks' (1990, p 177).

The second way in which the rock aristocracy have consolidated their position is through the symbolic articulation of this wealth. The acquisition of estates, large country mansions, and the appropriation of 'nature' – farms, fisheries, livestock, landscapes – presupposes a culture with ancient roots (Bourdieu, 1986). Not only does the purchase and display of these items signify a taste for luxury and distance from necessity, it communicates the exact opposite of the ephemeral life of the rock'n'roll hellraiser. It expresses 'the art of living of the aristocrat . . . indifferent to the passage of time and rooted in things which last' (Bourdieu, 1986, p 281). The audience no longer identifies with the rock aristocrat through links between shared life styles. Residues are retained – the south London accent, the faded torn jeans – but the relationship between artist and audience for the few global superstars becomes more like that between the monarchy and the people. This connection is visibly articulated when stars such as Phil Collins and Elton John are reported to be privately performing for royalty, photographed publicly socialising with the monarchy, and when the rock aristocracy gather to perform and fawn to their royal hosts at the Prince's Trust charity concerts.

Without the British aristocracy, landed gentry and monarchy to emulate, artists in the USA express their distance from necessity and taste for freedom by gravitating to the sun and leisure of California and the stars' colony of Beverly Hills. Here stars such as Madonna can hold court to the world's media and impress them with her tasteful collection of European art, a practice which symbolically affirms 'the quality of the person . . . in the capacity to appropriate an object of quality' (Bourdieu, 1986, p 281). At the same time the star may be visually recorded appearing with the president, often in The White House, articulating their status through an association with one of the symbols of the nation (Alberoni, 1972).

Between the pop pauper who looks like a star but is still on the dole, and the ageing rock star who looks like he's on the dole but is actually a star, are the webs of relationships which hold the process of artist development together. Here – poised midway between fortune and failure – the dynamic of success is negotiated through the intermediaries of the recording industry.

Collaboration and Conflict: Personal Relations and Motivations

The work of recording industry personnel has often been characterised as a 'collaborative' or 'collective' activity coordinated according to various conventions, shared goals, consensual values or commercial formulas. This has been a prominent theme in the work of writers associated with the 'production of culture perspective' which has grown out of Howard Becker's accounts of the various conventions governing the 'worlds' within which art is produced, and Richard Peterson's attempts to identify the constraints and variables which facilitate or inhibit cultural production (Becker 1974, 1976; Peterson 1976, 1982, 1985; Ryan, 1985). Useful as this approach is – and the synthetic and organic ideologies of creativity I identified earlier might be viewed as aspects of particular 'art worlds' within the recording industry – an emphasis on collaboration and coordinating principles tends to deflect attention away from the considerable conflict within the music business. Record company staff experience different levels of enthusiasm for the artists they work with, and in the following pages I shall describe some of the ways in which staff are influenced by their personal contact with an artist, their taste in music and – perhaps most significantly – the potential of a band or performer to reflect favourably on their reputation, status and career prospects. These tensions frequently disrupt the collaborative processes involved.

Record company staff form opinions of artists based on personal contact, and a number of staff I interviewed spoke of feeling 'demotivated' if their advice – which they pride in being based on years of experience – is not listened to or is dismissed out of hand. They can then be reluctant to motivate others in the company who will have to be involved in the artist's career and promotion.

The most obvious situation which de-motivates staff is when an artist simply refuses to cooperate. This often happens in the area of promotion and publicity where artists may refuse to do interviews or undertake a range of personal appearances. Staff may then feel that they cannot do their job properly, and as record companies have a roster of artists, particular acts may find that they are being marketed and promoted with a distinct lack of enthusiasm, or are simply being neglected. When I visited the office of one record label in New York they were engaged in promoting a 1960s influenced British rock band. The group's lead singer was refusing to do any interviews and the staff in the record company, already having difficulty placing the act's recordings and videos in the television and radio media, were noticeably irritated and complaining to each other about what they perceived as this performer's lack of cooperation.

Not only does an artist's refusal to do interviews annoy record industry personnel, but it can damage their reputation with journalists. As a result the publicist may tacitly let writers know that the lack of cooperation is coming from the artist and not the company. One head of press, when discussing this point, explained:

You travel thousands of miles and the artist turns round and says; 'Yeh, about the interview, I've decided I don't want to do it.' It's only happened to me once and it was enough miles for it to be a pain. You see the threat of that's always there. But, what can you do? I can't order them to do it . . . You are the person the journalist or features editor comes to and says; 'We really want to have an interview with so-and-so because so-and-so is a good journalist and we've got a new angle.' And you're thinking 'Yeh, it makes sense'. It fits in with some overall plan in your mind about a feature here and a feature there and it's on an upward curve. And the artist might say; 'I don't want to do it.' So then you have to go back to the paper and say; 'No, they can't do it'. You don't tell the journalist why they can't do it, but they can read between the lines. And then it affects your relationship with the paper.

When an artist does give an interview, what they say publicly can also affect their relationship with the record company staff. One marketing director, whilst acknowledging that what an artist says to a journalist and what gets reported in print is often a 'pose' and 'part of the game' admitted that:

> there are times when people in record companies find it extremely de-motivating to the point of getting very angry. I mean, I've heard artists slag this record company off – so-called artists maybe – and go into print and say very unpleasant things about us and how we did this and how we did that and how we did the other. On the other hand what they don't mention is; had we not done that they wouldn't have made that million pounds.

Hence, the way in which artists conduct themselves when dealing with company personnel, how they respond to the suggestions of staff, and what they say publicly, can affect their progress in subtle but decisive ways. The manager of a highly successful band when talking about how he sought to encourage staff in record companies to work for his artists remarked that, obvious as it might sound, the most effective policy was one of 'just being nice to people'. Emphasising this point he added: 'There are artists who are popular in record companies and artists who are unpopular. I've seen artists absolutely ruin themselves by being obnoxious to staff.'

Whilst staff may get demotivated by artists not cooperating, the musicians themselves may feel quite justified in refusing to participate in certain promotional activities. A number of publicity and marketing staff spoke with weary resignation about some of the questions artists are asked during interviews and the things they are expected to do when appearing on children's television, family entertainment programmes and quiz shows which are used to sell recordings in many countries. Although staff attempt to clarify what is expected prior to any interview or media appearance, there is always an element of uncertainty about what a specific activity might involve. One managing director who had previously coordinated international promotion for the labels of a European-based conglomerate spoke of some of the television work artists are expected to do across continental Europe in the following terms:

> You are sending off your artists into the jaws of potential ghastliness. You would be asking people to do things which seem bizarre over here, but which are perfectly acceptable over there . . . All sorts of dreadful misunderstandings occur. And they all stomp around saying; 'Are you kidding, I'm not going on that bloody awful TV show, I'm a real artist.' And you go; 'Yeh, I know you're a real artist, but the problem is that this is all there is. So if you want to sell records here you have to go on this TV show.' . . . The artist can feel genuinely compromised unless

you have been absolutely clear about it in advance, preferably in writing. Because then nobody can dispute that you haven't told them what to expect. Otherwise they'll go; 'You didn't tell me it was this, I'm leaving. I'm off. I'm never going to do this again'. And it can have terrible implications.

One act, whom this executive had worked with, had stormed off the set during the recording of a television show in Italy and refused to do any promotion in the country for three years. This offended the staff in the Italian division of the corporation and subsequently affected their promotion in that territory. Elsewhere, a member of artist development mentioned two members of one British band who sat ready to be interviewed at a Los Angeles radio station and on being asked the first question – what had they eaten for breakfast – promptly stood up and walked out.

Artists can also have quite genuine reasons for rejecting the advice of artist and repertoire staff. From the perspective of artists and their management the work of A & R can look quite different to that of a catalyst offering encouragement, providing constructive criticism and contributing creative ideas. A & R staff seem to be the most despised music industry workers amongst artists and their managers and are continually criticised – indeed they have acquired something of a reputation – for interfering and confusing things rather than contributing to and coordinating the production of material. The following remark, made by the director of a management company is typical:

> So many times I've been in a recording studio with an act and the A & R person, probably a junior one from some great conglomerate wanders in, listens for 30 seconds and says [adopts dopey voice]: 'The drums aren't loud enough in the mix, man'. It happened with one of my artists recently. We've actually had to have an A & R person taken off the case because I'm not prepared for an artist of mine to be badgered by some twatt who probably can't get the top off his milk bottles every morning.

In many respects A & R staff have a job to do and have to justify their own existence at the company, particularly if they are inexperienced and have no reputation to fall back on. This can result in relatively inexperienced staff feeling obliged to have an input, or make some kind of musical contribution which is not suitable. I was told one, possibly apocryphal, anecdote about an A & R person who kept dropping into a recording studio and making numerous irritating and unhelpful suggestions about how to improve a particular mix. Everyone in the studio became so irritated that they prepared for his next visit. A number of unused channels on the mixing desk were labelled 'vocal group', 'drum group' and 'fx send'. When the A & R person next came and suggested modifications to the vocals, he was sat down at the desk and told to try and adjust it himself. This he did, moving the bogus faders, exclaiming 'yeh, yeh, that's it!'

Taste in Music and the Taste for Success

A further factor which affects the relationship between artist and record company is whether staff actually like the music being produced. Artist and repertoire staff are initially employed because of their enthusiasm and knowledge of music and for their ability to identify talent and trends. When balancing the staff in their departments A & R directors sometimes seek staff with broad tastes, but more frequently tend to match the artist to the preferences of an A & R person. Marketing, press and promotion staff, although more concerned with visual presentation and not so close to the process of musical production in the studio, are also influenced by their taste in music and tend to gravitate to companies which suit their own preferred style of working.

Record companies which appear to be similar due to their size can have qualitatively different working environments and organisational cultures. To a visitor these can appear subtle and concealed, but can be detected in the physical arrangement of the buildings, in the reception area, in the internal office environment and in the way that staff dress, act and what they say. One member of the marketing department in a large formal corporation recalled how she had previously worked in a more 'laid back' environment at one of the labels of another conglomerate, but found the culture and music not to her taste, explaining that:

> It was much more, well, druggy, but just much more hip, trendy, cool speak, and music that I just couldn't get my neck around. At the end of the day if you love music you've got to be working with music that you love, not music that you couldn't give two fucks about . . . I'm an old fashioned girl. I much prefer rock music and AOR (album oriented rock).

Although staff in some companies seek to evade this issue by espousing a philosophy of 'professionalism', arguing that this enables them to 'work any product', there is no doubt that the way staff respond to the music being produced affects the way they work for an artist. It is easy enough to 'do a professional job' on a major artist such as Phil Collins where there is already a large demand for the artist and where a certain prestige is involved in being associated with him. It is quite another thing to do a professional job on a new artist where enthusiasm has to be generated within the company and amongst various media. One head of press provided an illustration of this when she described a situation which had arisen when an A & R person left the company and there was little enthusiasm amongst existing staff for an act which was still under contract:

> We had an act recently that none of us could get into. None of us liked the music. None of us could see where it was going. None of us could bring pressure to bear . . . because we didn't have faith in the act in the company generally. . . . It was an act signed by A & R as a developing act and that person left and it was sort of hanging around, and so they decided to try and carry on and develop it. And I couldn't understand it. I said; 'I'm sorry, it just does nothing for me, and that's the end of it'. So, the manager came in, rather heavy, and said 'the press office aren't giving me any support' and complained about me. Fine. I wasn't the only one who had no faith in it. And, I said; 'OK, we'd better put it out then. I resent it, but if it's going to help.' So we put it out, and I was really bitter about it. The act is dropped now.

This executive's attitude towards the act was indicative of feeling within the company generally. Not surprisingly when the material was released it disappeared without a trace.

However, there are more than just issues of taste in music involved here. An A & R person had left the company to further his career and this directly resulted in political changes and the redistribution of artistic rosters. From the artist's perspective such a movement of staff can seriously affect their progress. In the United States Lucinda Williams was signed to RCA by Bob Buziak who linked her with record producer Peter Moore because he was sympathetic to her idiosyncratic blend of country, folk and blues. However, Buziak left RCA and other staff had to be found to manage his acts. Lucinda was allocated a young executive who suggested that she worked with a 'hit producer', and exhibited a profound lack of knowledge and misunderstanding of the genre she was working in, seeking to transform her into a straighforward Top 40 artist. As Williams herself explained; 'When I first went to RCA they weren't acting like the usual major label because Buziak was there. When he left, what was expected of me as an artist changed . . . It's not that unusual. It happens a lot' (Cronin & Flanagan, 1991, p 57).

Managers, publishers and production companies who are presenting artists to record companies are continually monitoring the movements and relations between staff, and keeping track of how the personal preferences and prejudices of various senior record company executives and A & R personnel change over time. One manager made a distinction between the younger members of staff for whom musical taste and 'hipness' was an important motivation, and the older, more established personnel who may have mortgages and family responsibilities and who have developed a 'taste for success'. These executives are more concerned about maintaining their reputation and career, rather than just working with music they enjoy. However, their younger colleagues cannot be hip for too long before they themselves are going to have to establish a reputation for being successful.

Artist and repertoire staff establish their reputations through the artists they 'sign.' The critical and commercial success of an artist reflects favourably on the judgment of a particular A & R person. In a similar way, the reputations of staff throughout the recording industry are gained through the acts that they have been associated with, whether they were involved in a successful studio recording, marketing exercise or promotional campaign which resulted in front pages, rave reviews and influential features. In the case of managers, their association with an artist and their location as the person able to grant access to that artist can put them in a position to directly influence record company acquisitions and releases.

Maintaining Relationships and the Politics of Releasing Crap

As I mentioned earlier the releasing of recordings by record companies has often been characterised as merely throwing mud against a wall. Uncertain of what is going to be successful, record companies release as much material as possible, covering a range of musical genres, in the hope that some of this will stick. I hope I have shown so far in this book that there is nothing aimless about the way record companies go about acquiring acts, composing sounds and images and communicating these to various audiences. Artists are focused and sharpened in quite calculated ways and then aimed at some very specific targets. Many people also believe strongly in what they are doing and the recordings being released. A range of artists, record industry personnel, media figures and fans are often very disappointed and surprised when a particular recording is not successful.

However, this does not apply in every case. There are occasions when it is quite obvious to staff that a particular artist or recording is not going to be successful. Records are scheduled and issued, but staff are not even throwing them at the wall, let alone worrying about whether they will stick or not. This point was raised by a product manager when discussing how she tried to coordinate different departments and attempted to encourage staff to work for an act even if they had reservations:

> At the end of the day nobody is going to say; 'This is absolute crap', unless the vibe is from everyone; 'God, this is crap'. Basically we know when it's a good track, and we know when it's a difficult track. But if it's absolute crap, well, then A & R will know about it anyway. And sometimes, politically, you're just obliged to get on with it . . . Maybe the signing is; 'If you do this you might get another band'. I mean, deals are always there. And every major record company is dying to get their teeth into some major artist. A manager might have that relationship, or that artist . . . Believe you me, there is some crap we put out, but we are obliged to do it.

A lot of records are released in the hope and belief that they will succeed. However, there are occasions when staff know that a particular recording is not going to succeed, but are obliged to go through the motions. This is done to maintain a relationship with an artist or their manager, and was variously described as a 'political signing', 'grace and favour deal', 'courtesy signing' or 'public relations exercise'. If a manager represents a successful act, then that manager can often use the incentive of future access to that act to persuade companies to sign other artists. Alternatively, major artists themselves may be able to get deals for their friends, with senior record company staff issuing contracts merely to keep an artist happy and maintain a working relationship, rather than for any creative or commercial reasons. A marketing director at one of the labels of a conglomerate group remarked that it was often easier to put out a record, rather than fight with a manager who was important to the company.

However, managers are reluctant to employ this approach, and tend to use the power and influence which representing a successful act brings as a last resort, only orchestrating a political signing if nobody is genuinely interested in an act. This caution is based on the knowledge that staff within companies can get very resentful of these type of deals being introduced above their heads. Although senior executives try not to let details of a political signing known throughout the company, the information soon circulates, and staff respond to this. As Rudi Gassner, president of BMG Music International once remarked when discussing the acquisition of artists; 'You can't impose the artist on your people, because in the end they'll work against it, just to prove that they were right'.

In addition to releasing records as a 'courtesy' to a manager, artist or lawyer, recordings can be released to maintain relationships with staff in other geographical territories. International promotion and marketing staff in Britain are continually attempting to persuade sister companies, licensees and labels to release material in other territories and then persuade staff to work for these artists. Representatives of these companies are in turn trying to negotiate the release of their own artists' products in Britain. It is frequently obvious to staff at UK record labels that to release certain recordings from other territories at a particular moment is a complete waste of time. However, it is often tactically advantageous to release recordings and thus maintain reciprocal relations with staff in other countries, rather than to block their release. Of course staff in different regions may be well aware that little effort is being expended on their artists and may respond in a similar way. As Paul Rutten (1991) has observed when discussing how Dutch record companies license recordings around the world: a press release may state that a record has been released in ten countries, but in practice nothing may be happening in any of these territories.

So far I have been focusing on the way in which staff are motivated to work with artists, and how conflict arises due to the politics of personal relationships and social psychological factors, which undoubtedly lead to struggles and compromises in a range of collaborative work. I now want to turn to a wider, more structured web of tensions which arise between the different occupational groups I have been describing in this book.

Another One Bites the Dust: Reputations and Accusations

Uncertainty permeates the entire process of producing pop music, particularly during the early period for a newly-signed act when material has yet to be released. Everyone involved is aware that the record industry produces more failures than successes and that approximately one in eight of the acts signed by a record company will recoup their investment and start earning money for both themselves and the company. Artistic careers are dependent upon changing fashions, the contingencies of commercial markets and the responses of audiences. In turn the careers of record industry personnel are related to the success of the acts they are associated with, rather than just their experience or formal qualifications. As a result, positions are permanently insecure and staff are continually driven to assert the significance and legitimacy of what they are doing. This insecurity then feeds into a form of inter-departmental rivalry which can be found in many organisations.

Studies of businesses have highlighted the way in which organisations experience 'classification struggles' between different occupational groupings, such as production and publicity or engineering and marketing. Each division attempts to advance its occupational interests by imposing a scale of values which sets at the top of the hierarchy the activities for which it feels itself equipped. These struggles then become 'inseparable from conflicts of value which involve the participant's whole world views and arts of living' (Bourdieu, 1986, pp 309–10).

This is most noticeable in the recording industry in the broad division of staff into marketing and A & R. These are the 'two disciplines' around which the process of artist development is organised, and this division tends to result in the work of staff being split into two different media; sound and vision. As pop is composed and communicated, the music and images are closely related and usually develop together. However, the division of labour within the music industry has resulted in them being separated into two specialisms, with staff being drawn from different backgrounds which amplifies this separation and inflects it with different orientations and priorities.

This can result in a series of confrontations. Firstly, artist and repertoire staff assert that they lead the industry, and that any ultimate success is down to the artists they have 'discovered' and recorded. As I noted earlier, many A & R staff attempt to maintain a distance from the rest of the company in an attempt to protect and legitimate their position, and in order to maintain their credibility with contracted acts, potential new signings and music critics.

However, as promotional activities have become more complex, assumed greater importance and required higher levels of investment, marketing staff have become more directly involved with artists at an earlier stage, and increasingly emphasised the significance of their contribution. Many companies, responding to an increasing emphasis on marketing in the wider global economy, have attempted to make the informal dialogue between marketing and artist and repertoire more explicit by providing marketing with a formal veto on the artists who are signed.

A & R staff tend to be resistant to this challenge to their formal autonomy, and perceive these changes as a threat to their previously privileged role in proposing the artists to be acquired. At the same time A & R staff acknowledge the dilemmas they face and must negotiate in working with marketing. It is, after all, often the A & R person who must first communicate the significance of an act to the rest of the company and persuade others to work with and on behalf of that act. These dilemmas were acknowledged in the following remarks made by an artist and repertoire director at one of the labels of a major recording group. Talking about attempts to bring marketing and A & R closer together he asserted:

> It's very dangerous. Because everybody would like to be an A & R person. I try not to listen to anybody else . . . you have to be strong enough as an A & R person to thump your hand on the desk and say; 'This is the record, this is what we're going with whether you like it or not'. If you've got your marketing department telling you that your records are crap then you might as well resign. Now, whether they are right or not, who knows? Maybe the marketing department are deaf . . . If we've spent £150,000 making an album and then the marketing department turn around and say: 'We think this is a bunch of shit and we're not going to spend any money on it', well, you're in a terrible situation if you've got to that point and they don't love it. It happens, all the time.

This A & R director stressed his importance by responding that everybody would like to do his job. He asserted his autonomy not to listen to others and will to enforce his own judgment, but at the same time he tempered this with reservations and uncertainty that 'maybe marketing are right'. Marketing staff speak about this situation with a similar combination of assertiveness and uncertainty. One product manager in the marketing department of a major corporation described how she thought A & R and marketing should have the same view of an act, explaining:

> It wouldn't work if everybody was thinking that they should look a different way, be marketed in a different way, or the video should be done in a different way.

You'd end up nowhere . . . Sometimes we get bands who we think should not have been signed. But, there's nothing we can do about it because they've signed a contract, so we've got to deal with it . . . what's the point of them being all arty farty and signing up a band that there's no market for. How can you then go and spend thousands of pounds on campaigns and videos . . . if we get a bit of a duff album it would be great if we could go straight to A & R and say 'forget it, there's no way we're going to be able to market this. You've got to re-record it' . . . But then, who are we? We're a group of about ten people speaking for what we think they want out there, and we get it wrong.

This division between A & R and marketing can be widened to include the promotion division, who stress their significance in gaining radio and television exposure, and the publicity department (or freelance promotional outfit) who emphasise their importance in the early profile building and exposure of a new act. When I spoke to one press officer she held up a cassette tape and emphasized her contribution by declaring; 'This band do not exist until I start doing my job.' In a similar way one head of promotion at the office of a major corporation identified her department as the most important, and described her frustrations in a similar way to the product manager quoted above:

> We tend to lead as a department, because if there's no air play you rarely get a hit. If a bite starts happening and we say; 'Listen, Radio 1 are going to start playing this record', then everybody else comes round and starts putting in the rest of the jigsaw. But, if we come out and say; 'That's a dead duck, this is not going to happen', other departments might try, but the majority of it is how we lead . . . . Every time an A & R man releases a record he believes it's a hit. Now, if I challenged the A & R man and said; 'That's a piece of shit', he might come down. But it's always the same: 'When it left me it was a hit. And if it's not a hit it's nothing to do with me.' If it's a hit it's because it's a great record, nothing to do with what we've done in between.

In addition to working with artists, all divisions of the company are attempting to represent themselves as an indispensable component of the recording industry. The day-to-day work of dealing predominantly with one specific medium, whether the music, the image in the video, the radio media, or the press, tends to result in different staff assessing the potential of artists in different ways and developing their own agendas and goals rather than working towards a shared overall vision.

These divisions become most pronounced when there has been an unsuccessful act or recording. As the music business produces more failures than successes, this is frequent. Disputes continually occur with each side blaming the others for a failed recording or artist. Either artist and repertoire did not produce the music properly, or marketing put together the wrong type of image and campaign, publicity staff did not present the act properly to the press and journalists, or promotion failed to plug the act or record in the correct way through radio and television. The 'collaborative' process of artist development permanently teeters on this type of conflict.

Artists and the Struggle for Autonomy

Caught in the middle of this are the artists. It is newly-signed performers who are more subject to the collaborative processes of artist development than an act which has attained a degree of success. When a band or solo artist begins achieving commercial success they tend to use their proven commercial appeal to renegotiate the terms of their contractual relationship with the company. The artist becomes less financially dependent on the record company, and the company becomes more reliant on the income and prestige derived from their association with the successful artist. The company's control is limited by the fact that at some future point the artist may be contractually free and have the choice to stay or go elsewhere and earn a vast amount of money for a competitor. Not only is this a financial loss, but it is bad for a company's reputation to be seen 'losing' a successful artist. So, relations with successful acts have to be maintained.

The dynamic of commercial success is characterised by the struggle of artists for ever more autonomy. Acts attempt to get in a position where they can avoid the input of record company staff and the entire corporate jigsaw of artist development. This is not – as is sometimes implied – simply because artists want to be free of 'commercial' considerations to concentrate on their 'art'; Artists have already proved that they are commercial by reaching this position in the first place. Artists are primarily seeking the autonomy to direct the composition of their sounds and images without the interventions, divisions, compromises and conflicts which characterise the production of pop. Performers therefore attempt to gain greater control over their musical and visual material by licensing completed recordings, videos, photography and artwork to the record company and specifying precisely how the company should market and promote this.

In contrast, and far more frequent, is the dynamic of commercial failure. This is the complete opposite. The artist and their management, and the various record company divisions, all hold meetings, conduct inquests, apportion blame and undertake further experimentations and modifications. Meanwhile, the debts have been rising and the necessity of recouping the capital invested in an act increases the pressure on all involved.

The production of contemporary pop music emerges out of a continual tension between the collaborative practices I have described in earlier chapters, and the struggles of various staff to establish and maintain their reputations and assert the importance and legitimacy of their activities. Ultimately it is characterised by an attempt on the part of the artist to try and avoid the input of record company personnel completely and the entire process of artist development. Beyond the rhetoric of creative control, is the desire of artists to avoid the conflict, compromises and chaos which continually threaten to set the different divisions of record companies against each other and send the entire process of artist development into auto-destruct.

CONCLUSION

Commerce, Chaos and Cultural Change

This book began with an outline of the world markets for popular music, the corporate strategies and global dreams of the major transnational entertainment companies, and having passed through the jigsaw of artist development it has ended up with staff in different occupational groups living out a quite different logic at a local level in Britain; surveying the fragments of broken dreams and blaming each other for failed recordings. The new artist who has recently signed a recording contract confronts these different worlds simultaneously: an abstract, omnipotent corporation encircling the planet without appearing to stop at any identifiable source – ordering the industry according to market share statistics, sales figures, balances, budgets, unrecouped advances and returns on investment. And a day-to-day world of very specific human relationships between a relatively small number of people involved in composing and communicating the sounds and images of popular music. Here the grandiloquent logic of media synergy, and the bold rhetoric of a united global village is experienced as confusion, conflict and what one vice president of product development at the headquarters of a major entertainment group described as 'a mind boggling lack of coordination and communication'.

A similar point was implied in one of the first interviews I conducted for this book in the Spring of 1989. The director of a management company who had himself been to university in the 1960s but subsequently 'rejected all that stuff' and 'dropped out' – simultaneously dropping in to the recording industry – was intrigued that I should be carrying out a serious study of the production of pop music; 'I don't know how you're going to do it' he remarked, 'it will be like applying order to chaos'. During my research a number of staff in the recording industry referred to a phenomenological experience of chaos and disorder when trying to explain the routine and irregular activities and myriad personal relationships which surrounded them and informed their daily work. It is tempting, in the light of such comments, and when trying to sum up the complex practices I have been discussing, to search for equally complicated or chaotic causes. But, much of what I have been describing in this book arises as an active response – on the part of individuals and specific occupational groups – to the imperative of commercial success. This is the dominant criterion by which recordings, and also artists and music business personnel are ultimately judged. And, it is in response to this pressure that the strategies, tactics, dilemmas and dramas that I have been describing arise.

A number of writers have pursued this line of reasoning, and the production of popular music has often been described by reference to a conflict between commerce and creativity or art and capitalism (Cohen, 1991; Stratton 1982a, 1982b). There is of course, an important tension here, but there has been a tendency to treat the 'commercial' in popular music as if its meaning and influence was self-evident; occasionally coupled with a desire to identify, and extol the virtues of 'non-commercial' varieties of music (Wallis & Malm, 1984). Apart from the fact that most of the music which is audible at any one time is to a greater or lesser extent 'commercial', this approach tends to overlook the temporal dimension which cuts through the production of commercial music.

Staff in the recording industry are continually oriented to the future, to finding 'the next big thing', to producing tomorrow's sounds, to bringing into existence what is 'not yet' (Bloch, 1988). The personal reputation of recording industry personnel and the success of their companies, is dependent upon producing what is going to be commercially successful in three months, six months or even two years' time. The length of time between an artist signing a recording contract and the subsequent recordings being released and marketed is usually about nine months, but sometimes this period can be much longer. The pressure to come up with what is going to be financially successful in the future means that staff must take risks and invest personal belief and hope in what they are doing. They must adopt an anticipatory approach to the acts they sign and develop, rather than just respond to market indicators or reproduce existing styles.

In acquiring artists, staff in the recording industry are faced with the dilemma that what is commercially successful is always known in retrospect. It can never be adequately predicted. This is particularly acute during the period of artist development for new acts. Unlike the manufacturers of products like baked beans or toothpaste where a tried and tested product can be sold over and over again, the music industry is continually introducing new artists and simultaneously having to identify and construct an audience for their recordings. Despite constant attempts to establish a sense of brand loyalty to an artist, or to develop or imitate hit formulas, despite all of the marketing and promotional techniques and coping strategies I have described, the recording industry constantly produces more failures than successes. As Simon Frith (1983) has noted, it is precisely because record companies *cannot* control this process that they attempt to develop these strategies – as part of an attempt to order and regulate the production and consumption of popular music. Ultimately, the recording industry cannot 'control' or 'determine' what is going to be commercially successful. All entertainment corporations can do is struggle to monopolise access to recording facilities, promotional outlets, manufacturing arrangements and distribution systems, and be in a position to appropriate the profits.

In a similar way the meaning of 'creativity' – the practices involved in producing pop music and the values by which these activities and the resulting music is judged – are continually defined in retrospect; after its composition. And these are re-evaluated as different groups and individuals employ changing aesthetics and as new genres emerge which challenge or lead to a re-assessment of existing judgments – such as the different conceptions of what is good, innovative, authentic, true in rap, rock, soul, disco, world beat etc. If the recording industry is incapable of controlling what is going to be commercially successful, it certainly cannot, in any straightforward way, define what is creative. This does not, however, mean that the drive for commercial success does not come into conflict with creative activity. The most destructive consequence of the imperative of economic success is not that 'commerce' is simply bad for 'art' (judged from some detached, ascetic, purist position removed from the corporeal context in which the sounds and visions of pop communicate). It is the practical human cost involved. Commercial success is the dominant criterion by which artists, and personnel throughout the recording industry are assessed. As a result of this, a commercial failure – and the attendant debts, droppings and occupational divorces – can wreak havoc with the personal careers and lives of musicians, performers and record company personnel. At the same time, the high failure rates provide continual spaces for new artists and staff to participate in the composition and communication of popular music.

If the vagueness and changing nature of commercial criteria provides scope for artists and recording industry personnel to invest all kinds of idiosyncratic meanings, motives, desires and activities in what they are composing, the recordings have been commercially successful because audiences have actively responded to them. Enough research has been done to show that the reception and consumption of cultural items is not a passive process but is part of the way in which these sounds and images are given meaning. The drive for economic success, and the need to construct markets, immediately implicates the audience in the composition and communication of popular music. Artists are commercially successful because audiences have made them so, and as the act of consumption (like the act of production) involves a range of ethical, aesthetic and emotional investments (rather than a rational utilitarian choice), there is always something more than just the market exchange value involved in the relationship between the producers and consumers of commercial pop music.

The tension between commerce and creativity in the recording industry is not an abstract, unchanging conflict but is continually being negotiated and articulated in the working practices I have described in this book. The sounds, images and meanings of music and the criteria by which that music is judged are created together. The personnel involved in producing popular music – the artist, the A & R person, the studio producer, the press officer, the consumer – are simultaneously contributing to the aesthetic meanings employed to appreciate that music, and in the process defining what *is* commercial, and ultimately providing the contours of what 'popular music' means at any one time. The imperative of commercial success requires a market, but this market is not given, it is not simply 'out there', it has to be made. It is made in the process of artist development.

In suggesting that the sounds, visions and words of pop music are decisively defined and produced in the process of artist development I have described the music industry as a web of working practices, dialogues and articulated relationships, and identified a number (but by no means all) of 'habits of action' (Rorty, 1991) or 'orienting practices' (Bourdieu, 1986) which different staff employ as they negotiate these relationships. Within this context the cultural intermediaries I have referred to in previous chapters are involved in acts of making, of re-creating, of re-inventing, rather than a moment of discovery or a mechanical manufacturing operation performed on a cultural assembly line. The music industry is not organised around mechanical inputs and outputs nor the linear transmission of products along a straight line from producer to consumer. The process is far less stable, riddled with fluctuations and bifurcations. The pieces of the jigsaw of artist development frequently do not come together, the puzzle is often (usually) never solved because it is always being changed as it is being put together.

My approach throughout this book has been deliberately proposed in con-tradistinction to 'top-down' theorising which views changes in popular music (or the lack of changes in popular music) to be the result of the stultifying administrative regimes of a capitalist cultural industry, which merely provides endless repetition (Adorno, 1991; Attali, 1985); or which views the degree of diversity and 'innovative' trends in popular music arising as a reflexive response to a series of business cycles generated by the relative number of companies competing in the market at any one time (Peterson and Berger, 1975; Burnett, 1991). It has also been presented in contrast to the view which sees changes in popular music bubbling up from below as a result of the spontaneous eruption of creative activity or dramatic new proposals from inspired artists, entre-preneurs or subcultures (Chambers, 1985; Savage, 1991) – an argument which twists back to the top as these artists and subcultures are ultimately co-opted, absorbed and anaesthetised for a mass audience by the corporate entertainment business (Chapple & Garofalo, 1977; Harker, 1980). Although I prefer the latter explanations, if only because they are proposed by writers who usually have a passion for and greater understanding of pop music, (whereas the former seems to be a theory propounded by those who occasionally detest or are simply indifferent to it); I don't agree with either. Whilst not wishing to provide yet another 'model' which can be used as one more template to be held up to tie down popular culture, I think that greater attention needs to be paid to the day-to-day work of people in the industry itself, because, as I mentioned in my introduction – and as I have highlighted throughout this book – it is here where tensions between artists, consumers and corporations are mediated and find expression in a range of working practices, ideological divisions and conflicts. And, it is these which decisively shape the sounds and visions of contemporary pop music.

The critical question which needs to be addressed to the most successful pop music and recording artists of the past forty years is not about the way in which their purity, integrity and creativity has been co-opted and manipulated by the determinations of cynical corporate strategists (or their genius has flowered in spite of this); nor about the way in which they have spon-taneously emerged from, or been organically appropriated and defined by subcultures and audiences. It concerns the way in which artists have used the multi-media of popular culture at their disposal to constitute themselves as 'total star texts' (Dyer, 1991). The major artists in the history of pop – Elvis, The Beatles, Bob Dylan, The Rolling Stones, Abba, Stevie Wonder, David Bowie, Michael Jackson, Elton John, Prince, Queen and Madonna – have all composed themselves in this way, collaborating with a range of music business intermediaries and media personnel in the process. In doing this, these stars have been actively negotiating the tensions which continually arise between the global and abstract strategies of the corporations; the way in which these are turned into concrete daily policies and practices within the webs of these corporations; and the specific and local experiences which inform the reactions of consumers and audiences. I have tried to provide an indication of, and way into these tensions in this book.

Specifically, I have described how a particular faction of college-educated, white males from the rock generation of the late 1960s and 1970s have decisively influenced working practices in Britain, elevating a naturalistic aesthetic and accommodating their taste preferences, values and ideological dispositions to the business requirements of the recording industry. Alongside this are the multiple dimensions of the modern marketing process which encourages, and requires, artists to present themselves simultaneously in various media. This obviously limits the opportunities for composers and musicians who are not all round media manipulators and is done with the aim of maximising sales. But as marketing staff create a point of identification between artists and audiences, various possibilities arise for the communication and sharing of experiences which involve more than a simple commercial transaction between producers and consumers. I have also described how promotional strategies and tactics which have developed in response to the connections between the radio networks and record companies have influenced the way in which music is recorded and artists presented; setting up a number of divisions and resulting in rigid boundaries between black, brown and white music – distinctions which are continually challenged as artists and audiences refuse these categories. Throughout this book I have drawn attention to some of the ways in which women have been marginalised within the music business, and at the same time have actively established a presence in publicity departments (despite the widespread employment of 'feminine' skills by a range of male staff throughout the industry).

All of these working practices have been actively made. They do not simply or naturally fit or 'reflect' the business structures and commercial imperatives of the industry. Within the formal organisational systems and occupational categories, is the non-linear cultural world of the music industry which has been made and remade over the last thirty years. Corporate strategists are continually trying to order, regulate and perhaps co-opt what is produced; and artists and audiences are constantly offering fresh proposals; but it is within and across these tensions that the sounds and images of popular music are composed and communicated. By advocating alternatives, acquiring new habits and critically challenging existing practices, the webs I have described can be re-woven to create unfamiliar noises, novel identities, different working practices and new relations of producing pop.

APPENDIX 1

A Note About Recording Industry Statistics

During the course of writing this book I spent hours trying to obtain, and then grappling with various music industry statistics. I was intending to use some of these to illustrate particular points I was trying to make about the market shares and revenues of the large corporations, the consumption of music in different territories and the wealth and earnings of artists. In the end I have used statistics very sparingly and I have deliberately not littered the text with them. There are two main reasons for this: firstly most of the figures are usually at least a year old by the time they become available, and they will be even further out of date by the time this book is published. But, secondly, there are a number of problems involved in using and interpreting them, and here I simply want to highlight some of the difficulties involved and indicate the available sources for those who want to go and do some digging around.

Market Shares and Sales of Major Companies

The figures I cited in Chapter 1 are based on estimates which were given to me verbally in November 1990 by a member of staff at a trade magazine who divided the company shares at the time as follows: Warner Music 18 per cent, Polygram 18 per cent, Sony 17 per cent, EMI 11 per cent, MCA 8 per cent, BMG 6 per cent and Virgin 4–6 per cent. Very similar 'guesstimates' were made by various other people I spoke to, and comparable figures were sporadically reported for individual companies in the national and trade press. The acquisition of Virgin by Thorn-EMI immediately took their market share to about 18 per cent. I was unable to confirm officially, or further substantiate these figures despite hours of library visits, written requests and telephone calls to record companies, trade journals and business organisations. Although the major record companies place considerable importance on their market share, they are very secretive about revealing information. An accountant I spoke to at one of the transnationals told me that, although they were available 'somewhere', reliable figures could probably only be obtained after 'high level corporate detective work'.

These type of issues have also been highlighted by George Tremlett (1990) who discussed the problems of obtaining 'genuine statistics' in the music industry, and also quoted a figure of 70 per cent for the world share of retail sales of the top five companies for 1989, and stated that the 'majority of world sales' in 1988 were accounted for by eight companies. Larry Shore (1983), in an unpublished Ph.D thesis estimated that the majors accounted for about 70 per cent of the singles and 75 per cent of the albums distributed in the world during the late 1970s. Dave Laing (1986) puts the figures slightly lower, but suggests that five companies have regularly accounted for about two-thirds of the sales of musical products worldwide in recent years. Laing has also drawn attention to the problems involved in reading recording industry statistics, and noted the fluctuations and anomalies which occur depending on whether the calculation is based on retail sales figures or company turnover.

The best source of statistics for the recording industry is The International Federation of the Phonographic Industry (IFPI) which has offices throughout the world. A particularly useful publication is their *Statistical History of the World Recording Industry* covering the period between 1969 and 1990 (Hung & Morencos, 1990). In the United States the Recording Industry Association of America (RIAA) produces yearly, rather sketchy statistics, and in Britain the British Phonographic Industry (BPI) produces an annual report which contains a wealth of data about production and distribution patterns, retail and consumer sales and the top selling genres and artists. The trade magazines *Music Week* (UK), *Billboard* (USA) and *Music Business International* also regularly report various recording industry statistics.

Copyright Revenue

In Chapter 1 I drew attention to the problem of taking sales statistics alone as an indicator of musical consumption patterns – these have to be considered alongside the revenue derived from copyright. In the coming years money derived from the exploitation of copyrights may account for as much revenue – and eventually more – than straightforward consumer purchases. Unfortunately this data is currently dispersed amongst the numerous collecting societies who are responsible for administering rights in different geographical regions. However, there are indications that figures may become available in a more concise form as copyright legislation is harmonised around the world, and as these societies link their systems together through computer networks. At the time of writing this information could only be obtained by contacting the individual societies directly and obtaining their annual reports (if they produce them) or requesting information. The main organisations in Britain are; The Performing Right Society (PRS), The Mechanical Copyright Protection Society (MCPS) and Phonographic Performance Ltd (PPL). (A useful history of the Performing Right Society and copyright in Britain can be found in *The Harmonious Alliance* by Cyril Ehrlich (1989), Oxford University Press). The main collecting bodies in the United States are: The American Society of Composers, Authors and Publishers (ASCAP) and Broadcast Music Incorporated (BMI). (A useful historical study of the emergence and competition between these organisations can be found in Ryan (1985)). These societies should be able to provide lists of their sister organisations throughout the world.

Artists' Earnings

Established artists can receive royalties of somewhere in the region of 21–26 per cent on the sales of their recordings and anything up to 90 per cent of the rights revenue derived from the use of these recordings, and the whole of the revenue from performance rights (less admin costs) if they own their own copyright/ publishing. However, this is a very under-researched area – these figures I have just mentioned have come from individuals within the industry. This is an area where information is even harder to obtain or estimate than record company shares.

George Tremlett (1990) attempted to give some indication of the wealth of the major global artists, but his research is frustratingly partial, thwarted by the way in which multiple companies are registered around the world, earnings lodged in inaccessible off-shore tax havens, and the way in which the Companies Act enables returns reported in Britain to be 'modified' to reveal as little information as possible. It can be established, for example, that Queen Productions Ltd grossed £49 million between 1976 and 1988 from 'production royalties and income arising from live performances' and that Queen Music grossed a further £8 million between 1982 and 1988. Figures show that between 1982 and 1988 Philip Collins Ltd grossed £23,235,543 from 'royalties, performance and related income', and that as a director of Effectsound he grossed a further £12,064,193 between 1981 and 1989. But, these are only for companies registered in the UK. What percentage of total income they may represent when added to offshore companies, and other interests scattered throughout the world is almost impossible to ascertain. The earnings of artists are rarely reported in the press, and when they are it is often as part of a public relations exercise. When it is reported that X-singer has signed to xzy records for $1 million (or $50 million), this figure is often arrived at by accumulating all the advances and spending on their behalf that they would receive *should* they be successful and stay with the company for the length of the contract.

Appendix 2

World Sales of Records and Tapes 1990

	retail value $ millions	per cent of total
USA	7,541.1	31
JAPAN	2,981.8	12
GERMANY	2,273.9	9
UNITED KINGDOM	2,117.5	9
FRANCE	1,665.8	7
USSR (1989)	696.6	3
NETHERLANDS	643.0	3
CANADA	608.8	3
ITALY	581.8	2
SPAIN	521.5	2
AUSTRALIA	476.3	2
SOUTH KOREA	438.2	2
SWITZERLAND	287.9	1
SWEDEN	286.4	1
BELGIUM	240.7	1
BRAZIL	237.6	1
MEXICO (1989)	235.1	1
CHINA (1989)	215.8	1
SOUTH AFRICA	182.5	1
AUSTRIA	167.4	1
INDIA	166.7	1
FINLAND	161.0	1
DENMARK	154.6	1
TAIWAN	142.6	1
NORWAY	117.8	1
THAILAND	113.3	1
HONG KONG	82.1	–
TURKEY	77.2	–
INDONESIA	69.8	–
GREECE	69.2	–

	retail value $ millions	per cent of total
NEW ZEALAND	64.5	–
PORTUGAL	59.0	–
SAUDI ARABIA	51.1	–
ARGENTINA	48.8	–
SINGAPORE	46.2	–
VENEZUELA	44.5	–
IRELAND (1989)	36.5	–
CZECH & SLOVAK FED REP	32.9	–
COLOMBIA	31.8	–
MALAYSIA	30.8	–
CHILE	24.3	–
PHILIPINES	19.3	–
HUNGARY	19.1	–
NIGERIA	12.3	–
IVORY COAST	5.6	–
BOLIVIA	4.0	–
ECUADOR (1989)	3.7	–
PERU	3.0	–
URUGUAY	2.0	–
POLAND	not available	
TOTAL	24,050.0	

(Source: *World Records Sales 1990*. International Federation of the Phonographic Industry, Press Information, 1 October 1991.)

BIBLIOGRAPHY

The following bibliography lists the references cited in the chapters of this book. Anyone who wishes to consult a more detailed and extensive list of the less readily available sources that were used in putting this book together is advised to consult my Ph.D thesis (*The Discovery and Development of Recording Artists in the Popular Music Industry*, Southbank Polytechnic/CNAA, London, 1992).

The most extensive writings on the production and consumption of popular music in Britain are those of Simon Frith. From the mid 1970s, Frith, as one of the few academics to engage continually with the subject has provided an ongoing commentary on the Anglo-American recording industry, and an interrogation of what pop music means for the fan and critical observer. His writings include subjective celebrations and appreciations, critiques, empirical studies and commentaries which engage in most of the issues and debates within pop music. Much of this has provided the starting point for many of my discussions in this book (whether consciously acknowledged or unconsciously absorbed).

For an alternative perspective to the one presented here; Chapple and Garofalo (1977), and Harker (1980) emphasise how patterns of corporate ownership and control enables capitalist corporations to 'colonise leisure' and how popular music is absorbed and 'co-opted' by a ruthless and exploitative commercial system. In contrast to this are accounts which emphasise youth subcultures, the audience, and occasionally the performers, and highlight the way in which the sounds and images of popular music are 'appropriated' by various groups and individuals and used for the expression of subjective identities, symbolic resistance, and leisure pursuits in everyday life. See: Chambers (1985), Grossberg (1987, 1988, 1990), Hebdige (1979), McRobbie (1980, 1989). For an account of the issues which were facing the British recording industry and the changes it was undergoing during the middle of the 1980s see Qualen (1985).

Much of the most informative and perceptive writing about the way in which the recording industry and its personnel work on a daily basis is unfortunately spread in a fragmentary fashion through various biographies, ephemeral publications and profiles in the trade press. For useful case studies of individual record companies see; George (1985) on Motown and Gillett on Atlantic (1988). For an account of the frustrations and conflicts which an organic rock band encountered when making an album, which at the same time highlights many of the tensions I have discussed in this book see Stokes (1977); a similar insight can be found in a compelling account of the Billion Dollar Babies tour of the Alice Cooper Band written by Greene (1974). An insight into the personal, commercial and creative motives of one of the most enigmatic pop stars of the 1980s can be found in O'Brien's book on Annie Lennox (1991).

For further reading on the subjects of particular chapters: The best detailed information about the interests and orientations of entertainment corporations can be obtained in their company annual reports and in the music trade press (referred to in Appendix 1). For discussions of globalisation and 'world music' see Wallis & Malm (1984), Frith (Ed) (1989) and Robinson, Buck & Cuthbert (1991). The most detailed account of the history of sound recording is that of Read & Welch (1976). For a detailed exposition of the complexities and minutiae of recording contracts see Bagehot (1989). For a profile of the work of, mainly rock oriented, record producers see Tobler & Grundy (1982), and for an account of the emergence of music radio in Britain see Barnard (1989). For a detailed rambling account of the emergence of MTV see Denisoff (1988) and for a 'postmodern' response to music video see Kaplan (1987). For an account of the experiences of women in popular music and the recording industry see Steward & Garratt (1984).

An important collection of essays which covers most of the key debates in the production and consumption of pop and rock music is S. Frith & A. Goodwin (Ed), 1990, *On Record* (Routledge). Regular discussion and analysis of popular music from a variety of perspectives can be found in the journal *Popular Music* (Cambridge University Press).

Adorno, T. 1991: *The Culture Industry. Selected Essays on Mass Culture*. Ed. J. Bernstein, Routledge.

Adorno, T. & Horkheimer, M. 1979: *Dialectic of Enlightenment*. Verso.

Alberoni, F. 1972: 'The Powerless 'Elite': Theory and Sociological Research on the Phenomenon of the Stars' pp 75–116 in D. McQuail (Ed) *Sociology of Mass Communications*. Penguin.

Attali, J. 1985: *Noise. The Political Economy of Music*. Translated by Brian Massumi. Manchester University Press.

Bagdikian, B. 1989: 'The Lords of the Global Village'. *The Nation*, June 12th pp 805–820.

Bagehot, R. 1989: *Music Business Agreements*. Waterlow Publishers.

Baird, J. 1990: 'The Odd Couple of Epic's A & R'. *Musician*. August, pp 68–71.

Barnard, S. 1989: *On The Radio; Music Radio in Britain* Open University Press.

Barnes, K. 1988: 'Top 40 Radio: A Fragment of the Imagination' in S. Frith (Ed) *Facing the Music*, Pantheon.

Barthes, R. 1990: 'The Grain of The Voice' pp 293–300 in *On Record*. S. Frith and A. Goodwin (Eds). Routledge.

Bayton, M. 1989: *How Women Become Rock Musicians*. Ph.D. Thesis, Warwick University.

Becker, H. 1974: 'Art as Collective Action'. *American Sociological Review*. Vol 39 pp 767–776.

Becker, H. 1976: 'Art Worlds and Social Types' pp 41–56 in R. Peterson (Ed), *The Production of Culture*. Sage.

Benjamin, W. 1970: 'The Work of Art in the Age of Mechanical Reproduction' in *Illuminations*, Jonathan Cape.

Bennett, H. 1980: *On Becoming a Rock Musician*. University of Massachusetts Press.

Berg, A. 1989: *Goldwyn*. Sphere.

Berland, J. 1990: 'Radio Space and Industrial Time: Music Formats, Local Narratives and Technological Mediations' *Popular Music* Vol 9 No 2, pp 179–192.

Bloch, E. 1988: *The Utopian Function of Art and Literature*. Transl. J. Zipes & F. Mecklenburg. Massachusetts Institute of Technology Press.

Blumler, J. 1990. 'Elections, the Media and the Modern Publicity Process', pp 101–113 in M. Ferguson (Ed), *Public Communication, The New Imperatives*. Sage.

Bode, S. 1990. 'Video Stars.' *City Limits*, June 14th, pp 14–15.

Bourdieu, P. 1986. *Distinction. A Social Critique of the Judgment of Taste.* Routledge.

British Broadcasting Corporation (BBC). 1990: *Design Classics: The Sony Walkman.* Broadcast 19th June 1990.

British Phonographic Industry Ltd (BPI). 1988: *Annual Report.*

British Phonographic Industry Ltd (BPI). 1989: *Annual Report.*

British Phonographic Industry Ltd (BPI). 1991: *Annual Report.*

Bullough, H. 1991: 'When The Party's Over' *Music Week.* 2nd February pp 10–11.

Burnett, R. 1990: *Concentration and Diversity in the International Phonogram Industry.* University of Gothenburg.

Chambers, I. 1985: *Urban Rhythms.* MacMillan.

Chambers, I. 1988: 'Contamination, Coincidence and Collision: Pop Music, Urban Culture, and The Avant-Garde' pp 607–615 in C. Nelson & L. Grossberg (Eds) *Marxism and The Interpretation of Culture.* MacMillan.

Chambers, I. 1990: 'A Miniature History of the Walkman'. *New Formations*, Vol 11 Summer, pp 1–4.

Chanan, M. 1988: 'Piano Studies. On Science, Technology and Manufacture from Harpsichords to Yamahas'. *Science as Culture.* No 3. pp 54–91.

Channel 4 Television. 1991: *The Media Show.* Sunday March 10th 1991.

Chapple, S & Garofalo, R. 1977: *Rock'n'Roll is Here to Pay.* Nelson Hall.

Cohen, S. 1991: *Rock Culture in Liverpool. Popular Music in The Making.* Clarendon Press.

Connor, S. 1987: 'The Flag on the Road, Bruce Springsteen and the Live', *New Formations*, Number 3, Winter, pp 129–137.

Cosgrove, S. 1988: 'Idol Investment.' *New Statesman and Society.* 17th June, p 50.

Cronin, P. & Flanagan, B. 1991: 'The Phantom Zone', *Musician* August pp 56–58.

Cubitt, S. 1991: *Timeshift, On Video Culture.* Routledge.

Dalton, D. 1989. 'The Marketing Miracle Worker', *Europe Etc*, Music Week Publication, September 1989, p 10.

Dannen, F. 1990: *Hit Men. Power Brokers and Fast Money Inside the Music Business.* Times Books, Random House.

Davis, C. 1974: *Clive: Inside The Record Business.* Ballantine Books, Random House.

De Certaux, 1988: *The Practice of Everyday Life.* University of California Press.

Denisoff, R. 1975: *Solid Gold: The Popular Record Industry.* Transaction Books.

Denisoff, R. 1986: *Tarnished Gold: The Record Industry Revisited.* Transaction Books.

Denisoff, R. 1988: *Inside MTV.* Transaction Books.

Denselow, R. 1990: 'The Axeman Snoozeth'. *The Guardian.* 13th December p 27.

Dent, E. 1956: 'The Pianoforte and its Influence on Modern Music'. *The Score*, No. 18 pp 53–71. (Originally published in The Musical Quarterly, April 1916.)

Dilello, R. 1983: *The Longest Cocktail Party.* Pierian Press.

Dunphy, E. 1988: *The Unforgettable Fire: The Story of U2.* Penguin.

Durant, A. 1985: *Conditions of Music.* MacMillan.

Dyer, R. 1979: *Stars.* British Film Institute.

Dyer, R. 1991: 'A Star is Born and the Construction of Authenticity' pp 132–140 in C. Gledhill (Ed) *Stardom. Industry of Desire.* Routledge.

Ehrlich, C. 1976 *The Piano, A History.* J.M. Dent & Sons.

Eisenberg, E. 1988: *The Recording Angel.* Picador.

Ernst, D. 1977: *The Evolution of Electronic Music.* Schirmer Books.

Fabbri, F. 1991: 'Copyright: The Dark Side of The Music Business'. *World Beat.* Vol 1 No 1, pp 109–114.

Featherstone, M. 1991: *Consumer Culture and Postmodernism.* Sage.

Finnegan, R. 1989: *The Hidden Musicians. Music Making in an English Town.* Cambridge University Press.

Fiske, J. 1986: 'MTV: Post Structural Post Modern'. *Journal of Communication Inquiry*. Vol 10 No 1.

Flanagan, B. 1987: *Written in my Soul. Conversations With Rock's Great Songwriters*. Contemporary Books.

Fornäs, J. 1989: *Papers on Pop and Youth Culture*. Working paper 1/1989. Centre for Mass Communication Research, University of Stockholm.

Fox, T. 1986: *In The Groove: The People Behind The Music*. St. Martins Press.

Frederickson, J. 1989: 'Technology and Musical Performance in the Age of Mechanical Reproduction'. *International Review of Aesthetics and Sociology of Music*, Vol 12 pp 193–220.

Frith, S. 1976: 'The A & R Men', pp 25–44 in C. Gillet & S. Frith (Eds) *Rock File 4*. Panther.

Frith, S. 1978: *The Sociology of Rock*. Constable.

Frith, S. 1983: *Sound Effects. Youth, Leisure and the Politics of Rock'n'Roll*. Constable.

Frith, S. 1986: 'Art Versus Technology: The Strange Case of Popular Music'. *Media, Culture & Society*. Vol 8 pp 263–79.

Frith, S. 1987a: 'The Industrialization of Popular Music' pp 53–77 in J. Lull (ed), *Popular Music and Communication*. Sage.

Frith, S. 1987b: 'The Making of the British Record Industry 1920–64' pp 278–290 in J. Curran, A. Smith, P. Wingate, (Eds). *Impacts and Influences*. Methuen.

Frith, S. 1987c: 'Copyright and The Music Business' *Popular Music*. Vol 7, 1. pp 57–75.

Frith, S. 1988a: *Music For Pleasure*. Polity.

Frith, S. 1988b: 'Introduction' and 'Video Pop: Picking up the Pieces' in S. Frith (Ed). *Facing The Music*, Pantheon.

Frith, S. (Ed). 1989: *World Music, Politics and Social Change*. Manchester University Press/IASPM.

Frith, S. & Goodwin, A. (Eds). 1990: *On Record, Rock, Pop and The Written Word*. Routledge.

Garfield, S. 1986: *Expensive Habits, The Dark Side of The Music Industry*. Faber & Faber.

Garofalo, R. 1986: 'How Autonomous is Relative: Popular Music, the Social Formation and Cultural Struggle', *Popular Music*, Vol 6 No 1, pp 77–92.

George, N. 1985: *Where Did Our Love Go. The Rise and Fall of The Motown Sound*. Omnibus.

Giles, D. 1989a: 'Pulling The Plug', *City Limits* 6th April, pp 10–11.

Giles, D. 1989b: 'Who Leads The Press Gang?', *City Limits*, 3 August pp 16–17.

Gillett, C. 1983: *The Sound of the City*. Souvenir Press.

Gillett, C. 1988: *Making Tracks. The Story of Atlantic Records*. Souvenir Press.

Gilroy, P. 1987: *There Ain't No Black in The Union Jack*. Hutchinson.

Goodwin, A. 1987: 'Music Video in the (Post) Modern World.' *Screen*, Vol 28 part 3 pp 36–55.

Goodwin, A. 1990: 'Sample and Hold: Pop Music in the Digital Age of Reproduction' pp 258–273 in S. Frith & A. Goodwin *On Record*. Routledge.

Grant, K. 1989: 'GI Blues and Soul', *Melody Maker*. 11th November p 60.

Gray, H. 1988: *Producing Jazz*. Temple University Press.

Greene, B. 1974: *Billion Dollar Baby*. Atheneum Books.

Greig, C. 1989: *Will You Still Love Me Tomorrow*. Virago.

Gronow, P. 1983: 'The Record Industry: The Growth of a Mass Medium'. *Popular Music* Vol 3. pp 53–75.

Grossberg, L. 1987: 'Rock and Roll in Search of an Audience' pp 175–197 in J. Lull (Ed) *Popular Music and Communication*. Sage.

Grossberg, L. 1988. 'You [Still] Have to Fight For Your Right to Party: Music

Television as Billboards of Post-modern Difference'. *Popular Music*. Vol 7 No 3 pp 315–331.

Grossberg, L. 1990: 'Is There Rock After Punk?' pp 111–123 in S. Frith & A. Goodwin, (Eds), *On Record*. Routledge.

Grunfeld, F. 1974: *The Art and Times of the Guitar*. MacMillan.

Hardy, P. 1984: *The British Record Industry. IASPM UK Working Paper No. 3.*

Harker, D. 1980: *One for the Money: Politics and Popular Song*. Hutchinson.

Harron, M. 1988: 'McRock: Pop as Commodity', in S. Frith (Ed) *Facing the Music*. Pantheon.

Hearn, J. & Parkin, P. 1987: 'Sex at Work: The Power and Paradox of Organization Sexuality' in J. Hearn, D. Sheppard, P. Tancred-Sherriff, G. Burrell (Eds) *The Sexuality of Organization*. Sage.

Hebdige, D. 1979: *Subculture: The Meaning of Style*. Methuen.

Henderson, J. 1989: *The Globalization of High Technology Production*. Routledge.

Hennion, A. 1982: 'Popular Music as Social Production' pp 32–40 in D. Horn & P. Tagg (Eds) *Popular Music Perspectives 1*. IASPM.

Hennion, A. 1983: 'The Production of Success: An Anti-Musicology of The Pop Song'. *Popular Music 3* pp 158–193.

Hildebrandt, D. 1988: *Pianoforte: A Social History of the Piano*. Translated H. Goodman. Hutchinson.

Hirsch, P. 1970: *The Structure of the Popular Music Industry: The Filtering Process by which Records are Preselected for Public Consumption*. Institute for Social Research, University of Michigan.

Hirsch, P. 1972: 'Processing Fads and Fashions: An Organizational Set Analysis of Cultural Industry Systems.' *American Journal of Sociology*, Vol 77, No 4. pp 639–659.

Hoare, I. 1975: 'Introduction' to I. Hoare, C. Anderson, T. Cummings & S. Frith, *The Soul Book*. Methuen.

Horkins, T. 1989: 'A Woman's Work'. *Melody Maker*. 2nd December p 45.

Hosokawa, S. 1984: 'The Walkman Effect'. *Popular Music*, Vol 4. pp 165–180.

Houlton, R. 1967: 'The Process of Innovation: Magnetic Recording and the Broadcasting Industry in the USA'. *Bulletin of Oxford Institute of Economics and Statistics*, Vol 29 part 1 pp 41–59.

Hung, M. & Morencos, E. 1990: *World Record Sales 1969–1990, A Statistical History of the World Recording Industry*. International Federation of the Phonographic Industry.

Hymer, S. 1979: *The Multinational Corporation: A Radical Approach*. Papers edited by R. Cohen, N. Felton, M. Nkosi and J. Van Liere. Cambridge University.

Jensen, J. 1984: 'An Interpretive Approach to Cultural Production' in W. Rowland & B. Watkins (Eds) *Interpreting Television*. Sage.

Kaplan, E. 1987: *Rocking Around the Clock. Music Television, Postmodernism and Consumer Culture*. Methuen.

Kealey, E. 1979: 'From Craft to Art: The Case of Sound Mixers and Popular Music', *Sociology of Work and Occupations*. Vol. 6 No. 1. February pp 3–29.

Kealey, E. 1982: 'Conventions and the Production of the Popular Music Aesthetic'. *Journal of Popular Culture*. Vol 16 pp 100–115.

Kearney, R. 1988: *The Wake of Imagination*. Hutchinson.

Keen, B. 1987: 'Play it Again, Sony. The Double Life of Home Video Technology'. *Science as Culture*. Vol 1. pp 7–42.

Kelly, D. 1987: 'From C86 to Catch-22.' *New Musical Express*, 11th April pp 29–30.

King, A. (Ed). 1991: *Culture, Globalization and the World System*. MacMillan.

Laing, D. 1985a: 'Music Video: Industrial Product and Cultural Form'. *Screen*, Vol 26, No 2 pp 78–83.

Laing, D. 1985b: *One Chord Wonders. Power and Meaning in Punk Rock*. Open University Press.

Laing, 1986: 'The Music Industry and the Cultural Imperialism Thesis.' *Media, Culture and Society*. Vol 8 pp 331–341.

Lambert, D. 1980: *Producing Hit Records*. Schirmer/MacMillan.

Lambert, S. 1990: 'Are You Listening Carefully?' *Music Week*, 24th March 1990, pp 24–25.

Levitt, T. 1983:'The Globalization of Markets'. *Harvard Business Review*, May–June. pp 92–102.

Lewis, G. 1989: 'Creativity and the Making of Music Videos: An Interview with Lynn Kippax, Jr.' *Popular Music and Society*. Vol 13, No 2 pp 77–89.

Lipsitz, G. 1990: *Time Passages. Collective Memory and American Popular Culture*. University of Minnesota Press.

Lull, J. 1987: 'Listener's Communicative Use of Popular Music' pp 140–174 in *Popular Music and Communication*. Sage. (Second edition 1991).

Marcus, G. 1977: *Mystery Train*. Omnibus.

McGinley, P. 1991: 'Stylists: Putting Pop into Packages.' *Music Week*. 28th September pp 10–11.

McQuail, D. 1987: *Mass Communication Theory*, Sage.

McRobbie, A. & Frith, S. 1978: 'Rock and Sexuality' *Screen Education*. No 29, pp 3–19.

McRobbie, A. 1980: 'Settling Accounts With Subcultures: A Feminist Critique' *Screen Education* no 34, pp 37–49.

McRobbie, A. 1988: 'Peggy Sue Got Marketed'. *Times Higher Education Supplement*. 3rd June, p 24.

McRobbie, A. (Ed). 1989: *Zoot Suites and Second Hand Dresses*. MacMillan.

Meade, M. 1972: 'The Degradation of Women' pp 173-177 in R. Denisoff & R. Peterson (Eds), *The Sounds of Social Change*. Rand McNally.

Middleton, R. 1990: *Studying Popular Music*. Open University Press.

Millington, R. 1991:'Ad Nauseam, London's Pop Video Makers Have Become Commercial Travellers.' *The Sunday Times*. 7th April, London section, pp 8–10.

Morita, A. Reingold, E. & Shimomure, M. 1987: *Made in Japan: Akio Morita and Sony*. Collins.

Moss, C. 1990: 'All Men are Equal – But What About The Women?' *Studio*. November, pp 10–13.

O'Brien, L. 1991: *Annie Lennox*. Sidgwick & Jackson.

Ohmae, K. 1985: 'Becoming a Triad Power: The New Global Corporation'. *The McKinsey Quarterly*, Spring pp 2–25.

Ohsone, K. 1988: *The Case of the Walkman*. Sony's Innovations in Management Series. Vol 1. Sony Corporation.

Parish, C. 1944: 'Criticism of the Piano When it Was New'. *Musical Quarterly* Vol 30 pp 428–440.

Parsons, P. 1988: 'The Changing Role of Women Executives in The Recording Industry.' *Popular Music and Society*. Vol 12, No 4 pp 31–42.

Peterson, R. & Berger, D. 1971: 'Entrepreneurship in Organizations: Evidence From the Popular Music Industry'. *Administrative Science Quarterly*, Vol 16. No 1. pp 97–106.

Peterson, R. 1976: 'The Production of Culture. A Prolegomenon' pp 7–22 in R. Peterson (Ed) *The Production of Culture*. Sage.

Peterson, R. 1982: 'Five Constraints on the Production of Culture: Law, Technology, Market, Organizational Structure and Occupational Careers'. *Journal of Popular Culture*. Vol 16 Part 2 pp 143–153.

Peterson, R. 1985: 'Six Constraints on the Production of Literary Works', *Poetics*. No 14 pp 45–67.
Preston, K. 1989: *Scott Joplin*. Melrose Square Publishing, LA.
Qualen, J. 1985: *The Music Industry: The End of Vinyl?* Comedia.
Read, O. & Welch, W. 1976: *From Tin Foil to Stereo, Evolution of the Phonograph*. Howard W. Sams & Co.
Recording Industry Association of America (RIAA). 1991: *Inside The Recording Industry. A Statistical Overview 1990*. RIAA.
Reynolds, S. 1990: *Blissed Out*. Serpents Tale.
Robertson, R. 1990:'Mapping the Global Condition: Globalization as the Central Concept' pp 15–30 in M. Featherstone (Ed) *Global Culture*. Sage.
Robins, K. 1991: 'Tradition and Translation: National Culture in its Global Context' in J. Corner and S. Harvey (Eds) *Enterprise and Heritage*. Routledge.
Robinson, D. Buck, E. & Cuthbert, M. 1991: *Music at the Margins. Popular Music and Global Cultural Diversity*. Sage.
Robinson, N. 1991: 'Money Well Spent', *Music Week*. 30th March, p 6.
Rogan, J. 1988: *Starmakers and Svengalis*. Futura.
Rorty, R. 1991: *Objectivity, Relativism and Truth. Philosophical Papers Volume 1*. Cambridge University Press.
Rothenbuhler, E. 1987: 'Commercial Radio and Popular Music: Processes of Selection and Factors of Influence' pp 78–95 in J. Lull (Ed) *Popular Music and Communication*, Sage.
Russcol, H. 1981: 'Music Since Hiroshima: The Electric Age Begins' pp 199–207 in Battcock, G. (Ed) *Breaking the Sound Barrier*, Dutton, New York.
Rutten, P. 1991: 'Local Popular Music on The National and International Market'. *Cultural Studies*. October 1991, pp 294–305.
Ryan, J. 1985: *The Production of Culture in the Music Industry. The ASCAP-BMI Controversy*. University Press of America.
Ryan, J. & Peterson, R. 1982: 'The Product Image: The Fate of Creativity in Country Music Songwriting' pp 11–32 in J. Ettema & D. Whitney (Eds). *Individuals in Mass Media Organizations: Creativity and Constraint*. Sage.
Sabel, C. 1990: *Skills Without a Place: The Reorganization of the Corporation and the Experience of Work*. Paper presented to the British Sociological Association Annual Conference, Guildford, April 1990.
Sandall, R. 1991: 'Fancy Seeing You Here'. *Q Magazine*. April 1991, pp 50–52.
Savage, J. 1991: *England's Dreaming. Sex Pistols and Punk Rock*. Faber and Faber.
Schicke, C. 1974: *Revolution in Sound*. Little, Brown & Co, Boston.
Schlemm, W. 1982: 'On the Position of the Tonmeister (Sound Recordist) in the Musical Communication Process' pp 139–157 in K. Blaukopf (Ed) *The Phonogram in Cultural Communication*. Springer-Verlag.
Sheppard, D. 1989: 'Organizations, Power and Sexuality: The Image and Self-Image of Women Managers' pp 139–157 in J. Hearn, D. Sheppard, P. Tancred-Sheriff, G. Burrell (Eds). *The Sexuality of Organization*. Sage.
Shore, L. 1983: *The Crossroads of Business and Music*. Ph.D. Thesis, Stanford University.
Sklar, R. 1984: *Rocking America. How the All-Hit Radio Stations Took Over*. St. Martins Press.
Smith, M. 1989: 'The Tin Man', *Melody Maker*. 1st July p 44.
Stacey, J. 1991: 'Feminine Fascinations: Forms of Identification in Star-Audience Relations' pp 141–163 in C. Gledhill (Ed) *Stardom. Industry of Desire*. Routledge.
Steward, S. & Garratt, S. 1984: *Signed, Sealed and Delivered. True Life Stories of Women in Pop*. Pluto Press.

Stokes, G. 1977: *The Star Making Machinery. Inside The Business of Rock'n'Roll.* Vintage Books.

Stratton, J. 1982a: 'Reconciling Contradictions: The Role of The Artist & Repertoire Person in The British Music Industry'. *Popular Music and Society.* Vol. 8. No. 2. pp 90–100.

Stratton, J. 1982b: 'Between Two Worlds: Art and Commercialism in the Record Industry'. *Sociological Review,* Vol 30 pp 267–285.

Stratton, J. 1983: 'Capitalism and Romantic Ideology in the Record Business', *Popular Music.* Vol 3 pp 143–156.

Street, J. 1986: *Rebel Rock.* Blackwell.

Struthers, S. 1987: 'Technology in the Art of Recording' pp 241–258 in A. White (Ed) *Lost in Music: Culture, Style and the Musical Event.* Routledge.

Sutcliffe, P. 1989: 'Tears for Fears – The Sequel.' *Q Magazine.* September pp 60–66.

Sutcliffe, P. 1990: 'Busman's Holiday', *Q Magazine,* September pp 42–50.

Talbot, M. 1991: 'Is Research the Missing Link', *Music Week.* 2nd March pp 8–9.

Tankel, J. 1990: 'The Practice of Recording Music: Remixing as Recoding'. *Journal of Communication.* Vol 40 No 3 Summer pp 34–47.

Temple, J. 1983: 'Videopop'. *The Face.* No 45 pp 70–73.

Théberge, P. 1990a: 'Democracy and its Discontents. The MIDI Specification'. *Onetwothreefour.* No 9, Autumn, pp 12–34.

Théberge, P. 1990b: Musicians as Market Consumers of Technology'. *Onetwothreefour.* No 9, Autumn, pp 53–60.

Théberge, P. 1989: 'The "Sound" of Music. Technological Rationalization and The Production of Popular Music.' *New Formations.* Vol 8. Summer. pp 99–111.

Tobler, J. & Grundy, S. 1982: *The Record Producers.* BBC Books.

Toop, D. 1984: *The Rap Attack.* Pluto.

Tremlett, G. 1990: *Rock Gold. The Music Millionaires.* Unwin Hyman.

Vermorel, F. & Vermorel, J. 1985: *Starlust, The Secret Fantasies of Fans.* Comet.

Vignolle, J. 1980: 'Mixing Genres and Reaching the Public: The Production of Pop Music'. *Social Science Information* Vol 19, No 1 pp 79–105.

Vulliamy, G. 1977: 'Music and the Mass Culture Debate', in J. Shepherd, P. Virden, G. Vulliamy, T. Wishart (Eds) *Whose Music? A Sociology of Musical Languages.* Latimer New Directions.

Wale, M. 1972: *Voxpop. Profiles of the Pop Process.* Harrap.

Wallis, R. & Malm, K. 1984: *Big Sounds From Small Peoples,* Constable.

Webb, S. 1991: 'The Promo Dilemma: Money for Nothing?'. *Music Week,* 12th January, pp 14–15.

Wenner, J. 1973: *Lennon Remembers.* Penguin.

Williams, R. 1963: *Culture and Society.* Penguin.

Williams, R. 1990: *Television, Technology and Cultural Form.* Routledge.

Willis, P. 1990: *Common Culture.* Open University Press.

Wills, C. 1991: 'Into War With a Walkman', *The Sunday Mirror.* February 26th p 6.

Wise, S. 1990: 'Sexing Elvis' pp 390–398 in S. Frith & A. Goodwin (Eds), *On Record.* Routledge.

Wright Mills, C. 1953: 'Introduction' in T. Veblen. *The Theory of the Leisure Class.* Unwin.

Zeppenfeld, W. 1979: 'The Economics and Structure of the Record and Tape Industry: The Example of West Germany' pp 248–257 in H. Fischer & S. Melnik (Eds) *Entertainment: A Cross-Cultural Examination.* Communication Arts Books.

INDEX